The Mail&Guardian

A–Z of South African Politics

The Essential Handbook

2009

edited by
Rapule Tabane & Barbara Ludman

JACANA

For updates on the profiles of political figures, consult the *Mail & Guardian* website: www.mg.co.za

First published by Jacana Media (Pty) Ltd in 2009

10 Orange Street
Sunnyside
Auckland Park 2092
South Africa
+2711 628 3200
www.jacana.co.za

ISBN 978-1-77009-745-2

Set in Ehrhardt 11/14pt
Printed by CTP Book Printers
Job No. 000968

See a complete list of Jacana titles at www.jacana.co.za

Contents

Preface

A book like this one is the most awkward of creatures: bound in permanent-seeming covers, it must pretend to some kind of lasting authority, and yet its every judgement is subject to harsh review as history happens around it.

Journalists are used to building a picture incrementally over days and weeks – or, in the online world, over minutes and hours – but less so to committing themselves for the ages. The writers at the *Mail & Guardian* who contributed to this book have been tracking their subjects for years, adding here, subtracting there, reshaping and updating. In the early months of 2009, however, they faced a particularly acute challenge in fixing an image of a political landscape that was – and is – undergoing its most profound upheaval since 1994.

It is a job for a movie camera, once might argue, not a still photograph, or one for ephemeral blog posts and tweets rather than books. Yet it is precisely the difficulty of reducing this very fluid moment to the fixity of a directory that makes the book worthwhile.

At no time since the transition to democracy 15 years ago has a guide to the emergent reality of our politics been more necessary.

For the past decade the defining poles of our politics have been the opposing camps in the battle to define the future of the African National Congress, and since at least 2001 they have been most readily understood by reference to the two men who came to stand in for all the seething complexities that were tearing the party apart: Thabo Mbeki and Jacob Zuma. It was a caricature, no doubt, to reduce to a fist-fight the enormously complicated torsions within a liberation movement struggling to transform itself into a modern governing party, but as the investigation into corruption allegations against Zuma gathered momentum, and as Mbeki sought increasingly aggressively to freeze out the left wing of his party, along with its communist and trade union allies, the representation gradually became the reality.

The ANC's policy of cadre deployment – giving important public-sector posts, and sometimes private-sector ones, to its leading members – replicated the party's fault-lines across the entire state apparatus and some important boardrooms, too. The rationale was that people schooled in the party's vision of a new society were best placed to deliver thorough-going transformation of its most important organs, from the security services to Parliament and the public broadcaster. We now know just how badly crucial institutions, from the SABC to the Scorpions, were compromised, sometimes just by venal and incompetent leaders, but also as enmities, some of them dating back to the years of exile, others more recently discovered, coalesced around Zuma and Mbeki.

In the run-up to the ANC's December 2007 conference at Polokwane, and in its immediate aftermath, our entire polity began to resemble the set for an episode of the reality television show *Survivor*. Unfortunately the players had at their disposal spy agencies, state contracts and the economy, and there was no avuncular host to keep it all under control.

The principal questions during this long period were who would win, and just what would be left of their party, and the country, when they were done.

We know the answer to the first: Jacob Zuma was inaugurated just before this book went to press. The answer to the second is still unfolding, although there is a good deal of very mixed evidence in these pages to suggest that while he has not quite inherited scorched earth, he has an extraordinary rebuilding job to do, and a re-imagining job, too. So much of the Mbeki project was bound up in identity, in the rehabilitation of a scarred psychic and cultural body, that different approaches to that challenge struggled to assert themselves.

But with those answers come a host of new questions. Some of them are in the same register as the old ones. Who is Jacob Zuma really? Who, among all those who claim to have his ear, will really have influence with him? On whom will he draw to prosecute his own project, and what, beyond the fairly broad assertions of the ANC's policy documents, is that project?

We can't yet tell you the answers to those questions, but there are resources here to aid an understanding of Zuma's own unfolding responses to them, and perhaps to be less surprised by those responses.

In the absence of all-consuming combat, however, more interesting questions suggest themselves. What kind of economic model is appropriate for us in the middle of a dramatic rethink of the architecture of global capitalism? And who will have a say in building it? Will the emergence of the Congress of the People out of the ANC, however tentative and flawed, be the beginning of a broad, non-racial opposition coalition, or will the new party wither, leaving the Democratic Alliance to represent the 'majority of the minorities' while it struggles to attract African support? Will our basic constitutional architecture survive? Can an overwhelmingly dominant governing party overcome the ills of long incumbency – corruption, complacency, infighting – and use its hegemony truly to deliver on its promise of a better life for all? And, crucially, can it manage the growing pressure of inequality as a deepening recession threatens jobs, state revenues and spending plans?

We can't pretend to tell you the way through the maze of our politics and we can't promise a panacea for the anxiety that comes with uncertainty. But what this book does offer is a series of starting points that we think will help you begin the navigation; a jetty, if you like, thrown out into unfamiliar waters. Read along with us. It is going to be a remarkable year.

Nic Dawes

Acknowledgements

Thanks to Sewela Mamphiswana, Edwina van der Burg and Jane Franz Abbott from the Mail & Guardian and Russell Martin and Shawn Paikin from Jacana.

Contributors

Justin Arenstein, Adriaan Basson, Belinda Beresford, Maureen Brady, Stefaans Brummer, Matthew Burbidge, Shaun de Waal, Nic Dawes, Monako Dibetle, Lynley Donnelly, Maya Fisher-French, Drew Forrest, Lloyd Gedye, Primarashni Gower, Yolandi Groenewald, Ferial Haffajee, Sharon Hammond, Pearlie Joubert, Mara Kardas-Nelson, Qudsiya Karrim, Karabo Keepile, Matuma Letsoalo, Barbara Ludman, Percy Mabandu, David Macfarlane, Mmanaledi Mataboge, Thabo Mohlala, Rudo Mungoshi, Nosimilo Ndlovu, Faranaaz Parker, Cornia Pretorius, Ilham Rawoot, Mandy Rossouw, Sello Selebi Alcock, Reg Rumney, Lucky Sindane, Sam Sole, Rapule Tabane, Marianne Thamm, Niren Tolsi, Thembelihle Tshabalala, Stephanie Wolters, Percy Zvomuya

Useful Acronyms

ACDP	African Christian Democratic Party
ANC	African National Congress
ANCYL	African National Congress Youth League
Apla	Azanian People's Liberation Army
ARV	antiretroviral
AU	African Union
Azapo	Azanian People's Organisation
BBBEE	broad-based black economic empowerment
BCM	Black Consciousness Movement
BEE	black economic empowerment
CBO	community-based organisation
Codesa	Convention for a Democratic South Africa
Contralesa	Congress of Traditional Leaders of South Africa
Cope	Congress of the People
Cosas	Congress of South African Students
Cosatu	Congress of South African Trade Unions
CSIR	Council for Scientific and Industrial Research
DA	Democratic Alliance
DAC	Department of Arts and Culture
Daso	Democratic Alliance Students' Organisation
DBSA	Development Bank of Southern Africa
DG	director-general
EPWP	Expanded Public Works Programme
Fedusa	Federation of Unions of South Africa
FF+	Freedom Front Plus
Gear	Growth, Employment and Redistribution macroeconomic strategy
GGP	gross geographic product
HRC	Human Rights Commission
HSRC	Human Sciences Research Council
Icasa	Independent Communications Authority of South Africa
ID	Independent Democrats
Idasa	Institute for Democracy in South Africa
IEC	Independent Electoral Commission
IFP	Inkatha Freedom Party
JSC	Judicial Service Commission
KZN	KwaZulu-Natal

LRC	Legal Resources Centre
MEC	member of the executive committee (a provincial minister)
MJC	Muslim Judicial Council
MK	Umkhonto weSizwe
MP	member of Parliament
MPL	member of the provincial legislature
Nadel	National Association of Democratic Lawyers of South Africa
Nactu	National Council of Trade Unions
NaTIS	National Traffic Information System
NCOP	National Council of Provinces
NEC	national executive committee
Nedlac	National Economic Development and Labour Council
Naledi	National Labour, Economic and Development Institute
Nehawu	National Education Health and Allied Workers' Union
Nepad	New Partnership for Africa's Development
NGO	non-governmental organisation
NIA	National Intelligence Agency
NPA	National Prosecuting Authority
NUM	National Union of Mineworkers
Numsa	National Union of Metalworkers of South Africa
NWC	national working committee
OBE	outcomes-based education
PAC	Pan Africanist Congress
RDP	Reconstruction and Development Programme
SACBC	Southern African Catholic Bishops' Conference
Saccawu	South African Commercial, Catering and Allied Workers' Union
SACP	South African Communist Party
SADC	Southern African Development Community
SANDF	South African National Defence Force
SAPS	South African Police Service
Sars	South African Revenue Service
Sasco	South African Students' Congress
Saso	South African Students' Organisation
SMME	small, micro and medium enterprises
SRC	student representative council
Stats SA	Statistics South Africa
TAC	Treatment Action Campaign
TRC	Truth and Reconciliation Commission
UCT	University of Cape Town
UDF	United Democratic Front
UDM	United Democratic Movement
Unisa	University of South Africa
UWC	University of the Western Cape
Wits	University of the Witwatersrand

The New Cabinet

Government of the Republic of South Africa

President: Jacob Zuma
Deputy President: Kgalema
Petros Motlanthe

**Ministers and Deputy
Ministers**

1. Minister of Agriculture,
   Forestry and Fisheries:
   Tina Joemat-Pettersson
   Deputy Minister of
   Agriculture, Forestry and
   Fisheries: Pieter Mulder
2. Minister of Arts and Culture:
   Lulu Xingwana
   Deputy Minister of Arts and
   Culture: Paul Mashatile
3. Minister of Basic Education:
   Angie Motshekga
   Deputy Minister of Basic
   Education: Enver Surty
4. Minister of Communications:
   Siphiwe Nyanda
   Deputy Minister of
   Communications: Dina Pule
5. Minister of Cooperative
   Governance and Traditional
   Affairs: Sicelo Shiceka

Deputy Minister of
   Cooperative Governance and
   Traditional Affairs:
   Yunus Carrim
6. Minister of Correctional
   Services: Nosiviwe
   Mapisa-Nqakula
   Deputy Minister of
   Correctional Services:
   Hlengiwe Mkhize
7. Minister of Defence and
   Military Veterans:
   Lindiwe Sisulu
   Deputy Minister of Defence
   and Military Veterans:
   Thabang Makwetla
8. Minister of Economic
   Development: Ebrahim Patel
   Deputy Minister of Economic
   Development: Gwen
   Mahlangu-Nkabinde
9. Minister of Energy:
   Dipuo Peters
10. Minister of Finance:
    Pravin Gordhan
    Deputy Minister of Finance:
    Nhlanhla Nene

11. Minister of Health:
    Aaron Motsoaledi
    Deputy Minister of Health:
    Molefi Sefularo
12. Minister of Higher Education
    and Training:
    Blade Nzimande
13. Minister of Home Affairs:
    Nkosazana Dlamini-Zuma
    Deputy Minister of Home
    Affairs: Malusi Gigaba
14. Minister of Human
    Settlements: Tokyo Sexwale
    Deputy Minister of Human
    Settlements: Zou Kota
15. Minister of International
    Relations and Cooperation:
    Maite Nkoana-Mashabane
    Deputy Minister of
    International Relations and
    Cooperation (1):
    Ebrahim Ismail Ebrahim
    Deputy Minister of
    International Relations
    and Cooperation (2):
    Sue van der Merwe
16. Minister of Justice and
    Constitutional Development:
    Jeff Radebe
    Deputy Minister of Justice and
    Constitutional Development:
    Andries Nel
17. Minister of Labour:
    Membathisi Mdladlana

18. Minister of Mining:
    Susan Shabangu
19. Minister of Police:
    Nathi Mthethwa
    Deputy Minister of Police:
    Fikile Mbalula
20. Minister of Public Enterprises:
    Barbara Hogan
    Deputy Minister of Public
    Enterprises:
    Enoch Godongwana
21. Minister for the Public Service
    and Administration:
    Richard Baloyi
22. Deputy Minister for the Public
    Service and Administration:
    Roy Padayachie
23. Minister of Public Works:
    Geoff Doidge
    Deputy Minister of Public
    Works: Hendrietta
    Bogopane-Zulu
24. Minister of Rural Development
    and Land Reform:
    Gugile Nkwinti
    Deputy Minister of Rural
    Development and Land
    Reform: Joe Phaahla
25. Minister of Science and
    Technology: Naledi Pandor
    Deputy Minister of Science
    and Technology: Derek
    Hanekom

26. Minister of Social
    Development: Edna Molewa
    Deputy Minister of Social
    Development: Bathabile
    Dlamini
27. Minister of Sport and
    Recreation: Makhenkesi
    Stofile
    Deputy Minister of Sport and
    Recreation: Gert Oosthuizen
28. Minister of State Security:
    Siyabonga Cwele
29. Minister in The Presidency
    (1) National Planning
    Commission: Trevor Manuel
    Minister in The Presidency
    (2) Performance Monitoring
    and Evaluation as well
    as Administration in the
    Presidency: Collins Chabane
30. Minister of Tourism:
    Marthinus van Schalkwyk
    Deputy Minister of Tourism:
    Thozile Xasa
31. Minister of Trade and
    Industry: Rob Davies
    Deputy Minister of Trade and
    Industry (1): Thandi Tobias
    Deputy Minister of Trade and
    Industry (2): Maria Ntuli
32. Minister of Transport: Sbusiso
    Joel Ndebele
    Deputy Minister of Transport:
    Jeremy Cronin

33. Minister of Water and
    Environmental Affairs:
    Buyelwa Sonjica
    Deputy Minister of Water
    and Environmental Affairs:
    Rejoice Mabhudafhasi
34. Minister of Women, Youth,
    Children and People with
    Disabilities: Noluthando
    Mayende-Sibiya

The New Provincial Premiers

Eastern Cape: Noxolo Kiviet
Free State: Ace Magashule
Gauteng: Nomvula Mokonyane
KwaZulu-Natal: Zweli Mkhize
Limpopo: Cassel Mathale
Mpumalanga: David Mabuza
Northern Cape: Hazel Jenkins
North West: Maureen Modiselle
Western Cape: Helen Zille

Profiles

Achmat, Zackie

Abdurazzack 'Zackie' Achmat is the HIV-positive gay who caused all the trouble – or at least started much of it, as far as South Africa's government has been concerned. Achmat is best known as a founder of the Treatment Action Campaign (TAC), the organisation which he set up in December 1998 to campaign for better treatment for people living with HIV. In combination with other activist groups such as the Aids Law Project, the TAC has been the gadfly driving the government towards the provision of antiretroviral drugs. Repeated use of legal action, mass mobilisation and the media in order to garner local and international support led the TAC to become one of the world's most prominent activist groups. In 2004 Achmat and the TAC were nominated for the Nobel Peace Prize.

A relentless campaign by civil society, including court action, helped to force pharmaceutical companies to drop the prices of antiretroviral drugs and other medications needed to treat or prevent opportunistic infections associated with HIV. As part of this campaign, Achmat flew to Thailand and brought thousands of generic capsules of the anti-fungal drug fluconazole into South Africa. He accurately calculated that his well-publicised action and arrest would focus so much attention on the price difference between brand-name and generic drugs that pharmaceutical companies would drop their prices.

The TAC was also at the forefront of the campaign to force government to supply antiretroviral therapy to HIV-positive pregnant women to reduce the chance that their babies would be infected with the virus during labour and birth. Ultimately the TAC won the long and bitter case that ended up at the Constitutional Court. In the process the South African government and in particular minister of health Manto Tshabalala-Msimang acquired

1

international notoriety for their opposition.

Achmat started his activist career at the age of 14 when, in 1976, he set fire to his school in protest against the apartheid government; that earned him a three-month spell in jail. By the time he was 18 he had been jailed four times for his political activism. The skills he learnt as an anti-apartheid activist came in useful later against the government he had helped to bring to power when he and his fellow campaigners in the TAC welded together an international coalition to raise awareness and funding, and to put political pressure on pharmaceutical companies and the South African government.

In 2007 Achmat was at the receiving end of human rights laws when he was accused of genocide. The charge was laid at the International Criminal Court in The Hague by Anthony Brink, a South African lawyer and strong opponent of the use of antiretroviral drugs.

Openly gay for many years, in 1994 Achmat helped found the National Coalition for Gay and Lesbian Equality (now the Lesbian and Gay Equality Project). This organisation played a role in ensuring that South Africa's laws against homosexuality were removed and that freedom from discrimination on the grounds of sexual orientation was enshrined in the Constitution.

Although HIV-positive, Achmat refused to take antiretroviral drugs until the government made them available through the public health sector. He held firm to this decision even as he grew steadily sicker and weaker, and despite a plea to change his mind during a bedside visit from former president Nelson Mandela. Achmat started to take antiretrovirals in August 2003 after the TAC's national congress voted for him to start treatment and shortly before the government started its mass roll-out of antiretroviral treatment.

Achmat was born in Cape Town. In 1993 he received a BA from the University of the Western Cape and in 2005 the same university awarded him an honorary doctorate. He also received an honorary MA from the University of Cape Town in 2002, and an honorary doctorate of laws from the University of Natal in 2003. He is currently studying for an MPhil in law. In 2003 Achmat was awarded the Nelson Mandela Award for Health and Human Rights, and the Jonathan Mann Award for Global Health and

Human Rights. He has received a range of other awards, including being named as one of *Time Europe*'s 'Heroes of 2003'. In March 2005 Achmat had a heart attack. He married his partner, Dalli Weyers, in January 2008.

Date of birth: March 21 1962

Bham, Ebrahim

Moulana Ebrahim Bham is a Muslim cleric and secretary-general of the Jamiatul Ulama (Council of Muslim Theologians), a faith-based organisation that serves the South African Muslim community. Since its establishment in 1923 in what was then Transvaal, the council has extended to six branches across the country and is regarded as the voice of authority on all things Islamic, ranging from what foods are permissible for Muslims to consume to Islamic finance.

Bham is a graduate of the Jamiatul Uloom-il-Islamiyyah in Karachi. He holds an MA in Islamic studies from the same institution and has lectured and published widely on Islam. While the Jamiatul Ulama is governed by *shari'ah* (Islamic law), he is regarded as a liberal theologian who actively promotes interfaith dialogue and Muslims' participation in civic affairs. He believes in the principle of unity in diversity and has emphasised that Muslims can be integrated into the wider South African society without compromising their religious identity. During his tenure, he has expanded the council's role to include addressing socioeconomic issues such as poverty, HIV/Aids and education.

Bham is an executive member of the Muslim Aids Programme and a founding member of the Johannesburg Muslim School. He is part of the National Religious Leaders' Forum, which promotes interaction between religious groups and government. The council is also active in international aid relief efforts for victims of war and natural disasters across the globe.

Historically, the council has worked hard to be an influential presence in South African politics. During apartheid, the council objected vehemently to the Group Areas Act. Since 1993, it has lobbied for the legal recognition of Muslim marriages under Muslim personal law. The council has also made its religious views known to government through memorandums on pornography, abortion and capital punishment. It has consistently expressed its support for Palestine and condemned the Israeli occupation.

Bham acknowledges the progressive nature of the Constitution, which he says allows South African Muslims the freedom of religious expression and practice that other countries do not enjoy. However, he remains a vocal critic of the government's inefficiency in tackling crime and corruption and in addressing socioeconomic inequality.

Despite the Jamiatul Ulama's progressive views on many topics, it has come under fire for some of its conservative stances. The council owns and manages Radio Islam, a Johannesburg-based radio station that broadcasts Islamic-related content across the continent. In 1998, a complaint was successfully lodged against the station for prohibiting women's voices on air, which the council argued was against Islamic law. The Independent Broadcasting Authority ruled against the council and the station had to amend its policy. It now has a strong female staff and listenership.

In 1996, the Jamiatul Ulama obtained an interdict against several South African newspapers to prevent them from republishing Danish cartoons depicting the Prophet Muhammad.

In the wake of 9/11 and the American war on terror, there have been increasing claims of South African Muslims being involved in terrorist activities. Muslim clerics have been deported while en route to international conferences and some have been added to US terror lists. Along with other Muslim leaders, Bham has repeatedly called for evidence of South African terrorist activity, saying that many wild claims have been made by those who have a 'divisive agenda against Islam'.

Date of birth: September 20 1961

Block, John

John Fikile Block has been overlooked for the premiership of the Northern Cape by Luthuli House. A Zuma man through and through, he was voted the party's provincial chairperson in 2008 amid political infighting – some of it physical – between supporters of Thabo Mbeki and Jacob Zuma. However, the party prioritised its gender imperatives and appointed a woman premier, Hazel Jenkins.

In recent years, Block's reputation has been muddied in controversy.

In 2003 he resigned from his position as transport MEC amid allegations of fraud. Critics contend that he used state money for various private trips to Cape Town, including a jaunt to the jazz festival, and irregularly awarded tender contracts. A 2004 audit of Northern Cape transport found that under Block's leadership consultants were paid over R2-million for a parliamentary village that was never built. However, in 2008 he was acquitted of all four counts of fraud and repaid the money spent on his jazz festival trip. The whistle-blower was charged with misconduct and fired. Block's resignation and cooperation in court proceedings were touted as strengthening the ANC 'because all of us have respect for the law', according to then-ANC provincial chairperson and future rival Neville Mompati.

Block has vociferously supported Jacob Zuma both in court and publicly. At Polokwane there was speculation that his appointment as provincial chairperson over the more popular outgoing chairperson, Mompati, an Mbeki supporter, had much to do with his position within the Zuma camp. In the end, Block won with 255 votes, and Mompati secured 136. Several incidents of violence arose between Block and Mompati supporters throughout the election, with Mompati supporters alleging that they were selectively arrested during protests.

Block completed his matric through Damelin, completed an executive management course at the University of Cape Town, and studied African literature and history at Khanya College.

In November 2008 he was appointed MEC for education during a reshuffle within the provincial cabinet. He has been faced with a large budget shortfall within the department. According to his personal assistant, 'When he took over, we were in a very precarious position with regard to our budget, but he's been able to see us back on course. We had to re-determine the head of department's contract and he's been relieved [i.e. fired]. We now have a new head of department.' Block has focused primarily on service delivery since his appointment as both MEC and provincial chairperson. 'The ANC must be able to speed up the issue of service delivery,' his assistant said. 'To address the issue of service delivery, the issue of finances must be addressed first.'

Date of birth: February 10 1968

Buthelezi, Mangosuthu

To understand the IFP's past, the travails of the present and the uncertainty around its future existence, one need look no further than to a single link on its website. Under the 'biographies' link on www.ifp.org.za there is just a single profile: that of party president, Dr Mangosuthu Buthelezi. Even three weeks before a national general election it hadn't been updated to include other members of the party's hierarchy.

Buthelezi has loomed large over the party he founded as a cultural liberation organisation, with the blessing of the ANC, in 1975. And his has been a feudalistic grip that has led to a myriad of problems. Sycophancy masked as traditional respect for Shenge has only reinforced his hold on the IFP. It has also created subterranean competition to get into, and stay in, his inner circle; consequently, party elders have taken their eye off the political ball, especially with regard to updating policy and being truly creative in broadening the IFP's national appeal. This had led, since 1994, to the party's steadily declining electoral fortunes.

A stifling of internal democracy has hindered the party's modernisation efforts and subsequently contributed to a succession vacuum: there is no heir apparent with a national profile, as yet. While Buthelezi has, on occasion, threatened to resign – once during a post-mortem of the 2004 national elections when the party came away with an abysmal 6% of the national vote – it is clear the intention was to have the opposite effect: to rally and consolidate support.

None have felt the crack of Buthelezi's authoritarian knobkierie more than Ziba Jiyane. The former secretary-general and national chairperson of the party was engaged in spearheading a Youth Brigade-supported reform process within the IFP, which gained momentum between 2003 and 2005, when it came to a shuddering halt. Jiyane was increasingly ostracised by his fellow executive committee members – at one point, reportedly, they refused to speak to him – before he left to form the National Democratic Convention in 2005.

Despite remaining the traditional African 'Big Man' within the IFP, Buthelezi has, in more recent years, attempted to rebrand himself before the national public as the elder statesman of South African politics.

After losing two children in 2005 to HIV/Aids-related illnesses, he defied popular stigma and publicly announced the causes of their deaths. During the internecine succession battle between then-ANC president Thabo Mbeki and his deputy Jacob Zuma, he cautioned against the use of ethnicity in their factional mobilisation – although perhaps that had more to do with the methodology perceived to be the sole preserve of the IFP.

In 2009, after the South African government had refused to grant the Dalai Lama a visa to attend a local peace conference, Buthelezi instituted court proceedings to force the government to change its decision.

Buthelezi, who, remarkably for a Zulu man, eats no red meat, retains the ability to be urbane and a consummate gentleman. But he hasn't lost an irascible, petulant streak – especially when pushed on issues, or when he believes that he has been cornered. He came close to a televised altercation with the KwaZulu-Natal (KZN) MEC for local government, Mike Mabuyakhulu, during a Freedom Day event in eMacambini in 2008. The provincial Cabinet had decided to make the position of chairperson of the House of Traditional Leaders a permanent one, forcing Buthelezi to choose between that post and his leadership of the IFP in the national Parliament. Already smarting because the department had undermined his traditional power base by paying indunas and building them houses, Buthelezi felt it was another attempt to corner him. He duly responded with sharp finger jabs and a mouthful for Mabuyakhulu on the VIP platform at the event.

Proud of his lineage, which on his maternal side can be traced back to King Cetshwayo, Buthelezi was born in Mahlabatini. He joined the ANC Youth League in the late 1940s while studying at the University of Fort Hare. There he met activists like Pan Africanist Congress founder Robert Sobukwe and future ANC leader Z.K. Matthews. After being expelled for participating in student boycotts, he completed his social science degree at the University of Natal.

In 1953 he assumed his position as chief and was installed as chief minister of the 'self-governing' territory of KwaZulu in 1976, but consistently declined to accept autonomy for the homeland. In the 1970s and early 1980s he was extremely litigious, suing publications for everything from commentary to headlines. His stamina is legendary: his speech at the opening of the KwaZulu Parliament in 1993, at 18 days, remains a *Guinness Book of Records* achievement.

During the June 1976 uprising he travelled to Soweto to calm Zulu-speaking hostel dwellers, who were threatening to rampage through the township. Decades later, after internecine township violence between IFP self-protection units and ANC self-defence units, witnesses at the Truth and Reconciliation Commission linked Buthelezi to death squads. The TRC report was also damning of Buthelezi, but whether he played any role in the events has never been fully investigated.

The IFP entered the first democratic elections in 1994 at the last minute and garnered 10.5% of the vote and, as part of the Government of National Unity, three Cabinet positions. Buthelezi served two terms as home affairs minister. He contended that his efforts to turn around the department were crippled by the insubordination of ANC members under him.

Date of birth: August 17 1928

Cameron, Edwin

Consistently described as the best legal mind of his generation, Edwin Cameron made the journey to the highest court in the land in just under 10 years. He was initially nominated and recommended by the Judicial Service Commission (JSC) in 1999, but had to contend with disappointment after deputy president Thabo Mbeki, concerned about the racial composition of the budding court, intervened and suggested that the Cape judge and Harvard law graduate Sandile Ngcobo be appointed instead.

The following year Cameron, then an acting judge in the Constitutional Court and the first openly gay judge to declare he was living with HIV, went for the jugular at an Aids conference and criticised Mbeki's stance on HIV/Aids. He also vehemently criticised the Mbeki administration's failure to provide drugs timeously for people living with HIV. Later that year Cameron was elevated to the Supreme Court of Appeal, where he spent just under a decade accumulating a wealth of experience which he believes will stand him in good stead in his new role at the Constitutional Court.

In 2008, when nominations opened for a replacement for Eastern

Cape judge Tholakele Madala, Cameron was reluctant to make himself available for the position, saying he felt that he would not be elevated to the court while Mbeki was still president. But after much nudging from legal professionals and friends from across the race spectrum, he relented. He was interviewed in October in Cape Town but had to wait a little longer when the JSC failed to make an appointment after two other candidates withdrew from the race and disagreements surfaced in the JSC over the suitability of a third candidate. The situation also took a different turn on the political front when Mbeki was recalled by the ruling ANC and the party's deputy president, Kgalema Motlanthe, stepped in as caretaker South African president. The JSC eventually re-interviewed Cameron in Johannesburg in December 2008 and Motlanthe appointed Cameron to the highest court in the land on the eve of 2009.

Cameron was born in Pretoria and attended Pretoria Boys' High School. After landing an Anglo American scholarship, he pursued a BA degree in law and followed this up with honours in Latin at Stellenbosch University, both conferred with distinction. He briefly lectured in Latin and classical studies at the same institution before heading off to Oxford University on a Rhodes Scholarship in 1976. He continued to excel there, passing his studies with first class honours and bagging the law school's jurisprudence prize and the coveted Vinerian Scholarship given by Oxford to the best student in civil law.

He then enrolled with Unisa for his LLB, graduated with distinction again and was awarded the Johannes Voet Medal for best law graduate. He joined the Bar in 1983 and, three years later, moved to the University of the Witwatersrand's Centre for Applied Legal Studies. In 1989 he was appointed a professor of law at Wits and continued his work defending the defenceless in apartheid South Africa, including work on an HIV/Aids policy for the National Union of Mineworkers. He later founded the Aids Law Project, based at Wits University and tasked with taking up court cases on behalf of those afflicted with HIV/Aids.

He was closely involved in the submissions made by the gay and lesbian community at the multi-party negotiations in Kempton Park for a democratic South Africa and delivered a seminal paper that paved the way for equality in sexual orientation to be recognised in the new Constitution.

Cameron first acted as judge in the Johannesburg High Court in 1994 after becoming senior counsel; he also chaired a commission on illegal arms transactions instituted by former president Nelson Mandela. He became a permanent judge at the Johannesburg High Court in 1995 and was appointed to the Supreme Court of Appeal in 2000. A formidable lawyer with a wealth of experience, Cameron will be under consideration when the issue of leadership of the Constitutional Court comes up later in 2009.

Date of birth: February 15 1953

Chabane, Collins

As Limpopo minister of economic development, environment and tourism, Collins Chabane could have been the obvious choice for the position of premier after Sello Moloto, given his track record in the provincial government. But his election to the ANC's powerful national executive committee (NEC) and national working committee (NWC) automatically pushed him out of provincial politics and into the powerful post of minister in the presidency responsible for performance monitoring as well as administration.

A modest politician, Chabane is credited with driving Limpopo's economic growth to 6.5% after he took over as economic affairs minister in 2005. Under his leadership, Limpopo managed to attract prominent investors in the mining, agriculture, tourism and agribusiness sectors, which resulted in the creation of job opportunities in the poverty-stricken province. Eskom's R26-billion investment, which will see the power utility build its first power station since the 1980s near Lephalale in Limpopo, is but one of Chabane's success stories in his tenure as economic affairs minister.

Born in the dusty village of Xikundu in Venda, Chabane joined the ANC underground at the early age of 17 and went into exile in May 1980. In 1984 he was arrested and served six years on Robben Island for furthering the aims of a banned organisation. He joined ANC structures upon his release, serving the party in what was then the Northern Transvaal as provincial secretary until 1998. He was also a member of the ANC's provincial working committee, chair of its provincial disciplinary committee and political education group, and a member of the provincial constitutional committee.

After the 1994 elections, Chabane was elected to serve as an MP in the National Assembly, where he participated in the constitutional committee, joint committee on defence and intelligence, and the standing committees on finance and minerals and energy affairs.

In 1997 Chabane was sent back to Limpopo, where he was appointed an MEC in the office of the premier. A year later, he was named provincial minister of public works and leader of government business in the provincial legislature. One of Chabane's highlights as MEC for public works was the establishment of the Road Agency, the first institution of its kind in South Africa. Through this initiative, the provincial department managed to fast-track the upgrading of roads in the province. He also established Gundo Lashu, a labour-intensive road construction programme, which is seen as a local model for the current national Expanded Public Works Programme. Under Chabane's leadership, the Limpopo public works department won an award for the best provincial department in 2001 from the parliamentary standing committee on public accounts, the auditor-general and Absa Bank.

A former chancellor of Mbulaheni Rammano Training College in Venda, Chabane was elected on to the ANC's NEC during the party's watershed conference in Polokwane in 2007. Apart from membership of the NEC and NWC, Chabane also chairs the party's constitutional affairs subcommittee, and serves on the ANC's national deployment committee and the economic transformation subcommittee.

A trained aircraft technician, Chabane taught himself to play jazz while imprisoned on Robben Island.

Date of birth: April 15 1960

Coetzee, Ryan

Ryan Coetzee is not the most popular person in the Democratic Alliance (DA), but he is one of the brightest and most effective. To be fair, it was always going to be difficult for him: appointed as the party's strategy chief in his mid-20s by DA leader Tony Leon, and responsible for directing people many years his senior, he had to overcome some considerable resistance as he set about enacting Leon's plans to seduce and destroy the National Party.

It probably didn't help that he countered his critics with a brashness that seemed all too closely modelled on Leon's own, sometimes abrasive style, without the gravitas that the party leader brought to bear. He may have got up people's noses, but few contest that he was effective, building an exceptionally efficient spin operation, gathering the best polling data in local politics, and consolidating the white opposition vote behind the DA.

He is unrepentant about the party's infamous 'Fight back' campaign, pointing out that it achieved what was required at the time, the ultimate collapse of the National Party. And despite the fact that he was a crucial Leon lieutenant, he went out ahead of the changes in the party in 2006 with a strategy document that charted the path followed by Helen Zille once she took over from Leon. This paper argued that the DA had failed to attract black support in part because it had not taken cognisance of the depth of the wounds inflicted by apartheid. The policies might be right, he suggested, but the tone was all wrong – too combative, too dismissive of the terrible legacy of pain bequeathed by institutionalised racism. Deep and thorough changes were essential, Coetzee argued.

Now at the ripe old age of 36, he has been the DA's CEO for four years and an effective MP for five. But he has been involved in DA politics for far longer. At the University of Cape Town, where he earned a BA and an HDipEd, he was chairperson of the Democratic Party (DP) Youth and served on the DP's national council and regional executive. In 1993 he was already writing speeches for Leon. He went on briefly to teach but soon returned to politics.

These days, he has to help hold together an organisation that is far from united behind Zille's project of creating a non-racial, liberal opposition. He is surely helped in that by the fact that he is no longer simply one of 'Tony's cronies', and that he now has a decade of experience at the top of the party.

Zille, who sometimes seems isolated, and far out ahead of the rest of the party in her ambition to make it a viable choice for far more South Africans, needs all the enforcement help she can get as she insists on promoting relative outsiders to senior positions and maintaining a very different dialogue with civil society, the media and government from that of her predecessor. Coetzee, who is adept at managing expectations, surely knows that in the short term this project can only fail, and that its success between now and the 2011 municipal elections can best be measured by the extent to which the party is able to lay the groundwork for real change.

The Congress of the People presents powerful challenges – and opportunities – for the DA. If anyone can figure out how best to take advantage of them, it is Ryan Coetzee, backroom operator par excellence. **Date of birth:** January 8 1973

Cronin, Jeremy

Jeremy Cronin occupies an awkward position in the 'new' ANC.

Pushed to the margins of influence by Thabo Mbeki, and keenly aware that it could not survive outside the tripartite alliance, the South African Communist Party (SACP) has returned from the wilderness to the commanding heights in the vanguard of Jacob Zuma's campaign for the presidency. As deputy general secretary of the SACP, Cronin now finds himself defending some of the sleazier power plays of the post-Polokwane era. Everything in Cronin's background and record suggests that he must have deep misgivings about Zuma and some of those surrounding him, but he seems to hope against hope that the real policy shifts articulated at Polokwane will ultimately take effect, and that the Zuma project will give way to a left-democratic project.

There is no mistaking the deep contradiction that is now evident between Cronin's unquestioned reputation as a scrupulously ethical person and enormously hard-working, competent politician and some of the positions he has taken since Mbeki's defeat. That contradiction is only sharpened by the fact that he is a fine lyric poet and one of the few genuine intellectuals who remain in the upper ranks of the tripartite alliance.

Many of his friends and supporters in the ANC, the media and civil society were prepared to forgive him his public role in the excommunication from the SACP of Cosatu dissident Willie Madisha. He had to ensure, the charitable interpretation went, that the sensible left maintained some influence at a time when SACP general secretary Blade Nzimande, Cosatu president Zwelinzima Vavi and their acolytes were throwing themselves headlong into populism. The only way he could do so behind the scenes, it was suggested, was to make sure that he acted like a 'disciplined cadre' in public.

This explanation became harder to sustain in the immediate run-up to the April 2009 elections, when he wrote an appallingly revisionist op-ed defence of the government's decision to deny a visa to the Dalai Lama. 'Debunking the Dalai Lama' was factually unsound and extraordinarily crude, particularly coming from a gentle and thoughtful man who sacrificed seven of the best years of his life to imprisonment after his conviction in 1976 on terrorism charges for producing underground newsletters.

Less obvious, but equally worrying, is his signature careful prose in SACP statements backing the increasingly anti-democratic positions of the Zuma-led ANC. Even some of his staunchest fans now feel he is lending his intellectual dignity to a project that is otherwise bereft of it, and that it is his desire for a Cabinet post that drives him.

Cronin's appointment as deputy transport minister is a step below what he is capable of. He is hugely knowledgeable on the subject, and genuinely cares about it, which is why his transport portfolio committee in Parliament has been among the most effective in the legislature. He boldly took on the government to oppose the wasteful and grandiose Gautrain project and the chaos at the Road Accident Fund. He knows that public transport can be both socially and economically transformative, and it is clearly an area in which leftish policies of massive state support are critical.

Cronin joined the SACP at the University of Cape Town (UCT); he earned a BA there, and a master's degree at the Sorbonne in Paris, before returning to UCT to lecture in the philosophy department. In the mid-1980s, released from prison, he was active in the United Democratic Front but eventually went into exile, first in London, then in Lusaka, returning to South Africa in time to be involved in the SACP's contribution to the Codesa multi-party negotiations.

Although his willingness to help drape a negligé of respectability over the naked unpleasantness of the Zuma–Nzimande cabal is disturbing, he

remains one of the country's most talented politicians.
Date of birth: September 12 1949

Dandala, Mvume

Congress of the People (Cope) presidential candidate Mvumelwano 'Mvume' Dandala was not widely known to the South African public before the new political party chose him to be the face of its election campaign. A former bishop of the Methodist Church of Southern Africa, Dandala has a strong reputation within the churches as a peacemaker and vocal supporter of social justice.

His reputation as a virtuous man is believed to be the main reason behind Cope's decision to nominate him as a presidential candidate in a society whose morals were said to be declining. Political analysts describe him as an honest, trustworthy and highly skilled leader. Dandala exchanged the pulpit for politics just after he returned from Kenya, where he was general secretary of the All Africa Conference of Churches based in Nairobi.

The former cleric enjoys what many consider a disturbingly close relationship with former president Thabo Mbeki. A political analyst from the University of Cape Town once described Dandala as 'Mbeki's street-fighting sidekick in Southern African church politics'. Those who know him say Dandala, just like Mbeki, can be brutal when dealing with those who disagree with him.

Dandala ran into initial resistance when he was brought to Cope, as its president, Mosiuoa Lekota, and his supporters questioned why the new party needed a face other than its president for the elections.

During apartheid, Dandala was, together with some of his church colleagues, involved in the liberation struggle through his ministry to the people. When he was a young man pursuing his studies at the Federal Theological Seminary in Alice, Dandala became the local chairperson of the South African Students' Organisation (Saso). During this time he took an interest in developing programmes to assist communities with basic amenities such as building dams, school and clinics. He was the first black minister in South Africa to be pastor of a multi-racial congregation, in Empangeni, KwaZulu-Natal, from 1978 to 1982.

He then became superintendent of the north circuit of the Methodist Church in Port Elizabeth, at the time the largest circuit of the Methodist Church of Southern Africa. Here Dandala participated in reconciliation ministries among warring political factions. When the apartheid government declared a state of emergency in 1985 he was detained without trial.

Dandala was one of the ministers who launched the Malihambe Missions, whose policy was to send black and white ministers to work in pairs. His mediation and conflict resolution skills were in great demand during the political transition in the 1990s. He was at the forefront of helping to reduce violence in order to create an atmosphere in which elections could take place peacefully. This led – in the years directly after the 1994 elections – to his critical role in the disarmament of the ANC's self-defence units and the Inkatha Freedom Party's self-protection units, which were turning many townships into battlegrounds.

In 2002 Dandala received the National Order of the Baobab, silver category, for his role in the struggle against apartheid. Critics saw this, however, as a friendly reward from Mbeki for officiating at his inauguration in 1999. He has been compared to Mbeki in the way he speaks and carries himself – rational, soft-spoken, calm and intellectually engaging when he makes a point.

Dandala holds a diploma in theology from the John Wesley College of the Federal Theological Seminary and BA and MA degrees in theology from the University of Cambridge. In 2003 the University of Transkei granted him an honorary PhD and in 2005 he received another honorary doctorate in theology from Cameroon's Protestant University.

Born in Mount Ayliff, he is the son of the Rev. Killion Dandala, a Methodist minister in the small village of Dandalaville – named after his great-grandfather – in the Eastern Cape. Dandala's son is actor and television presenter Hlomla Dandala, one of the first celebrities to publicly support Cope when it was formed. His lawyer niece Thobeka Dandala was a founding member of Cope's leadership institute, the Cope College. His daughter Gqibelo Dandala works as an administrator at the United Democratic Movement's head office in Pretoria.

Date of birth: October 26 1951

De Lille, Patricia

Known for her passion on the topic of the multi-billion-rand arms deal and her strong disapproval of corruption in government, Patricia de Lille, the leader of the Independent Democrats (ID), has been prominent on the country's political scene for over 20 years.

She began in the trade union movement, joining the South African Chemical Workers' Union when working as a laboratory assistant for Plascon Paints in Epping, Cape Town, and in 1988 she was named national vice-chair of the National Council of Trade Unions.

She had joined the Pan Africanist Congress (PAC) early on, and in 1990 she was elected on to the party's national executive; she led the PAC's delegation in the constitutional negotiations that brought about South Africa's first democratic elections in 1994.

In October 1997 she read out in Parliament the names of ANC MPs who, she said, had spied for the National Party government. That bold act, relying on parliamentary privilege, led to a 15-day suspension and a court case – which she won. And she was the first MP to raise the alarm over the arms deal, a move which did not add to her popularity among many of her fellow parliamentarians, but which won her praise outside that august body.

De Lille broke away from the PAC in March 2003 and formed the ID, which won seats in Parliament and in the Western Cape provincial legislature for its first time round.

Born in Beaufort West, she was the third eldest of seven children, and matriculated from the local Bastiaanse High School. She has not had an easy run and has made a point of coming to the aid of the most vulnerable South Africans – women, children, people living with HIV. In one extraordinary case, she successfully approached the courts to improve the conditions of juveniles detained in appalling, overcrowded conditions at Pollsmoor Prison – even though one of the youths in question had murdered her sister.

But although her major image is of a clean and independent fighter, De Lille has come in for her fair share of criticism. She was accused of nepotism when her sister Sarah Paulse, who was said to be 'politically ignorant', was handed one of the ID's three seats in the provincial legislature, even though she had been ninth on the party's list. And there were other issues of dissatisfaction: disgruntled former ID members said that she ran the party in a 'dictatorial and undemocratic' manner, in direct contrast with the image of transparency and accountability on which she had grounded her party. De Lille refused to comment on the allegations, but told reporters that the dissenters had been fired from the party for fraud and corruption.

She has developed a significant public profile through appearances on television, in newspapers and on visits to informal settlements in the Western Cape, and has received a number of awards, including the *Rapport/City Press* Woman of the Year award. She has been chancellor of the Durban Institute of Technology, is an honorary colonel in the South African National Defence Force, and serves on the boards of the African Monitor, the Helen Suzman Foundation, the Nelson Mandela Children's Fund, Nazareth House and the Western Cape region of the National Association of People Living with Aids.

Date of birth: February 17 1951

Dlamini, Sdumo

Well known for his sharp tongue and strong support for Jacob Zuma, Sdumo Dlamini wasn't always the proud leader we see today. Dlamini was born in a rural village in Swaziland. His father died of TB when he was only four. Following his father's death the family moved to South Africa. Young Sdumo was forced to abandon his siSwati language, as he would not be accepted at school; he had to learn to speak isiZulu before entering school in South Africa.

His life began to change in 1984 when at the age of 17 he took a leading role in the first strike at his high school challenging corporal punishment, the system of education and the abuse of the school funds and fees. He only discovered, months later, that the strike had been spearheaded by ANC underground operatives when many of his comrades were arrested and detained.

From 1986 to 1988 he trained as a nurse, the first man in his area to opt for that profession. Failing to find a job, he moved to Durban and found work at Prince Mshiyeni Memorial Hospital in a KwaZulu government hospital. He later studied for diplomas in general nursing and midwifery.

He joined the National Education Health and Allied Workers' Union (Nehawu). Elected a shop steward, he later led six major strikes at the hospital, and moved up to become chairperson, first at branch level, then at provincial level.

In 2000 he was elected Cosatu provincial chairperson and six years later first deputy president. He also served on the provincial executive and provincial working committees of the South African Communist Party. He formally joined the ANC in 1990 and participates in its community programmes.

Following the decision to remove Willie Madisha, Sdumo Dlamini was unanimously elected to serve as Cosatu president until the 10th national congress planned for September 2009.

Date of birth: March 2 1966

Dlamini-Zuma, Nkosazana

Home affairs minister Nkosazana Dlamini-Zuma is one of the most successful but least popular women in South African politics. Her aggressive, no-nonsense personality and tough management style haven't gained her many bosom buddies in government. Instead, she has earned a few notorious nicknames, including Godzuma, based on the Japanese movie monster Godzilla, which destroys everything in its path.

Her entry into government was paved during her youth. She was strongly influenced by the Black Consciousness Movement but became an active member of the ANC while studying medicine at the University of Natal, from which she obtained a BSc in zoology and botany.

In 1976 her underground ANC activities attracted the government's attention and she moved to England. While abroad, she continued to juggle her ANC activism with her education. She completed her medical degree at the University of Bristol in 1978 and worked in hospitals across Britain.

The ANC sent her to southern Africa in the 1980s. She served as the movement's Florence Nightingale, addressing the medical needs of ANC cadres in Swaziland and Zambia while also developing post-apartheid health policy. While working in Mbabane Hospital in Swaziland, she met

Jacob Zuma, whom she married in 1982 and then divorced in 1997.

When she returned from exile in 1990 she played a leading role in negotiations for a democratic, non-racial South Africa. Given her medical expertise and political contribution to the ANC, it was no surprise that Nelson Mandela appointed her the country's health minister in 1994. She was successful in this role: under her direction, the country rapidly introduced free health care for pregnant women and children under six years, and implemented some of the world's toughest anti-tobacco legislation.

However, in 1995 she was embroiled in controversy over financial irregularities relating to the multi-million-dollar anti-Aids musical, *Sarafina II*. Zuma and key members in her department were investigated for corruption but she was cleared of all charges in 1999. In June that year she was appointed foreign affairs minister in then-president Thabo Mbeki's Cabinet.

Dlamini-Zuma has been faced with personal dilemmas in her career, which she has handled with integrity. She dismissed rumours that Mbeki offered her the position of deputy president after he fired her former husband. However, in the run-up to the 2007 Polokwane conference, Dlamini-Zuma was touted as the next president of South Africa if the party chose to elect a consensus candidate. It could have materialised had Mbeki and Jacob Zuma not chosen to fight to the bitter end – she had the support of the Mbeki camp, the ANC Women's League and even her former husband's backers.

During her nine years in office, Dlamini-Zuma has focused on improving relations with international and African communities. She has prioritised Mbeki's vision for an African renaissance and led the launch of the African Union in South Africa. She has also headed numerous peacekeeping missions in Lesotho, the Democratic Republic of Congo and Comoros. One of her priorities is tackling poverty and racism, which she highlighted strongly at the 2001 World Conference on Racism.

Her resolute support for Mbeki's soft diplomacy on Zimbabwe remains the most glaring blunder of her career. She has said that South Africa would 'never' condemn the Zimbabwean government. 'It is never going to happen as long as this government is in power,' she told journalists. A fiercely loyal Mbeki-ite, she has shared the flak for failing to take action against Zimbabwean president Robert Mugabe and for expressing support for his Zanu-PF party. She has also been criticised for positions South Africa has taken at the United Nations, siding with repressive regimes. South Africa's refusal to grant the Dalai Lama a visa in March 2009 was reportedly her decision.

Date of birth: January 27 1949

Duarte, Jessie

Jessie Duarte has been an activist during most of her adult life. A member of the activist Dangor family from Newclare, Johannesburg, she was much involved in the Mass Democratic Movement. She has long been a gender activist. She was an official of the Federation of Transvaal Women, and a member of the Southern Transvaal executive of the United Democratic Front in the late 1980s, and was repeatedly detained and restricted.

When Nelson Mandela was released, she served as one of his aides, but after 1994 she went into the new Gauteng provincial government as MEC for safety and security and spent much of her tenure promoting the concept of community policing forums.

She has been high commissioner to Mozambique and chief director for multilateral relations in Africa at the foreign affairs department but is now likely to be a near-permanent fixture at ANC headquarters, Luthuli House. Close to foreign affairs minister Nkosazana Dlamini-Zuma, Duarte rapidly changed sides from Thabo Mbeki to Jacob Zuma at the ANC conference at Polokwane in 2007 and so secured her political career.

Since that conference, Duarte, a member of the ANC's national executive committee, has achieved a new prominence as the party's national spokesperson. Her job keeps her on radio and television and in print every day. It's an often difficult task and Duarte is a defensive and prickly spokesperson. Privately, she is warm and articulate but feels that the media is so anti-ANC that she appears to be constantly on the attack.

Date of birth: September 19 1953

Ebrahim, Ebrahim

Beyond ANC president Jacob Zuma's coterie of advisers, hangers-on and wannabes, Ebrahim Ismail Ebrahim remains an influential member of a select inner circle. A veteran in foreign affairs, he is one of two deputy ministers of international relations and cooperation, along with Sue van der Merwe. The unobtrusive, quietly spoken Ebrahim is also coordinator for international relations at the party's Luthuli House headquarters. Together with the likes of ANC KwaZulu-Natal chairperson Zweli Mkhize and South African Communist Party general secretary Blade Nzimande, he is one of Zuma's most trusted lieutenants.

His relationship with Zuma was forged on Robben Island, where they shared a cell for 10 years. Ebrahim had joined Umkhonto weSizwe on its formation in 1961 and was serving a 15-year sentence after being found guilty of sabotage during the 1963 Natal sabotage trial. He had been tried with 18 others, including the late Billy Nair, after a spate of attacks on government installations had rocked the province.

After his release in 1979, Ebrahim was banned and his movements restricted to Durban. He left the country to continue working for the ANC in the frontline states bordering South Africa. In December 1986 he was kidnapped by South African security forces in Swaziland and brought back to the country. He was detained and tortured before being sentenced to another 20 years on Robben Island – this time, for high treason. He was released in 1991 and elected onto the ANC's national executive committee and its powerful national working committee.

During the Codesa talks to create a democratic South Africa, he was tasked with forming the umbrella Patriotic Front that brought together participating progressive civic, cultural, political and religious organisations in an attempt to reach consensus over the negotiations.

Ebrahim was elected an MP in 1994. In 1997 he was appointed the chairperson of Parliament's foreign affairs committee and also sat on the joint select committee on intelligence. He resigned from Parliament in 2002 to join the office of deputy president Zuma as a senior political and economic adviser. He has been, more or less, shadowing Zuma ever since.

Ebrahim was part of Zuma's mediation teams involved in brokering peace in Burundi (between 2002 and 2005) and in the withdrawal of

Rwandan troops from the Democratic Republic of Congo in 2002. Unassuming, but a skilled negotiator, he has also been involved in peace efforts in Kosovo and Sri Lanka.

Born in Durban, he holds both a BA and a BComm from Unisa. He was involved in the campaign that adopted the Freedom Charter in 1955. **Date of birth:** July 1 1937

February, Judith

Judith February thinks it is impossible to grow up in Cape Town 'without some sense that it is somewhat different to the rest of the country, not only in racial composition – though that too is changing – but also in people's attitudes towards politics and change'. This is perhaps the major reason that sparked her early interest in politics; ultimately, she was moved to want to contribute in some way to public discourse.

February is an all-professional woman and prefers to keep her personal life out of public view. Born in Cape Town, where she lives and works, February was admitted as an attorney in 1996 and practised law in Cape Town until 2000. She obtained her LLM in commercial law in 2000 from the University of Cape Town, where she had obtained her BA (law) and LLB degrees.

Since June 2000 she has been working at the Institute for Democracy in South Africa (Idasa), where she is the manager of the governance unit within the Political Information and Monitoring Service. The unit is tasked with monitoring the performance of South Africa's political institutions, with a focus on government, including corruption and its impact on governance, parliamentary oversight, constitutional law monitoring and institutional design. Members of the unit, including February, also write general political analysis for a number of publications.

February does consultative work for a New York-based group as part of the Stability Index on 25 developing countries. She is a member of the Council for Higher Education task team on academic freedom. February also sits on the boards of the Goedgedacht Forum for Social Reflection and the Parliamentary Monitoring Group.

'The law', she says, 'cannot be easily divorced from politics but it is important that the politicians show restraint when criticising judges and judgments.' February believes 'some of the rhetoric in recent years regarding judges and the courts has been unhealthy and unhelpful . . . and if left unchecked has the ability to undermine the judiciary. The court has a fundamental role to play in protecting the vulnerable in society . . .', especially in a young democracy like South Africa.

She has a modest vision of making some contribution to creative ways of writing and thinking about solutions to many of our democratic challenges. However, having spent a considerable amount of time dedicated to the importance of effective legislative oversight of the executive for socio-economic delivery and on monitoring the government's multi-billion-rand arms deal, February is sure to become central to any worthwhile analysis and discussion of the immediate future of South African politics.

Date of birth: October 8 1971

Gevisser, Mark

Mark Gevisser is the author of *The Dream Deferred*, former president Thabo Mbeki's biography, and winner of the 2008 Alan Paton Award. Gevisser is a graduate of Yale University, where he read comparative literature. After graduating, he worked in New York, writing for the *Village Voice* and *The Nation* before returning to South Africa in 1990, when the transition process had gathered pace with the release of Nelson Mandela.

Gevisser's analysis regularly appears in the *Mail & Guardian*, the *Sunday Independent, New York Times, Vogue* and other publications. One critic described his work as 'carefully researched and brilliant' and replete with probing psychological insight. Another analyst described him as the 'best scholar on Mbeki'.

One writer, referring to his biography of Mbeki, noted that it masquerades 'as a biography of one man, [yet] Mark Gevisser's book is in fact the best history we have thus far of South Africa's black intelligentsia. It is a national treasure.' Gevisser's former research assistant, George Ogola, now teaching journalism at the University of Central Lancashire, enthused that Gevisser 'overflows with confidence, [is] highly intelligent and yet distinctly unassuming. He is highly focused almost to a fault and a stickler for detail when working on something.'

Besides *The Dream Deferred*, Gevisser has also published two other books – *Defiant Desire: Gay and Lesbian Lives in South Africa*, a volume he co-edited with Edwin Cameron, recently appointed as a Constitutional Court judge, and *Portraits of Power: Profiles in a Changing South Africa*, a collection of his profiles that first appeared in the *Mail & Guardian*. A new book, *The Second Transition*, is due for publication late in 2009.

Gevisser has worked in film as a producer, scriptwriter and researcher. Some of his scripts were shortlisted for South African Film and Television and iEmmy awards. He co-produced a documentary with Greta Schiller, *The Man Who Drove with Mandela*, which won the Teddy Documentary Prize at the Berlin Film Festival in 1999. The film is about Cecil Williams, a South African gay and communist theatre director.

Gevisser is the founder of Trace, a heritage research and design company, and since 2002 he has worked in heritage development. He was joint head of the team that developed the heritage, education and tourism components of Constitution Hill, seat of the Constitutional Court, and he is the co-curator of the Hill's permanent exhibitions.

He also works as a political analyst and his clients include local and international organisations and companies.

Date of birth: November 11 1964

Goldstein, Warren

When South Africa's former chief rabbi retired after 17 years, the Union of Orthodox Synagogues made a surprising move in selecting a relatively inexperienced young rabbi – then only 32 years old – to lead the Jewish community.

Rabbi Warren Goldstein is the son of High Court judge Ezra Goldstein. At 17 he began his seven years of rabbinical studies at the Yeshiva Gedola in Johannesburg. At the same time he pursued a BA in law and philosophy through Unisa.

In 1996 he was ordained as a rabbi and completed his LLB through Unisa. He then began practising as a rabbi and studied towards his PhD at the University of the Witwatersrand's law school. His PhD thesis, which compared Western and Jewish law, later formed the basis of a book titled *Defending the Human Spirit: Jewish Law's Vision for a Moral Society*.

In addition to his community obligations, as chief rabbi Goldstein provides macro leadership to the Jewish community. He is an executive on the National Religious Leaders' Forum whose representatives, from various religious organisations, gather regularly to engage with government on issues of common relevance. The body also meets with the country's president twice a year.

Goldstein, who calls responsibility the basis of morality, views the Bill of Responsibilities, a document developed in association with the national department of education, as one of the successes of this forum. Based on the Bill of Rights, it outlines the responsibilities of South African citizens towards government and each other. The document, which has come under fire for its religious overtones and the omission of certain elements of the Bill of Rights, is undergoing curriculum development and will be incorporated into the 'life orientation' syllabus to be taught to high school students.

In October 2006 Goldstein, along with other stakeholders, established the Community Active Patrol, a Johannesburg-based anti-crime project for reducing contact crime. According to Goldstein, the aim of the project – which includes a call centre linked to police and armed response – is to allow people to reclaim public spaces without fear for their personal security, instead of retreating back into private spaces. He says the project has reduced contact crime drastically in the areas in which it functions.

For the chief rabbi, the Judaic principle of *tikkun olam* – or fixing the world – is made possible through a combination of dialogue and practical solutions. In 2007 he launched a discussion forum titled 'Enriching Tomorrow: Sharing Ideas for the Future', to which he invites prominent guests to share ideas on what the country needs in order to flourish. Former speakers include Graça Machel, Mamphela Ramphele, Ebrahim Rasool and Jacob Zuma.

Goldstein is a strong supporter of Zionism and the state of Israel, which has brought him into conflict with pro-Palestinian groups, such as the Palestine Solidarity Committee and the trade union federation Cosatu, as well as a section of the South African Jewish community which, although strongly supporting the right of Israel to exist, is critical of some of the actions the state uses to secure its survival.

Date of birth: June 21 1971

Gordhan, Pravin

For more than a decade, Pravin Jamnadas Gordhan collected the money that oiled the wheels of government. Now, as finance minister, he can have a say in how to spend it.

Gordhan, commissioner of the South African Revenue Service (Sars) since 1998, has arguably been the best in the country's history. His department has been so efficient at shaking money out of South Africa's corporate and individual taxpayers that – until this year, when it fell slightly short – it has beaten the minister's target year after year. Gordhan is credited with a range of innovations that have made this possible; prominent among them is a structure devolving authority and accountability throughout the organisation.

A year before he was appointed, Inland Revenue and Customs and Excise were combined into a new department. Gordhan established anti-smuggling teams and built close links with the country's neighbours in the Southern African Development Community in an attempt to halt the constant flow of untaxed goods across South Africa's porous borders. These operations were so successful that Gordhan was elected, and thereafter repeatedly re-elected, chairperson of the World Customs Organisation.

To improve the collection of taxes, Sars opened service centres throughout the country, with staff primed to answer taxpayers' queries. Separate compliance centres were set up to handle audits and investigations. Computerisation has not only made it easier to spot tax dodgers but has transformed the way taxpayers hand over their hard-earned cash. Like the banking sector, Sars, under Gordhan, has shown a great affection for cyberspace. The department encourages taxpayers to fill out returns with its eFiling ('e@sy filing') software and to use internet banking facilities for payment.

The job of Sars commissioner was not such a giant leap for a man trained as a pharmacist; both tasks require an eye for detail, a gift for precision. Born in Durban, Gordhan earned a bachelor's degree in pharmacy from the University of Durban-Westville and went to work at the King Edward VIII Hospital. At the same time, he was active in the Natal Indian Congress and the Durban Housing Action Committee, which became part of the South African National Civic Organisation. Repeated detentions cost him his job but not his activism; he continued working both under ground, for the South African Communist Party, and above ground, in the United Democratic Front.

In 1990 he was arrested and charged with treason for his involvement in the ANC's Operation Vula, according to which senior ANC officials in exile were sent back to South Africa to link up with activists inside the country. A year later, having been granted amnesty, he chaired the management committee at the Codesa negotiations which established a democratic South Africa; in 1993 he was co-chairman of the Transitional Executive Council set up to supervise national elections and install the new government; and in 1994 he went to Parliament, where he was chair of the constitutional committee. Three years later, he was drafted to the newly constituted Sars as deputy commissioner and in 1999 he was named commissioner.

His elevation to the finance ministry may come as a relief to hard-pressed taxpayers. Only weeks before his new job was announced, he was talking about the 'sponginess in the South African fiscal system' and was clearly working out ways of expressing just a bit more.

Date of birth: April 12 1949

Hanekom, Derek

Derek Hanekom has always been a 'son of the soil', and has a deep passion for agriculture and land. His views on agriculture are seen as supporting the ANC's Polokwane declaration to revive a struggling rural economy. He has been in and out of Cabinet since 1994.

Hanekom started off his career in the Cabinet two years after 1994, after the National Party (NP) left the Government of National Unity. The NP's Kraai van Niekerk had filled the portfolio and Hanekom stepped into the void. The portfolio suited him perfectly. Prior to the ANC coming to power he had been the architect of the ANC's draft land reform policy and had been pushing for land reform and especially restitution. Before 1994 he spent four years as coordinator of the ANC's agriculture desk.

During his term as minister, he oversaw a number of land reform bills. When his controversial Extension of Security of Tenure Act – which granted tenure to farm labourers and was hated by many commercial farmers – was adopted in 1997, he broke into a jive in Parliament, and one newspaper labelled him the 'minister of toyi-toyi'.

Hanekom has always been seen as a champion of the rural world. It was his vision to promote sustainable subsistence farming, rather than pushing commercial farming, that made him unpopular with the Mbeki regime. His successor, Thoko Didiza, was much more in line with Mbeki's policy, and Hanekom was shifted out of Cabinet in 1999 shortly after Mbeki took office.

As an ordinary MP he still pursued rural land issues vigorously and was quite vocal on the agricultural and land affairs portfolio committee. He also used his free time to study for a master's degree in agricultural economics at the University of Pretoria. He was appointed a deputy minister in 2004, and has worked hard in his portfolio of science and technology. Hanekom's return to his old passion of agriculture under a Zuma government was widely touted, but it did not happen.

Hanekom worked on a kibbutz in Israel where he learned the trade of farming. His first arrest came after participating in a peaceful candlelight demonstration at John Vorster Square police headquarters in Johannesburg in 1976. A decade later, he served three years in prison for leaking information to the ANC about South African Defence Force support for the Mozambican rebel movement Renamo. Although the official charge was illegal possession of secret state documents, Hanekom had turned the family farm into a transit point for ANC recruits en route to exile. After his release he lived in exile in Zimbabwe, working on development projects and coordinating the Popular History Trust. He returned to South Africa in 1990.

Date of birth: January 13 1953

Hermann, Dirk

Dirk Hermann is the deputy general secretary of South Africa's largest independent trade union, Solidarity. He is the best-known of the union's leadership as he constantly features in public debates about affirmative action and employment equity.

A largely white, Afrikaner trade union, Solidarity has its roots in the

Transvaal Miners' Association, formed over 100 years ago, which later became the South African Mine Workers' Union. The union in its former incarnation strongly protected the rights of white mineworkers under apartheid. It supported a policy of separate development and separate employment areas for white and black employees, enjoying significant government support.

With the advent of democracy and major reform to South Africa's labour laws, the union was faced with the choice to change or to become increasingly irrelevant to its members, many of whom no longer came exclusively from the mining sector, but included workers from the iron and steel industries, transport workers and parastatal employees. The organisation officially became Solidarity in 2001 and has significantly shifted focus: it is no longer just a trade union but has become a social 'movement', as Hermann has put it. Still representative of a largely white base, Solidarity has repositioned itself as a vocal protector of minority groups, particularly the Afrikaner community, representing on the whole highly skilled artisans, engineers and technicians in various sectors.

The body has created various ancillary organisations, among them AfriForum, its civil rights initiative, which actively campaigns for the rights of minority groups in South Africa. It has also created the Sol-Tech training college, the Solidarity Investment Company, the Solidarity Retirement Fund and a development institution, the Solidarity Growth Fund. It set up a Helping Hand Fund, an aid organisation that began in response to a mine liquidation that left over 6 000 employees destitute. The fund has since become an official section 21 company funded mainly by union members working to alleviate poverty in minority groups, mainly poor white communities. In 2008 the union also started its own not-for-profit medical aid fund, Solvita, to provide for its members, as the cost of private medical care in the country has become increasingly expensive.

Hermann joined Solidarity in the late 1990s as a sector organiser. Having done his doctoral thesis on the influence of affirmative action on the alienation of the 'non-designated group' in South Africa, Hermann is a vocal critic of the ANC government's affirmative action policies, particularly in the face of South Africa's ballooning skills shortage.

He has written three books, the most recent of which, *The Naked*

Emperor: Why Affirmative Action Has Failed, was published in 2007. Hermann has also addressed academic conferences on affirmative action and trade unionism in the new South Africa.

He argues that while the need for affirmative action can be understood in its historical context, in reality it has failed to distribute wealth or knowledge to the largely poor, ill-educated black majority, while a small percentage of the black middle class is the only group that has been effectively empowered. He has also frequently questioned the alienation of skilled white workers through policies like affirmative action which serve to deprive South Africa of much-needed skilled labour.

Born and raised in Heilbron in the Free State, Hermann was an avid sportsman in his school years, achieving provincial colours for athletics and rugby. He studied law at Potchefstroom University. After graduation in 1993, he obtained three postgraduate qualifications: honours in industrial psychology and industrial sociology and a postgraduate diploma in labour law, which he completed at the University of Johannesburg, as well as a master's degree in labour sociology. He was the 1996 recipient of the Potchefstroom University council medal for academic achievement and community development, as well as the Abe Bailey travel scholarship for leadership and academic development.

Date of birth: January 13 1972

Hogan, Barbara

Public enterprises minister Barbara Hogan was appointed minister of health on September 26 2008, a move widely welcomed after the controversial tenure of her predecessor, Manto Tshabalala-Msimang. Hogan has the reputation of being tough and in command of her brief; in an interview conducted shortly after her elevation to Cabinet, she said that her managerial and finance skills had played a role in her appointment.

Once in office Hogan quickly started to make a clean break with the ministry's unfortunate past. In her first public speech as minister, she made it clear to delegates at an international HIV conference in Cape Town that HIV causes Aids, that TB and HIV need to be treated together, and that she is interested in scientifically proven and evidence-based strategies against HIV. Her speech was greeted with delight as a sign that South

Africa's government was finally coming in from the healthcare cold as far as the international research and policy arena was concerned.

She appointed well-respected advisers to assist her. One of them, Aids activist Fatima Hassan, is a member of the Treatment Action Campaign and the Aids Law Project, both of which organisations had been involved in successful court actions against the government on HIV-related issues.

Hogan's first few months in power were eventful, with the spread of cholera in South Africa and a crisis in the Free State, where possible financial mismanagement led to a moratorium on starting new patients on antiretroviral therapy.

She has said that the biggest challenges she faces are boosting the morale of healthcare workers and creating a functional healthcare system that is responsive to the people using it despite the strains it operates under as a result of the HIV/Aids epidemic. Hogan has also stepped into office at a time of regulatory upheaval in South Africa with debates raging over the way forward for the public and private health sectors. Speaking out against the refusal to grant the Dalai Lama a visa in March 2008 did not earn her any friends in government although she won wide public support for her human rights stand. But government rebuked her and she later backed down and apologised.

Hogan matriculated from St Dominic's Convent in Benoni; while at school she was elected deputy junior mayor. She qualified in development studies at the University of the Witwatersrand while playing an active role in anti-apartheid activities, which included feeding information to the ANC in Botswana and organising consumer boycotts. She joined the ANC in 1976 after the Soweto uprising.

In 1981 she was detained on charges of treason and spent a year in solitary confinement. In 1983 she became the first woman in South Africa to be found guilty of treason and was sentenced to 10 years in jail. During her imprisonment Hogan studied economics and accounting science. She was released in 1990, a week after the ANC was unbanned.

After her release Hogan worked to develop the ANC's structures and became secretary-general for the organisation in the PWV region, now Gauteng province. From 1990 to 1992 she was on the ANC national executive committee and participated in the Codesa talks, which negotiated the end of the apartheid era. In 1993 she was appointed to the Development Bank of Southern Africa as part of a team looking at policy development in relation to public works. She became an MP in 1994. She was chairperson of the finance portfolio committee from 1999 to 2004 and has held the same position on the standing committee on public accounts and the auditor-general standing committee.

Hogan is married to former Robben Island prisoner and anti-apartheid activist Ahmed Kathrada.

Date of birth: February 28 1952

Holomisa, Bantu

Major-General Bantubonke Harrington Holomisa, founder of the United Democratic Movement (UDM), has been part of South African political life since the late 1980s. He was a military leader in the Transkei, where he was the first to free political prisoners.

He was born the son of Thembu chief Bazindlovu Holomisa in the Mqanduli district; his primary schooling was in the area and he matriculated at Jongilizwe College for the sons of chiefs. He joined the Transkei Defence Force a year later and speedily rose through the ranks to become major-general.

Detained by the unpopular chief minister Kaiser Matanzima, he led a bloodless coup shortly after his release to unseat Matanzima and install Stella Sigcau, a Pondo princess and daughter of a former Transkei president, in his place. Eight months later, accusing Sigcau of corruption, Holomisa staged a second coup – with the approval of the ANC, which was still banned in South Africa – and installed himself as leader. The move was not popular with the South African government, which backed an unsuccessful counter-coup, allegedly with the connivance of Sigcau, to remove him.

After the first democratic elections and the dissolution of the homelands, Holomisa and Sigcau both secured high-level government posts: Holomisa, who topped the list for the ANC's national executive committee, became deputy minister for environmental affairs and tourism and promptly waged war on plastic bags; Sigcau was made minister of public enterprises, but was not seen to accomplish very much.

Holomisa testified before the Truth and Reconciliation Commission that Matanzima had given Sigcau a R50 000 bribe. The allegation cost him his job and his position in the ANC; it was believed that the ANC leadership felt they needed to back Sigcau in order to secure the vote of traditionalists in Transkei, now part of the Eastern Cape. Was Holomisa, as some claimed, 'arrogant and politically immature' to accuse Sigcau in public? Indeed, she later admitted to the R50 000, but insisted it had been a loan. Or was he simply naïve and principled?

By 2004, when former president Nelson Mandela asked him to 'come back home' to the ANC, it was too late; Holomisa had founded the UDM and had other fights on his hands. The party received significant support, especially in the Eastern Cape, with membership being upwards of 200 000 nationwide. But over the years floor-crossing shrank the ranks of his MPs. He opposed the system of floor-crossing, took it to the Constitutional Court, which ruled that Parliament had to write legislation for the practice, and suspended eight of his top elected officials whom he suspected of floor-crossing intentions after Parliament passed an enabling law. Parliament abolished the system in 2008, after many UDM MPs, and other members of smaller parties, had defected to the ANC.

Holomisa has a keen interest in sport. He has managed several sports teams, including the Tembu Royals football team. His golf handicap is 14, and he supports Kaizer Chiefs.

Date of birth: July 25 1955

Howard, Randall

Randall Howard is general secretary of the South African Transport and Allied Workers' Union (Satawu) and is also a member of Cosatu's national executive. He started his career at the old Transport and General Workers' Union (TGWU) in 1986 and has risen to become one of South Africa's most prominent trade union leaders.

Born in Bontheuwel, but raised in Greenhaven, Cape Town, Howard first worked in several jobs before joining the freight company South African Container Depots. It was here that he became an active trade unionist. He was elected a shop steward after joining the TGWU and then became chairperson of the Western Cape branch.

In 1988 he was dismissed from his job and became a full-time organiser with TGWU. He was subsequently elected branch secretary, then national deputy general secretary and, in 1994, general secretary. He held this position until the merger of TGWU with another union in 2000. At Satawu's founding congress Howard was elected general secretary and in this capacity is a member of the central executive committee of Cosatu.

His strength in the labour movement is seen in his cunning strategic decisions. He is quite a vocal trade unionist and can be seen at the forefront of many Satawu strikes, leading the charge. He has been particularly critical of South African Airways (SAA) and has always been quick to point out any flaw in the national carrier's handling of labour relations.

Howard was also one of the biggest critics of Mbhazima Shilowa when Shilowa left the ANC to form the Congress of the People (Cope), calling him a hypocrite and an embarrassment to trade unionists. Howard represents Cosatu at ANC–Cosatu–South African Communist Party tripartite alliance meetings, as well as at meetings of Nedlac at management committee and executive committee levels.

He was elected president of the International Transport Workers' Federation in 2006 and is vice-president of the International Workers' Federation for Africa.

Howard and his union led the campaign in 2008 against a Chinese ship bearing arms to Zimbabwe; they motivated dockworkers all over Africa to refuse to handle the load of weapons. His actions won wide praise.

The Freedom of Expression Institute nominated Howard to serve on the SABC board two years ago, but he did not make the cut after Thabo Mbeki's ANC changed the final list and excluded him.

Date of birth: August 8 1961

James, Wilmot

The media were intrigued when well-known social scientist Wilmot James threw his lot in with the Democratic Alliance (DA) and announced that he would contest the 2009 election as a DA parliamentary candidate, second only to chief strategist Ryan Coetzee.

James was born in Paarl, in the Western Cape. A consummate academic and educator, he comes from a family of teachers, many of whom were members of the Teachers' League of South Africa, an extension of the Non-European Unity Movement. One of his early memories, he says, is of standing in a doorway as a terrified child, watching as protesters marched from Paarl to Mbekweni, shortly after the Sharpeville Massacre in 1960.

James matriculated from Athlone High School, then studied sociology and history at the University of the Western Cape. In 1976, he was arrested by police for his student activism and put in 'cold storage' at Victor Verster Prison for three weeks.

In 1977 he received a Fulbright Scholarship, which enabled him to study further at the University of Wisconsin-Madison, where he received the MS and PhD degrees in sociology. His scholarly credentials are impressive and include research, teaching posts and visiting fellowships at institutes such as the Open University in the UK, the ESRC Genomics Research and Policy Forum at the University of Edinburgh, and the California Institute of Technology. He has written and edited numerous books and essays on history, sociology and politics.

In 1994, he took leave of absence from his teaching post at the University of Cape Town (UCT) to work with the Independent Electoral Commission in preventing threats to freedom and fairness in the electoral process. He was later asked to head the Institute for Democracy in South Africa (Idasa), a body that promotes reconciliation and good governance. In his four years as executive director, he worked closely with former UCT vice-chancellor Mamphela Ramphele.

James became dean of humanities at UCT in 1999 but served for just over a year before leaving to study biology. He later set up the Africa Genome Education Institute to further public understanding of science and biology.

He has served on various government task teams, mainly in the areas of migration and immigration, and was chairman of the Immigration Advisory Board of South Africa. He stepped down from this position in April 2006, citing frustrations over the delay in setting up a new board.

James gained invaluable international experience during his 12 years as a trustee at the Ford Foundation, which runs programmes to reduce poverty, strengthen democracy and foster education. His term at the foundation ended in May 2008. Freed of the foundation's restriction on political involvement, he joined the ranks of foundation members now in politics, including former Nigerian president Olusegun Obasanjo.

James says he joined the DA because its values align with his own and because he has faith in its leader, Helen Zille. His years of dedicated study and policymaking will serve him well; he sees his role in Parliament as a national spokesperson on science and technology, forwarding the ideal of public service and advancing the sciences and science education for all South Africans.

Date of birth: July 5 1953

Jansen, Jonathan

South Africa's most coruscating and most compassionate public intellectual might well have been cooling his vigorous heels in Pollsmoor by now if his early years on the Cape Flats had taken a different turn. Now the country's doyen of education – and due to assume the vice-chancellorship of the University of the Free State in mid-2009 – Jonathan Jansen spent the 1960s and 1970s avoiding recruitment by the local Americans gang.

The allure of the gangsters lost out to the energies of the evangelical church, in which Jansen became a preacher in his mid-teens. In a sense, he hasn't stopped preaching since then. A typical couple of days in March 2009 saw him addressing the Union of Jewish Women, advising the Finnish government on its education spending, consulting with some NGOs, and spending time with a mission community in Cape Town.

Social justice animates all he does, and the seeds of that were sown early. Born in the small town of Montagu in the Western Cape, he learnt as a child that his family had lost their property in the town to whites, courtesy of the Group Areas Act. His grandfather went blind at this time – an affliction, Jansen has written, that his relatives believe was psychosomatically induced by this brutal apartheid dispossession.

He has also written of his own anger towards whites during childhood. But his political education took a decisive turn during his studies for a BSc at the University of the Western Cape, where figures such as Allan Boesak and Beyers Naudé, and exposure to the influence of black consciousness founder Steve Biko, were powerfully formative. He completed a teaching diploma and a BEd through Unisa, and taught science for seven years at deprived Western Cape schools. It was there, he says, that 'the connections between teaching and social injustice became apparent'.

In 1985, Jansen became one of the first recipients of a scholarship scheme for black South Africans that Bishop Desmond Tutu set up with the United States. He proceeded to complete an MSc at Cornell and, in 1991, a PhD at Stanford University's school of education.

Returning in 1995 to South Africa, where he became professor of education at the University of Durban-Westville, he quickly established a formidable academic reputation, deepening it when he subsequently entered the Afrikaner stronghold of the University of Pretoria, where he was dean of education from 2000 to 2007.

One measure of his local and international standing is his CV, which in its abridged form runs to 14 closely typed pages. But he has never been solely an ivory-tower academic. His trenchant contributions to education and other socio-political debates have become a major feature of the post-apartheid public terrain, whether in the form of his weekly column in *The Times* online newspaper or his annual assessment of the matric results. Some government bureaucrats have sound reasons for trembling as Jansen pens that yearly public appraisal of their performances. Wiser government heads, however, have realised that Jansen is a rare national resource: despite his insistence on speaking uncomfortable truths to power, the government has taken to presenting him with challenges that would make most others run a mile.

These have recently included chairing a ministerial committee on the fraught issue of school and teacher evaluation and development; restoring the corruption-ridden Durban University of Technology to working order; and currently doing the same at the longstanding basket case that is the Mangosuthu University of Technology.

But in 2009 he confronts an even thornier challenge when he becomes vice-chancellor of the University of the Free State, which has regularly made headlines for all the wrong reasons – racism in university residences, and the like. Jansen's seven years at another bastion of Afrikanerdom, Pretoria University, produced his profound meditation on socio-political change, *Knowledge in the Blood: Confronting Race and the Apartheid Past* (Stanford University Press), so his first experience of guiding transformation from the driver's seat could provide the country's universities with a sorely needed model of tertiary governance.

Date of birth: September 29 1956

Jara, Mazibuko

The co-managing editor of *Amandla!*, a Cape Town-based political journal published by the collective Amandla Publishers, Mazibuko Jara is an independent researcher, writer and development consultant. He is the former chief spokesperson of the South African Communist Party (SACP), but fell out of favour with the SACP leadership after publicly questioning the party's support for Jacob Zuma in his court cases and his campaign to become ANC president. He was expelled from the Young Communist League, where he was deputy national secretary, for refusing to support Zuma's presidential ambitions, but continues to be a member of the SACP.

He joined the SACP in 1992, when he was a student at the University of Natal in Durban, where he earned an engineering degree. He also holds a master's degree from the University of the Western Cape. He was an activist in the Young Christian Students and the South African Students' Congress (Sasco) and the media spokesperson and strategist for the SACP from 2000 to 2005.

In defiance of the SACP's stance on Zuma, Jara wrote a document titled 'What Colour is Our Flag: Red or JZ?', a critique of the SACP approach on the support the party pledged for Zuma. In the document, which was leaked to the media in 2006, he questioned the modus operandi of SACP general secretary Blade Nzimande. Jara argued that Nzimande's support of Zuma's presidential ambitions was motivated by a desire to 'share the spoils' that come with being in power. He also questioned whether Zuma could be regarded as part of the left and working-class forces in the ANC. The document put additional strain on Jara's relationship with SACP leaders, in particular with Nzimande.

Jara's professional work includes time as a student engineer-in-training at Eskom power stations in Mpumalanga and as a project coordinator and national director at the Lesbian and Gay Equality Project. He was involved as an activist and researcher with several NGOs in the areas of human rights advocacy, HIV/Aids, lesbian and gay equality, community development, local government transformation, financial sector transformation, and social and economic justice as well as land and agrarian reform.

As part of his passion for human rights, he founded the Employment Equity Alliance, which was a lobbying alliance of various NGOs in support of the Employment Equity Act. The alliance joined the fight, which was ultimately successful, for the legal protection of lesbian and gay people, people living with HIV/Aids, and women and people living with disabilities, from unfair discrimination in the workplace. Jara also served as a board member of the Aids Consortium and the Treatment Action Campaign.

A dissident communist, he has extensive global experience working with alliances and coalitions that are critical of corporate-led, finance-dominated modes of globalisation and articulate alternatives consistent with the principles of social justice and ecological sustainability.

Jara is working towards a master's degree in land and agrarian studies at the University of the Western Cape. In addition to his part-time position at Amandla Publishers, Jara is a research associate at the Cooperative and Policy Alternative Centre. He is a member of the Cape Town district executive committee of the SACP.

He was born Mazibuko Kanyiso Jara at Rabula village in the Keiskammahoek district of the Eastern Cape. He is married to Nolene Morris, CEO of Bloem Water.

Date of birth: October 30 1973

Jeenah, Na'eem

When it comes to religion and revolution, Na'eem Jeenah is the man to talk to. He has crafted a multi-tasking role in South Africa as a journalist, community leader and author, but first and foremost as an activist. His sometimes contentious views range from Islamic politics to feminism and human rights.

He was born in Durban and began his life in activism at the age of 14, when he joined the Muslim Youth Movement. In 1985, while national president of the Muslim Students' Association, he was arrested for distributing anti-government pamphlets, spending only a few hours in jail. He and his first wife, Shamima Shaikh, co-authored a book entitled *Journey of Discovery: A South African Hajj* after the couple's pilgrimage to Mecca. Shaikh, also an activist and author, died in 1998.

By that time Jeenah had acquired certificates in computer training and news editing, and completed leadership and Islamic leadership programmes at institutions including the University of Malaysia and the International Islamic University in Islamabad. He had been president of the Muslim Youth Movement in Johannesburg and founded its gender desk; chief editor of *al-Qalam*, a monthly national Muslim newspaper; and southern African regional coordinator of SANGONet, an information portal for local NGOs. He was also a talk-show host on the Johannesburg Muslim community radio station, The Voice, a job that lasted till 2003.

He earned an MA with distinction in religious studies at the University of the Witwatersrand and went on to begin his PhD in political studies, which he hopes to complete by the end of 2009.

He married fellow activist Melissa Hoole, an artist and co-founder of a Brisbane solidarity group called Fair Go for Palestine, in 2005. His career as an author continued, with his booklet on *Religion and Schools* published in 2005, and he is working on *Islamic Feminisms in South Africa*. In 2008 he was listed as one of the *Mail & Guardian*'s '100 young people you should take to lunch'.

Still very much the activist, Jeenah was director of operations at the Freedom of Expression Institute and organised and addressed several seminars and workshops focusing on issues relating to youth development, journalism and Islam. He has also been a delegate at numerous international and local conferences held on such subjects as Muslim youth, youth leadership and the United States–Islamic relationship. He is spokesperson for the Palestine Solidarity Committee of South Africa.

Religious issues play a major part in his activism, and he has been a coordinator of Masjidul Islam in Brixton, Johannesburg, since 1998. He has also done work in promoting inter-faith relationships and activities and is the director of the Afro-Middle East Centre in Johannesburg, which aims to conduct research into the Middle East and relations between Africa and the Middle East.

Date of birth: August 8 1965

Jim, Irvin

Firebrand unionist Irvin Jim has a way of shooting his mouth off, without much provocation.

Born in the industrial town of Port Elizabeth in the 1960s, Jim had an early introduction to the hardship of workers in the area. He completed courses, but not a diploma or a degree, at the Port Elizabeth Technikon and the University of Port Elizabeth, going to work at the Firestone Tyre Company in 1991. Two years later he was elected local shop steward for the factory workers. He also joined the South African Communist Party in the Eastern Cape and served for two terms as the party's deputy provincial secretary. He became known as a unionist who speaks his mind, even if it is to the chagrin of the ANC leadership in the province.

Within the National Union of Metalworkers (Numsa) he rose to the position of provincial chairperson, a post he served in for five years before being elected in 2008 as the union's general secretary. For the first time he left the Eastern Cape and moved his base to Johannesburg, where Numsa headquarters are situated. He represented Numsa at various international conferences, including that of the International Metalworkers' Federation, and championed negotiations across various sectors, ranging from collective bargaining and labour laws to restructuring, outsourcing, retrenchments and plant closures.

He served on the first board of directors of the Numsa Investment Company, which partners bodies like the burial society Doves, and through these partnerships he made money for the trade union, with Doves being the preferential burial society for Numsa members who take out burial policies.

Jim was involved in the 2002 Volkswagen jobs crisis that led to the layoff of 1 200 workers when the workers went on strike to oppose job losses. He is also a member of the Uitenhage Despatch Development Initiative, set up to deal with the legacy of mass dismissals at the Volkswagen plant in Uitenhage.

He is a staunch opponent of inflation targeting and trickle-down economics and used his platform as newly elected general secretary of Numsa to criticise finance minister Trevor Manuel and Reserve Bank governor Tito Mboweni. He believes the government should play a more interventionist role in the economy.

He was brought in by Cosatu heavyweights to replace Silumko Nondwangu, who had been seen as too close to the cause of Thabo Mbeki when the whole of the trade union federation was supporting Jacob Zuma. Shortly after his election as general secretary of Numsa in 2008, Jim took aim at Manuel, describing him as the architect of an economic policy that has created wealth for a few and left the bulk of South Africans still poor. He feels Manuel should, as finance minister, devise bailout plans in the same way as the US has done to protect jobs following the global financial meltdown. Firing back, Manuel told Jim that the general secretary fails to 'grasp the complexities of the metals industry'.

Date of birth: February 1 1968

Jordan, Pallo

Zweledinga Pallo Jordan is a historian and scholar who comes from one of the country's most academically accomplished families. His father, Dr A.C. Jordan, was a novelist and academic, the first African to lecture at the University of Cape Town (UCT) in 1946; his mother, Phyllis Ntantala Jordan, has been a teacher, researcher and lecturer. Her autobiography, *A Life's Mosaic*, has recently been reissued.

His parents were active in the Non-European Unity Movement, an organisation he joined at the age of seven, selling *Torch*, a newspaper the movement produced. His membership of the ANC followed just over a decade later, in 1960. After matriculating, he went to UCT and then left for further study at the University of Wisconsin, where his father had secured a position.

In 1977 he was appointed head of Radio Freedom, an ANC radio station run from Luanda, Angola, and in 1979 director of the ANC's first internal mass propaganda campaign. The ANC then became more alive in the public imagination as posters, postcards, T-shirts, stickers and comic books proliferated on the streets of many world capitals. It was a publicity role that he would play again before and during the 1994 elections as the ANC's spokesperson.

In the 1970s and 1980s, Jordan wrote scholarly articles on the student protests of 1976, socialism, the Soviet Union and its relations with the region, and other related subjects. During that same period Jordan's intellectual input was used elsewhere in the organisation. For instance, he accompanied then-ANC president Oliver Tambo, Mac Maharaj, Chris Hani, Thabo Mbeki and James Stuart to a meeting attended by white business in Zambia in 1986. He was also part of the ANC delegation that travelled to Dakar, Senegal, in 1987 and to Paris in 1989 for talks with the apartheid establishment, sponsored by the Institute for a Democratic South Africa (Idasa).

Elected to the National Assembly in 1994 as number five on the ANC list, Jordan was appointed to the Nelson Mandela Cabinet as minister for posts, telecommunications and broadcasting in the same year, and in 1996 he became minister of environmental affairs and tourism. But when Thabo Mbeki became president in 1999, Jordan was overlooked.

In 2004 he was appointed minister for arts and culture, a seemingly appropriate post for one who is concerned with cultural production and development. He is particularly passionate about the role of public libraries (previously much neglected) in a post-apartheid South Africa and in 2008 made R200-million available for that sector. Under his administration the department of arts and culture embarked on a nationwide consultative imbizo in a move to update national policy in that area. But in a surprise move, Jacob Zuma did not reappoint him to Cabinet.

Jordan is not without detractors. The Democratic Alliance accused Jordan of running a 'poorly performing department', calling on the minister to indicate whether he has instituted a 'turnaround strategy' for the facilities under his aegis. They also reminded Jordan that his department received a qualified audit opinion for the year 2007/8. His opponents point out that it was under his watch that the ferry belonging to Robben Island was attached in August because of a R26-million debt owed to the boat builder.

An independent left thinker, he challenged conventional wisdom in the movement long before it was considered acceptable, and as a result he is one of the most senior ANC members ever to have been detained by the organisation's security apparatus. Jordan was held in Lusaka for six weeks after criticising the movement's security wing for turning a search for apartheid spies among exiles into an inquisition.

In 2003, he said 'democracy ... is about the right ordinary people have to participate in society's decision-making processes'. When Mosiuoa Lekota and others left the ANC to form the Congress of the People, he was one of the more articulate people who defended the ANC's record.
Date of birth: May 22 1942

Kodwa, Zizi

A former spokesperson for the ANC Youth League, Zizi Kodwa is general manager in the office of ANC president Jacob Zuma, who may be said to owe Kodwa a debt of gratitude. For it was Kodwa who, hand-in-hand with former Youth League president Fikile Mbalula, first mounted an open challenge to Mbeki's hegemony in the party at a time when the president was treated with a great deal of respect and regarded with trepidation. The two famously said that then-president Thabo Mbeki was not indispensable and started a debate about succession, insisting that ANC tradition holds that whoever is deputy president automatically becomes the next president. It was an argument meant to favour Zuma but was refuted by some ANC veterans.

Kodwa is a fun-loving young man who organised numerous Youth League bashes during his tenure and even hosts an annual big party on his birthday in January.

He attracted notoriety when he managed the rowdy crowd outside the Johannesburg High Court daily during Zuma's rape trial in 2006. The crowd sang, waved toy AK47s and insulted the woman who accused Zuma of rape. Kodwa, who called the Zuma rape accuser 'Lucifer', often got caught up in mob frenzy and also made the controversial remark that 'we need to hit the dog [the National Prosecuting Authority] so hard that its masters are forced to come out'.

Born in Langa, Cape Town, he joined the struggle at the age of 15 through membership of the student movement at Masiyi Senior Secondary School. He participated in student representative councils

(SRCs) and in more militant organisations such as the Congress of South African Students (Cosas), which was banned and later reincarnated as the Township Student Congress.

At the University of the Western Cape he became a member of the South African Students' Congress (Sasco) and was elected SRC president. He was determined to fulfil the demands of both studying and politics and accomplished this, being elected SRC president and graduating with an honours degree in development studies.

Kodwa worked in different capacities in the Youth League's Western Cape branch and was later elected on to the organisation's national executive committee. He was a member of the Youth League until its national congress in Mangaung in 2008.

Date of birth: January 19 1971

Langa, Pius

As chief justice of South Africa and head of the Constitutional Court, Pius Nkonzo Langa sits at the pinnacle of South Africa's judiciary, with one of his tasks being to transform the Bench to reflect the country's demographics. He also chairs the powerful Judicial Service Commission (JSC), which is the constitutionally appointed body responsible for the initial selection of judges, forwarding its recommendations to the president for approval.

Langa came to the court as an ANC member who had played an active role in the multi-party transitional talks and had served on the party's constitutional committee. Having initially served as deputy president of the court, then as deputy chief justice, Langa has been chief justice since 2005. He succeeded Arthur Chaskalson, the first president of the Constitutional Court and the first incumbent of the combined position of Constitutional Court president and chief justice after a constitutional amendment in 2001 combined the position of leader of the country's highest court with that of leader of the entire judiciary. He will relinquish his position in October 2009.

Langa was born in Bushbuckridge to deeply religious parents – Langa senior was a priest. Forced to leave school at the age of 14 because his parents could no longer afford to pay the fees, he faced a bleak future until a 'miracle' in the form of a bursary allowed him to complete his studies. A year of unemployment was followed by his first job, in a shirt factory. Three years later he moved on to the department of justice, where he worked as an interpreter and messenger while simultaneously pursuing a law degree by correspondence. He earned a BJuris degree in 1973 and an LLB in 1976 through Unisa. After a stint as a prosecutor and then a magistrate, he was admitted as an advocate of the Supreme Court in Natal in 1977. He became a senior counsel in 1994 shortly before his appointment by then-president Nelson Mandela as a member of the first group of Constitutional Court justices.

His term as chief justice has been relatively smooth, though it has been marred by controversy over a high-profile case of alleged judicial misconduct involving Cape judge president John Hlophe, who was accused of giving judgment in a case in which he had an involvement with one of the parties. When the case was brought before the JSC, Langa's casting vote reportedly saved Hlophe from potential impeachment, drawing criticism from members of the legal fraternity and the public.

The decision would return to haunt Langa when, in his absence, Hlophe was accused, in a press statement made by the judges of the Constitutional Court, of attempting to 'improperly' influence two judges (one of them an acting judge) to rule in favour of ANC president Jacob Zuma in his long-running battle with the National Prosecuting Authority over allegations of corruption, tax evasion and racketeering. The Constitutional Court referred the matter to the JSC's complaints committee. Hlophe meanwhile lodged a counter-complaint against 13 acting and permanent Constitutional Court judges and won a High Court judgment, but lost on an appeal heard by a full, nine-judge Bench of the Supreme Court of Appeal. He also brought a defamation suit against the judges, seeking R10-million.

The matter has cast doubts in some minds about the independence of the judiciary and has led to fears of an imminent constitutional crisis as Hlophe supporters call for the impeachment of the Constitutional Court judges. Entering the fray, ANC secretary-general Gwede Mantashe labelled the judges of South Africa's highest court parties to a 'counter-revolutionary' agenda.

Date of birth: March 25 1939

Lekota, Mosiuoa

Once a leading light in the Black Consciousness Movement and, a decade later, the United Democratic Front (UDF), Mosiuoa 'Terror' Lekota has had a turbulent political career in post-liberation South Africa.

Removed from the Free State premiership by his own party in 1997, he clawed his way back into Thabo Mbeki's first Cabinet as defence minister in 1999, remaining in the portfolio until the demise of Mbeki's presidency nine years later. Despite being an 'inzile' with strong non-racial convictions – he has publicly defended the struggle role of whites under apartheid – he seemed to have reconciled himself with Mbeki's racially divisive political style and became more and more closely identified with his leadership. In 2002, for example, he aligned himself with Mbeki's long battle to stifle persistent questions about South Africa's multi-billion-rand arms procurement when he misleadingly represented a report by the public protector, auditor-general and National Prosecuting Authority to Parliament as a vindication of government's clean hands. As ANC chair, he was also accused of being Mbeki's authoritarian enforcer in meetings of the party's national executive committee (NEC).

In the build-up to the ANC's December 2007 conference in Polokwane, Lekota emerged as Mbeki's battering-ram, publicly accusing Jacob Zuma of being a tribalist. In terms of his own political future, it was a miscalculation – booed and heckled from the floor, he was rejected as Mbeki's candidate for the secretary-general's post and failed to make the party's NEC.

There was little surprise, therefore, when he resigned from the Cabinet after Mbeki was forced out as president in September 2008. But the irrepressible Lekota was already planning his next move: after publicly crossing swords with the ANC treasurer-general Mathews Phosa, he fronted a media conference in Johannesburg where he announced that a national convention would soon be held to launch a new party to fight the 2009 elections. Speaking of his disillusionment with the new ANC leadership and its attacks on the Constitution in defence of Zuma, he said the new movement should be seen as the real ANC. Asked why he could not accept the outcome of the Polokwane conference, he said

Mbeki supporters had been systematically hounded out of the party in its aftermath.

The new party – launched at a convention in Sandton and ultimately called the Congress of the People (Cope) – is the most significant split in the ANC since the emergence of the Pan Africanist Congress in the late 1950s. As a predominantly black party led by figures with a liberation struggle background, it has prospects and is pinning its hopes on the 2014 elections.

Lekota's role in Cope is, however, problematic. He lost a bid to become the party's presidential candidate although, as leader of the party, his face was on the ballot. Many Cope supporters would prefer the party to be led by former Gauteng premier Mbhazima Shilowa. They are uncomfortable with Lekota's close association with Mbeki, fearing that this could count against Cope at the polls. In addition, Lekota did not earn himself much respect in the defence portfolio, where he was widely seen as an absentee minister who did little to halt the deepening neglect of the South African National Defence Force. The 2008 defence department report highlighted the loss of skills and desperate measures to retain critical personnel by diverting operational budgets to bolster salaries, as well as the shortage of basic equipment, such as tank ammunition and soft-skin vehicles.

Lekota was born in the Senekal district of the Free State, matriculating from a Catholic mission school, St Francis College, in Mariannhill, KwaZulu-Natal. His nickname 'Terror' comes from his prowess as a striker in semi-professional soccer. He enrolled for a social science degree at the University of the North but was expelled because of his membership of the South African Students' Organisation (Saso). He became an organiser for this black consciousness organisation after founder Ongopotse Tiro went into exile, and was sentenced to eight years on Robben Island for conspiring to 'commit acts capable of endangering maintenance of law and order' – largely, organising rallies on campus in support of Frelimo in Mozambique.

Once on Robben Island, he opted for non-racialism. The UDF was launched in the year he was released, and Lekota was elected national publicity secretary. Three years later he and 21 other UDF leaders were charged with treason. After a lengthy trial, five of the accused, including Lekota, were sentenced to 12 years, but in 1989 they were released after an Appeal Court review.

Lekota moved quickly up the ranks of the ANC – chief of intelligence, an ANC election commissioner, a member of the NEC and the national working committee, and, in 1994, Free State premier. He did not keep that job long: clashing with leaders of the provincial ANC, he was 'redeployed' as chairman of the National Council of Provinces. After his surprise election as national ANC chairman, he was named minister of defence in Mbeki's first Cabinet.

Date of birth: August 13 1948

Love, Janet

Janet Love is national director of the Legal Resources Centre (LRC), whose lawyers provide free legal services to the poor, both individuals and communities, on a range of crucial matters, from constitutional issues to land, from housing to the status of refugees.

Although not a lawyer, she is well versed in the Constitution, having served as a member of Parliament's constitutional committee in the 1990s, when South Africa's final Constitution was being drafted.

Love joined the ANC in 1976 and left South Africa for exile two years later, joining Umkhonto weSizwe and undergoing military training. Two years after her return in 1987 she was appointed communications officer for Operation Vula, the ANC's campaign to send senior ANC members in exile back to South Africa to link up with activists inside the country.

She was involved in the Codesa negotiations to establish a new, democratic South Africa in the early 1990s, and as an MP during the 1990s she served as chair of the portfolio committee on agriculture, water affairs and forestry, leaving the National Assembly to act as special adviser to the minister. She moved on to the Reserve Bank, spending five years as head of strategic analysis and support in the currency department. In 2006 she assumed her present post at the LRC. A year later she was elected on to the ANC's national executive committee.

Love earned a BA in political science and industrial sociology from the University of the Witwatersrand and holds two postgraduate diplomas: in economics from the University of London and in public administration and development management from Wits.

Date of birth: December 21 1957

Mabandla, Brigitte

Brigitte Mabandla first made it into government in 1995 as deputy minister of arts and culture and went on to briefly occupy the hot seat at the housing ministry before being elevated to the arduous position of looking after the justice and constitutional development portfolio. She was appointed minister of public enterprises in Kgalema Motlanthe's Cabinet after Alec Erwin resigned in solidarity with Thabo Mbeki in 2008 but was not reappointed after the April 2009 elections.

Her record as justice minister was nothing to write home about, although some of her former aides have argued that her initial replacement, Enver Surty, went on to reap the benefits of her work. They argue that she has always been passionate about access to justice and set the ball rolling for some of the projects, such as mobile courts, that were unveiled by Surty. As her ANC background in exile suggests, she is passionate about the rights of children and women. Hence her work as minister on a project to increase the number of women judges and her passionate plea to judicial officers not to be lenient in their sentencing of rape offenders.

Mabandla's time in the justice portfolio in 2008 was marked by controversy. With her indecision and inability to take a firm position on issues, her director-general actively waded into an area very much reserved for politicians and in the process waged a turf war with former national prosecutions boss Vusi Pikoli. The Ginwala inquiry into Pikoli's fitness to hold office showed her director-general to be ambitious. Mabandla's kindly nature also allowed former president Thabo Mbeki to use her name to pull the wool over the eyes of South Africans by giving the excuse of a breakdown in relations between Mabandla and Pikoli as the reason for suspending him. Not only did she quietly encourage this but she remained silent at the inquiry, declining to take the stand to explain publicly where things went wrong between her and Pikoli. All she could muster, as Pikoli's testimony revealed, was, 'Vusi, this is all about integrity, and one day I will talk.'

She stood by when some of the country's judges went to war with one another and did not say a word during the battle between Cape judge president John Hlophe and the Constitutional Court judges and during the fallout which led to repeated attacks on the judiciary. She also did not utter a word when Luthuli House launched a tirade against the judiciary in defence of ANC president Jacob Zuma.

In her last portfolio she flexed some muscle against the chief executive of South African Airways (SAA), which has benefited from cash injections from government for a long time with no real prospect of a turn-around. SAA has created such a headache that MPs booed when finance minister Trevor Manuel announced in his budget speech that the airline would be receiving billions of rands.

Mabandla holds an LLB from the University of Zambia. She taught English and law at the Botswana Polytechnic and law at the Botswana Institute of Administration and Commerce in the 1980s. She also served as legal adviser to the ANC's legal and constitutional affairs department. On her return from exile she joined the University of the Western Cape's Community Law Centre as coordinator of projects on women's and children's rights.

Date of birth: November 23 1948

Madisha, Willie

If awards were anything to go by, William Mothipa 'Willie' Madisha would definitely scoop the 'moemish of the year' award for South African politics in 2008. Not that he flopped as leader of one of the biggest trade unions on the continent or leader of the biggest teachers' union in the country or influential member of the South African Communist Party (SACP), but he was sacked from all three positions in one year – South African Democratic Teachers' Union (Sadtu) president, SACP central committee member and Cosatu president. Madisha was fired from all three positions in the first half of 2008 for talking to the media about an alleged R500 000 donation to SACP general secretary Blade Nzimande, and for disobeying a Sadtu and Cosatu resolution to support Zuma's candidacy for ANC president. Madisha had publicly backed Thabo Mbeki for the presidency at the ANC's 2007 national conference in Polokwane, while the trade union federation had adopted a resolution supporting Jacob Zuma.

Madisha's expulsion came at a time when the winds of political change were sweeping over the South African political landscape. It signalled the intensification of a campaign to rid Cosatu of leaders who backed Mbeki's failed bid for a third term as ANC president at Polokwane in 2007. Madisha subsequently resigned as a member of the ANC. His announcement was met with much delight from many political quarters, including the ruling party's breakaway formation, the Congress of the People (Cope). Madisha is one of the many political stalwarts from the ruling party who joined Cope after the resignation of Mbeki as president.

Born in the former Northern Transvaal (now Limpopo province), Madisha moved to Tshwane, where he grew up in Atteridgeville. Here, he became a member of the United Democratic Front while he studied to become a teacher at the Transvaal College of Education. Madisha rose to popularity in 1996 when he became Sadtu president and was subsequently voted Cosatu president in 1999. His trade union career spans many years and is deeply rooted at regional level, where he served on various positions before shifting into mainstream structures and politics. In March 2009 it looked as if he was going back to his roots: he announced he would be a 'consultant' to a new, independent trade union federation.

Date of birth: August 7 1959

Madlala-Routledge, Nozizwe

Nozizwe Madlala-Routledge, named deputy speaker of the National Assembly in September 2008, resigned from Parliament in May 2009 after being redeployed as chair of the ANC caucus. It was not the first time her career had been halted. She had returned to the back benches after losing a power battle with her former boss, then-minister of health Manto Tshabalala-Msimang.

Madlala-Routledge was deputy minister of defence from 1999 to April 2004, after which she was appointed deputy minister of health. She was removed from this post on August 8 2007, the eve of National Women's Day. She had previously refused a request from president Thabo Mbeki that she resign. The ostensible reason for her departure was a trip she made to an international Aids conference in Spain. She had applied for approval but flew off before it was received – it was denied the day after she left. On hearing the news she returned to South Africa immediately but was fired for failing to get authorisation and for not being a team player. After being sacked Madlala-Routledge was ordered to pay the health department R312 000 for the cost of the trip, a move which led the Treatment Action Campaign to launch a fundraising campaign to cover her costs.

It is widely believed that Madlala-Routledge's unceremonious removal from her post and the criticisms she faced were due to other factors. These include her outspoken views on HIV/Aids – she had criticised Aids denialism at the highest levels – which conflicted with those of Tshabalala-Msimang. In 2006 Madlala-Routledge took a public HIV test and called on others to follow suit – a stand that was interpreted as a criticism of Mbeki.

Another high-profile area of conflict was the state of the maternity ward at Frere Hospital in the Eastern Cape, which, after an unannounced visit, Madlala-Routledge described as a national disgrace. This was criticised by Tshabalala-Msimang after her scheduled visit to the same hospital – which was reportedly preceded by a general sprucing up of the facility in preparation for the health minister.

While Tshabalala-Msimang was on extensive sick leave, Madlala-Routledge began the process of unblocking the state's responses to the HIV/Aids epidemic. Although transport minister Jeff Radebe was appointed acting health minister, he delegated powers to Madlala-Routledge. She continued a consultative process with healthcare workers and activists that resulted in the launch of the National Strategic Plan 2007–2011. However, the deputy health minister faced inertia and obstruction within her own department – she told a press conference that officials were told not to liaise directly with her, but rather to go through the departmental director-general.

Madlala-Routledge is a Quaker and has been a member of the South African Communist Party (SACP) since 1984. She was a member of the SACP delegation to the Codesa talks, which negotiated the birth of a democratic South Africa. Her appointment as deputy minister of defence followed her service on the portfolio committee on land affairs and the committee on the improvement of quality of life and status of women.

Madlala-Routledge completed her schooling at the Inanda Seminary in Durban and studied at the University of Natal and the University of

Fort Hare. In 1979 – the same year that she joined the ANC – she obtained a diploma in medical technology. She worked as a medical technologist for six years before moving to a full-time position as an organiser for the Natal Organisation of Women. As a result of her anti-apartheid activities, Madlala-Routledge was arrested and spent time in solitary confinement.

In 1989 she gained a postgraduate diploma in adult education from the University of Natal and in 1994 obtained a social science degree, majoring in philosophy and sociology, from the same institution. She received the Peacemakers in Action award from the Tanenbaum Center for Interreligious Understanding in New York in 2002.

Date of birth: June 29 1952

Magwaza-Msibi, Zanele

Political analysts, and the party itself, have punted Zanele Magwaza-Msibi as the new face of the Inkatha Freedom Party (IFP). And it has nothing to do with her broad smile – almost the antithesis of the dourness associated with the IFP – or a sometimes bling fashion sense.

Magwaza-Msibi is the first female chairperson of a party long considered a bastion of Zulu patriarchy. As the IFP tussled with the demands of modernisation and reconciling president Mangosuthu Buthelezi's almost feudalistic control of it – a tension as yet unresolved – Magwaza-Msibi emerged as a somewhat surprise choice as chairperson in 2007. In 2008 she also rose above stalwarts like secretary-general Musa Zondi and national organiser Albert Mncwango to become the party's KwaZulu-Natal (KZN) premiership candidate in the 2009 general elections.

Yet, while Magwaza-Msibi has shattered the IFP's gender mould, she remains baked in the party's furnace of social conservatism, traditionalism and unquestioning loyalty to Buthelezi. When Buthelezi announced that he would not hold public office after the elections in 2009, she was one of the first to proclaim that the party would attempt to convince him otherwise.

Magwaza-Msibi has, however, proved an adept administrator. Since 2000, when she assumed office as executive mayor of the Zululand District Municipality, the municipality has received unqualified reports from the auditor-general during the entirety of her tenure – an exception in the province. In 2006, the Zululand District also won a provincial award for the municipality with the most effective service delivery in KZN.

Magwaza-Msibi has been critical of the ANC-led provincial government for wasteful expenditure, and a lack of accountability and transparency. She has been especially critical of the provincial department of agriculture, accusing the KZN government of covering up audit reports relating to over-expenditure amounting to R125-million in 2006. There was also R80-million unaccounted for and the IFP has instituted legal action to gain access to the reports.

Born in rural Makhosini, she is a former primary school principal with a BA degree from the University of Zululand. She also holds a diploma in further education (management) from the University of Natal and a diploma in local government from the University of Durban-Westville.

Magwaza-Msibi joined the IFP in 1975 and moved up to the executive committees of both the IFP Youth Brigade and Women's Brigade by 1988. She also served as deputy chairperson of the Youth Brigade from 1998 to 2003 and later as national secretary of the Women's Brigade before assuming the position of national chairperson of the party.

Date of birth: February 1 1962

Mahumapelo, Supra

The ANC's provincial secretary in North West province, Supra Obakeng Ramoeletsi Mahumapelo, has been described by his detractors as 'brutal' and as someone who politically isolates those he disagrees with.

Mahumapelo led a campaign in the province to have former president Thabo Mbeki re-elected for a third term to lead the ANC. His faction of Mbeki supporters known as 'the Taliban' was up against the Jacob Zuma faction, called 'Mapogo', and managed to take control of several regions in the province, imposing its power in the provincial executive committee (PEC) as well as in ANC structures. The Taliban appeared to want to control premier Edna Molewa. Mahumapelo's intermittent skirmishes with the premier on governance matters were widely seen as a sign that none of his political comrades, no matter how close he is to them, should expect to escape his wrath in cases of differences of opinion.

Despite his loyalty to Mbeki, Mahumapelo still seemed to retain his power as a local strongman when he was re-elected provincial secretary in 2008 – beating Matlosana mayor China Dodovu by 507 votes to 306, the biggest majority at the conference. The provincial Umkhonto weSizwe Military Veterans' Association failed in its bid to prevent the accession of Mahumapelo to the strongest position in the North West. The veterans' association accused him of running the provincial ANC like a bantustan.

He is, however, still seen by staunch Zuma supporters as disinclined to reach out to his opponents after the national and provincial leadership battles. Pressure has been mounting on Mahumapelo to prove his loyalty to the ANC after being accused of conspiring with the Congress of the People and amid rumours within the ANC that he would be joining the new party.

Mahumapelo became politically active as a 19-year-old student, recruited to work underground for the ANC in Moruleng outside Rustenburg. He worked for the party during school holidays. It was while studying at Technikon Northern Transvaal in 1989 that he was elected to the national executive committee of the South African National Students' Congress (Sansco). He was expelled a year later for political activism, but was readmitted the following year.

After obtaining a national diploma in commercial practice, Mahumapelo worked for Eskom's procurement division in Witbank before being appointed as the ANC's provincial deputy elections coordinator in the then Western Transvaal. He became a political adviser to the MEC for transport in the North West, Phenye Vilakazi, and his predecessor, Johannes Tselapedi.

Mahumapelo served for nine years from 1996 as the ANC's provincial political education secretary and became ANC Youth League chairperson in the province two years later. His steady rise to political power in the ANC saw him elected to the party's PEC in 2002 when he lost his first bid to become the province's secretary, then a member of the provincial legislature in 2004, chief whip of the North West legislature in 2005, and provincial secretary in the same year.

He holds a master's degree in political economy from the University of Port Elizabeth. He was also sent on study tours by the ANC to Cuba and China where he did short courses on political systems.

Date of birth: June 7 1968

Makgoba, Malegapuru William

Malegapuru William Makgoba once said: 'People have tried to shoot me and they always miss.' This statement is an apt illustration of how as a scientist, commentator and university leader, Makgoba never appears to lose a battle.

Makgoba hails from rural Sekhukhuneland in Limpopo. He matriculated at Hwiti High School in Polokwane with, among others, Olive Shishana, president and CEO of the Human Sciences Research Council. He was one of a handful of black students to attend the University of Natal, where he completed his training as a medical doctor.

After working at the McCord and King Edward VIII hospitals in Durban he became the first African, in 1979, to win an Oxford Nuffield Medical Fellowship. Makgoba obtained his DPhil from Oxford in 1985 and then spent 15 years at institutions both in the UK and US before he was headhunted by the University of the Witwatersrand.

Here he became a symbol of the transformation battles then raging within higher education when, shortly after his appointment in 1994 as a deputy vice-chancellor at Wits, 13 senior academics at the institution accused him of falsifying his curriculum vitae. The saga, which made international headlines, led to Makgoba's 'relegation' to a research position and prompted the exodus of the 13 academics from Wits. But it also contributed to establishing the media savvy and vocal Makgoba as a public intellectual who does not shy away from controversy.

The tumultuous time at Wits prepared Makgoba well for his next job. In 1998 he became president of the Medical Research Council (MRC). His time at the MRC coincided with the emergence of then-president Thabo Mbeki's denialist position on the link between HIV and Aids. After Makgoba refused to endorse Mbeki's dissident view on HIV/Aids, his relationship with the head of state collapsed. Such was the nature of the breakdown at the time that he spoke out publicly against a campaign of vilification from the president's office against scientists who did not want to appease Mbeki. Makgoba was internationally recognised for the firm stance he took in the debate surrounding the pandemic.

But by 2002 Makgoba was ready to move on. He became vice-chancellor of the University of Natal at a time when the higher education sector was preparing for far-reaching restructuring. Natal University, for instance, was preparing to merge with the University of Durban-Westville (UDW). A bitter leadership battle ensued between Makgoba, vice-chancellor of Natal, and Saths Cooper, vice-chancellor of UDW. But Makgoba won the race and was installed as the vice-chancellor of the new University of KwaZulu-Natal (UKZN) in 2005.

As UKZN vice-chancellor, Makgoba appears to have focused more on university affairs and less on national matters. In higher education circles this has been seen as a symptom of the merger difficulties, which have required Makgoba to be inward- rather than outward-looking. It has been for his handling of UKZN university matters, in particular academic freedom, that Makgoba has attracted public attention. Following criticism against Makgoba for allegedly stifling open debate at the institution, several academics have faced disciplinary action and a number have left UKZN. But Makgoba, with his trademark composed demeanour, has not been moved by attacks on his leadership style.

With Makgoba's term ending soon, he may be looking towards new challenges again, which do not exclude eyeing a position in the post-Polokwane ANC government.

Date of birth: October 29 1952

Makgoba, Thabo

A man who sees himself as an activist for God, Thabo Makgoba, the Anglican Archbishop of Cape Town and Metropolitan of the Anglican Church of Southern Africa, often speaks out on issues close to him, interpreting them in a Christian context. He has spoken for peace in Somalia and the Democratic Republic of Congo, and for an end to hostilities in Gaza. Along with other church leaders, he called for former president Thabo Mbeki to step down as the mediator in Zimbabwe, and urged a United Nations arms embargo on Zimbabwe.

Makgoba grew up in Alexandra township and Pimville, and began work in the church when he was 17 years old. He earned a BSc at the University of the Witwatersrand, and then moved to St Paul's Theological College in Grahamstown, where he studied to be an Anglican minister.

Before working full-time for the church, he returned to Wits to do his master's in educational psychology and also lectured part-time. But this wasn't to last. He felt God calling him to the Church to try to instil hope and to show the possibility of a future without the pain of prejudice, crime, hatred and racism. Wrestling with God in the context of these painful social experiences as well as of poverty and gangsterism has constituted his journey of faith, as he describes in his book *Connectedness*, published in 2005, and yet he had been able to catch glimpses of hope.

He started his life in the ministry in Johannesburg, as a curate at St Mary's Cathedral and chaplain at Wits University. He was made Archdeacon of Sophiatown in the late 1990s and then Bishop of Grahamstown in 2004. On New Year's Eve 2007, he became the Archbishop of Cape Town.

The issues closest to his heart are the spiritual development 'of all God's people', teaching theology, and working with 'all marginalised'. His key values include upholding the sanctity of life and the dignity of difference, which he feels can be applied to numerous economic and socio-political subjects, such as HIV/Aids, free and fair elections, and the maturing of South Africa's democracy.

Makgoba is also a blogger (http://archbishop.anglicanchurchsa.org/), who discusses issues of political and social significance, such as Gaza and the crisis in Swaziland, Barack Obama's election, and how the Southern African Development Community 'has failed and is morally bankrupt'. And now and then, he adds a byte about his dog, Toffee.
Date of birth: December 15 1960

Malema, Julius

When the time came for firebrand Fikile Mbalula to finally admit that he was too old for the ANC Youth League and step down as its president, there was a collective sigh of relief from some in the ANC and outside to see the back of the young man, who had no guard for his mouth. Enter his successor, Julius Malema, and the unthinkable happened – things got worse. The mood of the rowdy and chaotic conference where Malema was elected was captured in an iconic photograph in which a Youth League member pulled down his pants to show his buttocks to the camera. It turned out to be a prescient warning to the ANC of what this 27-year-old would bring to the party – Malema would become the one constantly flashing his buttocks, figuratively, to South Africans and, lately, even to senior members of his party.

Malema is probably the best-known politician in South Africa, after ANC president Jacob Zuma. His gaffes provide fodder to many columnists and talk-show hosts, and his uncompromising and arrogant attitude feeds the frenzy.

Although he is seen as the ANC court jester who should not be taken too seriously, he has managed to emasculate important public institutions like the Human Rights Commission. His pledge to 'kill for Zuma' landed him in trouble with the commission, whose members at first hesitated as to how to deal with him and then had a discussion with him about his comments. He was sent home with an 'understanding' that he would not use that phrase again because it incites violence, but he was not punished in any way and not made to apologise.

Although some elders in the party, like arts and culture minister Pallo Jordan, insist that Malema's outbursts were not tolerated by the party leadership and that he had been reprimanded, only when Malema called on education minister Naledi Pandor to sort out a university strike with her 'fake American accent' did the ANC finally call him to order. After a flurry of statements Malema publicly apologised for his behaviour towards the minister and retracted the statement.

But during election time he took aim at everyone who dared to suggest that Zuma, who he says is like a father to him, might not be fit to be the president of the country.

In this regard he engaged in a public spat with Democratic Alliance leader Helen Zille, who called him an uncircumcised boy. Even ANC treasurer-general Mathews Phosa stepped into the resulting fray and criticised Zille, perhaps hoping that some of the attention Malema attracts would rub off on him.

But Malema has also been on the receiving end. He was the butt of a joke by a radio DJ who phoned Malema pretending to be newly elected American president Barack Obama. In the recorded conversation Malema made a fool of himself by saying to 'Obama' that he did not have questions for the American president because 'you phoned me'. The real embarrassment for Malema came, however, when he later insisted that he had not spoken to the fake Obama, although the soundbite was already doing its rounds.

Malema hails from rural Limpopo, where he passed his matric exam with a double G in woodwork and an H in maths, another embarrassing public relations disaster for the Youth League when these results were leaked to newspapers. Gauteng education minister Angie Motshekga came out in support of his poor matric record, proclaiming that academic qualifications are not important when you want to become a South African leader.

Malema is the kite the ANC flies to test public reaction to possibly controversial ideas. He was the first to mention the possibility of firing former president Thabo Mbeki. His remarks and the ANC's lack of will to restrain him were also mentioned as one of the key reasons why senior ANC members left the party to start the Congress of the People.

He may be billed as unsophisticated and his outbursts may provide journalists with unbeatable quotes and headlines, but Malema's most impressive achievement is that he has managed to force senior leaders and organisations to dance to his tune. When it came to selecting leaders for Parliament, however, Malema might have seemed a shoo-in, but the ruling party put its collective foot down and denied him the ultimate prize: to speak his mind under the comforting security of parliamentary privilege. **Date of birth**: March 3 1981

Maloyi, Nono

Patrick Dumile Nono Maloyi is the ANC's chairperson in the province that still bears the scars of Jacob Zuma's victory at the Polokwane conference in December 2007. Chairing an obviously divided North West province, Maloyi is well placed to be the ruling party's answer to problem child Supra Mahumapelo, his provincial secretary and staunch Thabo Mbeki supporter, who has seemed to have had the upper hand.

As a young man from Potchefstroom, Maloyi started his political career in the Congress of South African Students (Coasas) in 1983. He became youth chairperson of the Ikageng News Congress when he was 17 in 1985 and was arrested during apartheid South Africa's state of emergency the following year. Maloyi skipped the country for Zimbabwe and later moved to Lusaka, Zambia, where he joined other ANC exiles, only returning to South Africa in 1992.

He became a prominent leader of the ANC Youth League in the North West, holding positions such as provincial secretary in 1994 and chairperson in 1996. When Maloyi realised that his role as a youth leader was drawing to a close at 34, the ambitious politician began to spread his wings much wider. Barely out of youth politics, Maloyi was elected to the National Council of Provinces in 1999 and began serving on Parliament's portfolio committee on justice in 2004.

He was one of the many ANC MPs who were found guilty of fraud in what became known as the Travelgate scandal. Those involved colluded with travel agents to use travel vouchers for purposes other than the business of Parliament. Maloyi's case involved R150 000 in service benefits and mileage claims. After the widely publicised scandal, Maloyi was redeployed to the North West legislature as chief whip, a move opposition parties called his reward from the ANC for committing a crime; they dubbed him a 'Travelgate refugee'. He represented the North West on the national ANC chief whips' forum, a body composed of ANC chief whips from the national and provincial legislatures.

Maloyi was elected ANC chairperson of the North West at a conference at Sun City in 2008 marred by violence. Police had to intervene to keep order. After the conference his efforts to play the role of a good leader and extend an olive branch to rivals and tripartite alliance partners Cosatu and the South African Communist Party to mend their fractious relationship did not bear any fruit. Instead factionalism prevailed afterwards, resulting in stabbings and assaults in some regions of the North West.

A Zuma supporter, Maloyi witnessed the defection to the Congress of the People of his long-time colleagues Lolo Mashiane and Nikiwe Mangqo, who were on the provincial executive committee (PEC). He faces the challenge of leading a PEC that he is reluctant to trust, as he fears there are leaders within the ANC sympathetic to Cope. There is no love lost between his PEC and ANC head office, Luthuli House; the provincial ANC leadership was labelled 'fraudulent' by the party's secretary-general, Gwede Mantashe.

Date of birth: May 5 1968

Manamela, Buti

Buti Manamela, the national secretary of the Communist Party's youth wing, the Young Communist League of South Africa (YCL), has been known for his shooting-from-the-hip kind of public speaking since he assumed office when the party's Youth League was re-established in 2003.

His political activism began in the early 1990s when at the age of 12 he helped recruit members for the ANC Youth League and the South African Students' Congress (Sasco). Because of his age, Manamela did not qualify to be a member of either organisation, so he was given minor responsibilities that included blocking the township entrance with other comrades to ensure that residents honoured stayaways and consumer boycotts. 'I was 13 when I sneaked in my membership form,' he told the *Mail & Guardian*.

A staunch communist, Manamela idolises the late SACP secretary Chris Hani and singles him out as his biggest influence in choosing politics instead of a glossy career. He rose in the political ranks through the presidency of the SRC in 1997 at Phagameng High School in Modimolle, was elected Phagameng branch secretary at 15 and then continued to lead student bodies while studying electronic engineering at Mamelodi College.

Those critical of his rise to the leadership of the YCL say the firebrand leader never participated in the resurrection of the YCL but was 'fetched from the catalogue and brought to lead' by SACP leaders who knew him from the South African Commercial Catering and Allied Workers' Union, where he was a regional organiser. He seems to have used that opportunity quite well, considering that he has made it to the 2009 national list of nominees to occupy a seat in Parliament on the ANC ticket.

Manamela was one of the young leaders from the YCL and its tripartite alliance partner, the ANCYL, who played a prominent role in ensuring that Jacob Zuma would come out victorious as the ANC president at the party's conference in Polokwane in 2007. Surprisingly, he mentions former presidents Nelson Mandela and Thabo Mbeki as his political icons, despite being one of the louder voices demanding Mbeki's recall as the president of South Africa in September 2008. He even put a deadline on Mbeki's axing when he told journalists at a press conference that the then-president would be out of office in four days' time because he was 'incapable of leading the country'.

An outspoken Zuma supporter, Manamela is known for criticising the courts of law whenever they rule against the ANC president, calling the prosecutors in Zuma's case the 'terrible twins', and the judges that ruled against Zuma were reminded that they had served under apartheid.

Putting his foot in his mouth gained Manamela increasing popularity, and he has found a way to use it to his advantage. Just after the Congress of the People was formed after a breakaway from the ANC, Manamela called its leaders baboons and refused to apologise despite widespread condemnation.

Manamela made his mark in student politics, and while he advocates better education and skills to empower youth, he abandoned his electronic engineering studies in favour of politics. He wants the government to prioritise the 'quality and accessibility' of education and skills development. His ideas on curbing unemployment include the proposal that the South African National Defence Force be opened up for national service in order to give young people career options and to prepare for any future 'foreign invasion'.

The man who believes that only communism and socialism could work for South African people says communism is not about glorifying poverty and that communists can also live luxurious lives, as long as efforts are made to ensure that no one lives in poverty.

Date of birth: July 10 1979

Mandela, Nelson

Grey-headed and frail, Nelson Mandela has almost entirely withdrawn from public life. In 2008 he made one of his rare public appearances at the concert marking his 90th birthday in Hyde Park, London, and his increasingly abstract status as a world symbol was underscored by the torrent of tributes from celebrities and other public figures who can have little knowledge of the real man.

The inspirational revolutionary turned peacemaker remained active in the years immediately after he stepped down as South Africa's president in 1999, particularly in promoting children's welfare and the fight against HIV/Aids. In 2003 he launched the 46664 Aids fundraising campaign, named after his Robben Island prison number, and a year later flew to Bangkok to address the 15th International Aids Conference. As in the case of Inkatha Freedom Party leader Mangosuthu Buthelezi, his high-profile Aids stance appears to have been spurred by personal tragedy – his son Makgatho Mandela died of the disease.

Mandela also continued to take a public stand on geopolitical issues, for example accusing former US president George W. Bush in 2003 of 'undermining the United Nations' by invading Iraq. The mounting horrors in Zimbabwe have been particularly close to his heart. In 2007 he urged Zimbabwe's president Robert Mugabe – to whom he was never close – to step down 'sooner rather than later ... with a modicum of dignity' before he was hounded out of office like former Chilean dictator Pinochet. In June 2008, at the height of the crisis after Zimbabwe's presidential election, Mandela condemned the 'tragic failure of leadership' in that country. Mugabe, predictably, made no response.

Also in 2007, Mandela and his wife Graça Machel helped convene a group of world leaders, including Archbishop Desmond Tutu, former US president Jimmy Carter and former UN secretary-general Kofi Annan, to apply their wisdom to some of the world's most intractable problems. 'The Elders', as they were dubbed, made a brief and ineffectual intervention in Zimbabwe in a bid to ease that country's humanitarian and human rights crisis.

But Mandela's public statements have become increasingly infrequent, and when they happen they generally come from 'his office'. From time to time he is sucked into public controversies not of his own making, when his advisers, lawyers or other minders speak for him. An example was the dispute with his friend and attorney of more than 30 years, Ismail Ayob, over Ayob's alleged selling of prints signed by Mandela without his authority; the case went to the High Court. Initially claiming that he was a victim of a vendetta by Mandela's inner circle, chiefly advocate George Bizos, Ayob later apologised and agreed to pay R700 000 into a trust for Mandela's children.

Mandela's personal disappointments in his post-prison years, which also include the collapse of his marriage to Winnie Madikizela-Mandela and her misbehaviour while a deputy minister in his Cabinet, must have scarred this sensitive man. It is a fair assumption that he has been similarly wounded by the policy aberrations, unseemly scramble for loot and power, and infighting in the ANC – but he has given no sign of it.

Those who speculate that he is distancing himself from the ANC or even supports the breakaway Congress of the People underestimate the depth of his attachment to the Congress movement. He made this clear in an address at an ANC rally on his 90th birthday when he called on members 'to celebrate the achievements and reaffirm the values of a great organisation, one that has led for almost 100 years ... the struggle has been my life and the ANC led that struggle'. He made no reference to the factional upheavals in his party, which would reach a brutal climax mere months later with Thabo Mbeki's removal as party leader and his replacement as South Africa's president.

By the same token, it would be wrong to see his February 2009 appearance with Jacob Zuma at a rally in Mbeki's Eastern Cape birthplace as an endorsement of the ANC's new leadership. Mandela is a very old man who does not want to be drawn into the party's internal conflicts. It would be quite unrealistic to expect him to repudiate the movement to which he has devoted his life.

It has been an active one. Born into the Thembu royal family at Qunu in the Transkei, he fled to Johannesburg to avoid a traditional marriage, qualified as a lawyer and in the mid-1940s went into practice with Oliver Tambo, who would later lead the ANC in exile. With businessman Walter Sisulu, they founded the ANC Youth League, which radicalised the ANC; Mandela became its president in 1950.

He was volunteer-in-chief for a campaign to defy apartheid laws; was banned throughout the 1950s; and went on trial for treason during much of that time. Discharged, he went underground; he was the first overall commander of Umkhonto weSizwe, the ANC's armed wing. Mandela was captured in 1962 and jailed for 27 years, but even in prison he worked for the movement. Men would arrive in prison as black consciousness activists; they would leave as ANC stalwarts, ready to build a multi-racial society.

In the mid-1980s, he began secret talks from prison with the apartheid government, and in 1990 he was released, the liberation movements were unbanned, and four years of negotiations to establish a new South Africa began.

Date of birth: July 18 1918

Mangena, Mosibudi

Former president Thabo Mbeki surprised many, including those within his party, when he appointed Mosibudi Mangena to his Cabinet in 1999 as deputy minister of education. Most felt it was premature to appoint someone who was not from the party ranks to such a crucial position. Moreover, Mangena's party, the Azanian People's Organisation (Azapo), had fared particularly badly in past polls, with Mangena surviving as its sole MP. But those close to Mbeki said he looked at the bigger picture and wanted to tap into the skills of people who were not necessarily members of his party but were patriotic and keen to lend a hand in the building of a new democratic society.

Unlike other opposition MPs who used Parliament as a platform to score narrow political points as well as lambaste government policies, Mangena was always principled and gave balanced views about government's weaknesses and failures.

Like any other deputy minister, Mangena was overshadowed by his senior, Kader Asmal, who was then enjoying time in a sustained spotlight as he pushed through policies that were to transform the face of education in the country. Some of these policies included the controversial mergers of tertiary institutions and the much-vaunted outcomes-based curriculum.

But Mangena's star began to shine after he was appointed minister of science and technology in 2004, the new ministry created to drive government's key policy objective of focusing on mathematics and science as gateway subjects. Mangena was a good choice, not only because he holds a master's degree in applied mathematics from Unisa, but also because as a deputy minister of education, his remit had been to promote the two subjects, particularly at school level.

Soon after his appointment, Mangena forged links with and mobilised key science and research organisations to share his department's vision and strategy. These included the Council for Scientific and Industrial

Research, the National Research Foundation, the South African Agency for Science and Technology Advancement, and university-based research units. Mangena also ensured that there was good coordination and close collaboration among the organisations and increased their funding so that they could improve their research capacity and innovation.

He also embarked on a crusade to demystify maths and science and to raise public awareness about their significance and relevance to daily life. A particular focus was put on increasing the numbers of youth and women in science. To achieve this he launched a number of initiatives, including internship programmes; he also set up a database and other services to cater for unemployed science and technology graduates.

To interest learners in science at school level, the department introduced programmes like the National Science Olympiad for grades 10 to 12, Primary Science Day, National Science Week and Women in Physics.

He has successfully driven another, somewhat spectacular strategic project, SumbandilaSat, a science satellite to be launched into orbit in 2009.

Mangena's involvement in the liberation struggle goes back to the 1970s when he first joined the black consciousness-aligned South African Students' Organisation (Saso) while studying at the University of Zululand. As was common at the time, he was expelled for his political activities. In 1972 he convened a Black People's Convention chapter in Pretoria and was subsequently elected national organiser at its founding congress.

He was arrested and detained under section 6 of the Terrorism Act and in 1973 was sentenced to five years' imprisonment on Robben Island, the first black consciousness (BC) activist to arrive at the notorious prison. On his release he was banished to Mahwelereng township near Potgietersrus.

In 1981 he fled to Botswana with his family, with a mandate to set up a BC body in exile, which became known as the Black Consciousness Movement of Azania (BCMA). In 1994, when BCMA and Azapo merged, he was elected president of Azapo, a position he still holds.

Mangena has published three books; the latest is entitled *A Quest for True Humanity*. After the 1999 general elections, he became Azapo's sole representative in the National Assembly.

Date of birth: August 7 1947

Mantashe, Gwede

ANC secretary-general Gwede Mantashe has been at the centre of all ANC activities since the Polokwane conference and has shown a steady hand, although he has also been mired in controversy. First, Mantashe came in for a great deal of criticism in July 2008 after he accused the country's top judges of being elements of counter-revolutionary forces seeking the destruction of ANC president Jacob Zuma. Mantashe's attack on the judiciary came after the Constitutional Court lodged a complaint with the Judicial Service Commission, alleging that Cape judge president John Hlophe had improperly tried to influence the court's judges in relation to aspects of Zuma's corruption case.

Mantashe also took the rap after his controversial decision in November 2008 to bring back former ANC spin doctor Carl Niehaus as party spokesperson despite Niehaus's shady past. Barely three months after his appointment, Niehaus confessed to the *Mail & Guardian* to having forged the signatures of top ANC politicians on a letter in order to secure a loan from a Johannesburg businessman who hoped to use the letter to ensure favourable treatment from the Gauteng government on property deals. As if that were not enough, even after the *Mail & Guardian*'s exposé, Mantashe insisted he would find an alternative job for Niehaus within the ANC.

A former trade unionist, Mantashe was elected to the ANC's most powerful position in December 2007. During the same year he also became chairman of the South African Communist Party. He had served as a unionist for more than 30 years, eight of them as general secretary of the National Union of Mineworkers (NUM). In 2006, a year after he left the NUM, he was appointed executive director of the Development Bank of Southern Africa and head of the technical task team of the government's Joint Initiative for Priority Skills Acquisition (Jipsa). He resigned from both positions after his election as ANC secretary-general.

Union leaders have praised Mantashe for the role he played as NUM general secretary. When he left the NUM, it had over R70-million in reserves from subscriptions paid by members. Under Mantashe's leadership, the NUM established the Mineworkers Investment Company and the Mineworkers Development Agency, to promote self-employment strategies by providing mineworkers with access to essential training and skills development programmes. Mantashe also initiated the J.B. Marks Education Trust, a bursary scheme intended to help children of mineworkers in their studies. By 2000 the bursary scheme had produced 425 graduates and it approved 220 new scholars in 2006.

In his farewell speech to Mantashe in 2006, Cosatu general secretary Zwelinzima Vavi described Mantashe as a peasant, a worker, an organic intellectual, a Marxist and an African communist, who was passionate about the broad liberation movement. 'Last year [2005], I took my family to Gwede's house in the rural Cala. I saw some of his family and brothers. I came back understanding why Gwede Mantashe was what he is. For the first time, I understood why he feels so passionately about family and why he repeatedly quotes Karl Marx about the importance of family. I listened to an account of his father and great-grandfathers from him and his brothers, and understood why he would always mix Marxism with concerns for cows, goats and sheep. I understood why he was a communist and a worker because he came from a village of migrant labourers and peasants.

'There is no electricity in his homestead, no clean running water or proper sanitation. I understood why he had a passion for development.

'I also came to understand why he had a passion for both formal and informal education. He developed his own capacity by enrolling and studying part-time. Through his level of dedication he has grown from an abrasive trade unionist to one of our greatest organic intellectuals.'

Mantashe obtained an honours degree in commerce from Unisa in 2002 and is studying for a master's degree in commerce at the University of the Witwatersrand.

Date of birth: July 18 1956

Manuel, Trevor

Trevor Manuel wears well-cut jackets, but they do nothing to conceal the broad spread of his shoulders. The seams aren't strained, but there is the barest hint of tension in the fabric. Is it intentional, this signal of just-constrained force? Like most things about the world's longest-serving finance minister, it seems certain to be so. The physique of a retired prize-fighter is a not inconsiderable asset in the private confrontations of the Cabinet room, the International Monetary Fund or the ANC's national executive committee, or on the public stage of the National Assembly, the press conference and the hustings. Manuel certainly knows how to use it.

His wife, Maria Ramos, cuts a very different figure: slim, diminutive, perfectly contained in a Chanel suit. A *Mail & Guardian* headline once referred to the former Treasury director-general and Transnet CEO as an 'Amazon'. 'It is the first time I've seen a four-foot Amazon,' Manuel joked, not at all disapprovingly.

But if the Trevor Manuel of 2009 conveys an impression of physical and political heft, and if he clearly has an appetite for confrontation, we should not forget that he began his political career as an escape artist, and it is in fact his combination of force and guile that makes him the most remarkable of the ANC's big beasts. In the 1980s he was a worthy inheritor of Nelson Mandela's 'black pimpernel' moniker, criss-crossing the Cape Flats, and later the country, under the noses of the police, as the United Democratic Front generated the most coherent resistance yet to the apartheid regime. Key aides today, like his spokesperson, Thoraya Pandy, and Logan Wort, now a general manager at the South African Revenue Service, were among his troops then.

His apparent ability to survive the post-Polokwane street-fighting in the ANC required a combination of guile and sheer power that only he could bring to bear. Here, at number four on the party's electoral list, amid the vanguard of Jacob Zuma and the left wing, is the man who implemented the most successful and, for many, the most loathed of Thabo Mbeki's policies.

Manuel may not have invented the Growth, Employment and Redistribution Strategy (Gear) – Ramos, along with Treasury staff and private-sector advisers like Iraj Abedian worked out the detail – but he drove it through a reluctant ANC, and indeed government, against intense resistance. Derided by the South African Communist Party (SACP) and the union federation Cosatu as the '1996 class project', Gear dramatically reduced state debt by keeping expenditure on a tight rein, and gave the bond market new confidence in South Africa. Manuel has always insisted that inflation hurts the poor most, and that government borrowing constrains the capacity of the state to spend on services, making it beholden to financiers. 'It *was* a class project,' he told the *M&G* in 2008, 'a working class project.' SACP general secretary Blade Nzimande would beg to differ, and it is from him that comes some of the staunchest resistance to Manuel staying on in Zuma's government as a senior economic minister.

Even Manuel's admirers concede that the fiscal restraint of the late 1990s may have cut too deep, choking off investment in crucial infrastructure – notably electricity and transport – just as the neglect of the late apartheid years was beginning to tell. Manuel counters that the discipline was essential, and the steep reduction in debt service costs, along with a boom in tax revenues, enabled him to open up the taps to fund vastly expanded infrastructure programmes, as well as welfare spending, from 2003 onward. Even unemployment, the most intractable of South Africa's problems, began to fall.

The resurgent SACP and Cosatu have long complained that the Treasury under Manuel has had far too much power. It must not be so in a new government, they insist. A new law that gives Parliament much greater say in the budgeting process is one constraint, but there will be others, they say – not least a new planning division in the presidency with oversight of all economic departments.

Manuel's greatest frustration, however, has been his lack of ability to force better value for money out of other departments. Year after year he has cajoled Parliament to insist that education, health, transport and other ministries demonstrate that they are spending taxpayer money wisely and well. He has had little joy.

And he has been reluctantly forced to sign off on some of the least defensible investments the government has made: the arms deal, which he resisted but ultimately put his signature to; the Gautrain, which he felt was colossally wasteful; and bailouts for South African Airways and the Pebble Bed Modular Reactor.

If, after Polokwane, he seemed briefly to give up on fighting for his job, that quickly changed. His resignation when Mbeki was forced out sent markets briefly into a tailspin. It was, his team assured us, a communication error, but not before a useful message about the value of Trevor Manuel had been sent.

Of late he has been saying what he no doubt does not believe, backing the government's refusal to grant the Dalai Lama a visa, for example, just as he backed the arms deal and allowed it to appear as if he tolerated Mbeki's position on HIV. It is part of the escapologist's toolkit, this dissembling, and something he knows he has the political capital to get away with.

There are many in the ANC who believe he should be deputy president, but he has instead come in as a minister in the presidency, responsible for the powerful National Planning Commission. Make no mistake, he thinks he must stick around to save the country and his own legacy; and make no mistake, he will survive. He has been part of government since 1994, cooling his heels for two years as trade and industry minister before replacing Nedcor CE Chris Liebenberg as finance minister

Ramos's current position as CE of the Absa banking group presents conflict-of-interest problems, and the ANC's loony left are still baying for his head, but Zuma himself, along with Kgalema Motlanthe, Mathews Phosa and Gwede Mantashe, knows how vital a stabiliser he is. Manuel's greatest battle is only just beginning.

Date of birth: January 31 1956

Mapisa-Nqakula, Nosiviwe

Nosiviwe Noluthando Mapisa-Nqakula was not any more successful than her predecessor Mangosuthu Buthelezi in sorting out the mess at the home affairs department, which she took over in 2004, and now she has been appointed minister of correctional services. She presided over a government department many South Africans regard as dysfunctional and corrupt. As home affairs minister, she was on a continuous collision course for most of her term with the parliamentary portfolio committee that provides oversight of her department, on issues including staff incompetence, unsafe borders, poor treatment of refugees, and, most recently, the British government's decision to insist on visas for South Africans travelling to the UK because of that country's concern about the abuse of South African passports by non-South Africans. She was one of the three worst performers listed in the Democratic Alliance's annual performance report card for 2008.

Mapisa-Nqakula was born in Cape Town, attended the Mount Arthur High School and obtained a diploma in primary teaching from the Bensonvale Teacher Training College. After being employed as a teacher and youth worker, she contributed to the founding of the East London Domestic Workers' Association in 1982. She also studied project management, psychology, human relations, community development and communications through various institutions such as Canadian University Students Overseas, a Canadian non-profit organisation that assists with the development of Third World countries.

In 1984 Mapisa-Nqakula underwent military training with Umkhonto weSizwe (MK) in both Angola and the Soviet Union, then worked in the military arm of the ANC and became involved with women's issues. The ANC appointed her to a commission that investigated unhappiness within MK ranks in the 1980s.

She returned to South Africa in 1990 to help rebuild ANC structures and worked with schools to assist students from disadvantaged communities who had dropped out of school as well as with women's organisations inside and outside the country.

She rose to the position of secretary-general of the ANC Women's League, which she filled from 1993 to 1995. Eight years later, she demonstrated her impressive ability to marshal political force when she beat MK veteran Thandi Modise for the presidency of the Women's League, vacated by Winnie Madikizela-Mandela. She defeated her more fancied opponent convincingly, apparently by securing the backing of the respected Madikizela-Mandela.

Some of the controversial decisions taken by the Women's League under her leadership include the resolution to back Jacob Zuma for the ANC presidency and Kgalema Motlanthe as his deputy, despite the league's earlier intention to nominate a woman. She lost her Women's League presidency in 2008 after failing to make it to the nomination stage for re-election.

Selected as an ANC MP in 1994, she was appointed to the defence committee and was later chairperson of the committee on intelligence. Her appointment as ANC chief whip after Tony Yengeni's resignation drew praise from MPs across the political divide; she was the first woman to hold what is believed to be the most powerful position in the ruling party in parliamentary affairs. She was implicated in the Travelgate scam, which involved politicians cashing in their official travel vouchers or using them for purposes other than government business, but it did not seem to affect her career. She took over the position of deputy minister of home affairs from her husband, Charles Nqakula – who was appointed safety and security minister – in 2002 and was subsequently named the department's minister in 2004. The home affairs department is currently engaged in a multi-billion-rand turn-around and continues to be under mounting pressure to get its house in order.

Date of birth: November 13 1956

Maseko, Themba James

Themba Maseko is the government's über-spokesperson. Responsible for communicating the progress government makes on its delivery agenda, he also leads the task of broadening government's interaction and communication with the South African public and coordinating the communications strategy of all government departments. He is, in addition, ultimately responsible for managing the brand 'South Africa' internationally through ancillary organisations like the International Marketing Council as well as increasing previously disadvantaged South Africans' access to broad, diverse media through institutions such as the Media Development and Diversity Agency.

With a history in the field of education and time done in the private sector, Maseko has fitted well into his role as CEO of the Government Communication and Information System (GCIS), taking over from its former head, Joel Netshitenzhe. Netshitenzhe was given the unenviable task of re-engineering the state's communication machinery back in 1998. He was responsible for the creation of the post-Cabinet meeting media briefing, as well as media briefings by the relevant Cabinet clusters created to tackle various government plans of action through cross-departmental groupings.

Maseko, as the new leader of the GCIS, has done well in continuing and strengthening the department's work. He is generally accessible and is a good facilitator between the media and government. Under his watch networking sessions between the media and government have taken place in an attempt to smooth the largely acrimonious relationship between the two.

His work has met with some success, but ultimately, as observers have pointed out, though Maseko and the GCIS are able to influence how government departments communicate, they cannot be responsible for the end result. Government's response to incidents such as the power failures – or 'load shedding' – in early 2008 which shut down the country's mines is a case in point. Its reaction was uncoordinated and slow on the uptake, with departments like public enterprise and minerals and energy unable to coordinate the messages being sent out to the public at large.

The reasons for the blackouts – a combination of insufficient capacity, poorly managed coal stockpiles at the power parastatal Eskom, ageing and poorly maintained distribution infrastructure, and the under-valuation of electricity as a commodity long maintained by government as part of its industrial development policy – were identified after weeks of interrogation by an irate civil society and the media at large.

However, when former president Thabo Mbeki stepped down, the GCIS managed to slip seamlessly into communicating for what is essentially a very different administration, under interim president Kgalema Motlanthe.

With challenges such as these, Maseko has proved to be an excellent replacement for Netshitenzhe, not surprisingly for someone who is a consummate activist and politician in his own right.

Born and bred in Johannesburg, Maseko attended Immaculata High School in Diepkloof, Soweto, obtaining his matric in 1982. He has a degree in sociology and law from the University of the Witwatersrand, along with an MBA from De Montfort University in the UK, earned in 2002.

In the 1980s and 1990s he was active in politics chiefly through student organisations like the South African National Students' Congress (Sansco), the Azanian Students' Organisation (Azaso) and the National Education Coordinating Committee, which he served as general secretary from 1991 to 1993.

In 1994 he became an MP but left in 1995 to become superintendent-general of the Gauteng education department. He did a short stint in the private sector as managing director of the Damelin education group and CEO of Sifikile Investments, then went back to government as director-general of the department of public works, a position that he left in 2006. He took up the mantle at the GCIS in 2007.

Date of birth: January 27 1964

Mashatile, Paul

Paul Shipokosa Mashatile, Gauteng's ANC chairperson, was appointed the province's fourth premier on October 7 2008 after the shock resignation of Mbhazima Shilowa, who shortly thereafter joined the breakaway party, the Congress of the People, as its first deputy president. After the 2009 elections, the premiership was sensationally taken away from Mashatile and given to Nomvula Mokonyane, while he was redeployed to national office as deputy arts and culture minister.

Previously Mashatile, who holds a postgraduate diploma in economic principles from the University of London, served as MEC for housing, safety and transport after joining the Gauteng legislature in 1994 and then became MEC for economic development of the country's richest province.

The last few years of Mashatile's term as provincial finance minister were mired in controversy. In 2006 the *Mail & Guardian* revealed that he had declared an interest in the listed IT company, Business Connexion; this had contracts with the Gauteng Shared Service Centre (GSSC), which answered to him as finance minister. Later he said he had been offered but never taken up a R50-million stake in the firm. Gauteng's integrity commissioner, Jules Browde, cleared Mashatile of any conflict of interest in 2006.

A year later the *M&G* revealed that the study fees of Mashatile's nephew were paid by government consultant Donny Nadison, who had two contracts with the Gauteng Economic Development Agency (Geda), a statutory body that reports to the provincial finance minister. Nadison claimed he sponsored a number of young people through his New Africa Youth Trust and had 'mentored' Mashatile's nephew. Mashatile backed up the argument, saying that Nadison had facilitated funding for a number of students from previously disadvantaged backgrounds, including his nephew. He had no powers to award tenders and was not involved in any of Nadison's Geda tenders.

In August 2007 the *M&G* reported that Mashatile's daughter Palesa was employed by Business Connexion as the company awaited the outcome of two multi-million-rand tenders from the GSSC. The *M&G* also outlined Mashatile's connection with the so-called 'Alex mafia' – former activists from Alexandra township who have risen to positions of influence around him in Gauteng. It was revealed that Geda and the Gauteng Enterprise Propeller, which also reported to Mashatile, had awarded tenders to a security company which has Mashatile's friends as directors. Mashatile accused the *M&G* of a witch-hunt against him.

One of the more sensational storms around Mashatile was his department's R96 000 bill for more than 200 people at the exclusive French restaurant in Sandton, Auberge Michel, in 2006. At the end of 2008, shortly before he became premier, questions were asked about the legality of a private equity fund – the Gauteng Fund – set up with government money by Mashatile in the provincial treasury to attract foreign investment to fund government projects.

Although having ingratiated himself with the 'Zuma camp', Mashatile is seen as politically closer to businessman and former Gauteng premier Tokyo Sexwale, who ran a short campaign as the 'third way' candidate for the ANC's 2008 presidential election in Polokwane.

Mashatile cut his political teeth as a youth activist in Johannesburg's Alexandra township during the 1980s. He actively participated in the underground structures of the ANC and South African Communist Party, serving as Transvaal secretary until 1992. He was also secretary of the United Democratic Front in the Southern Transvaal from 1985 to 1991 and was detained for almost four years without trial under successive states of emergency.

Date of birth: October 21 1961

Masondo, Amos

Amos Masondo has one of the tougher jobs in the country: executive mayor of Johannesburg, the country's fastest-growing metro, South Africa's financial powerhouse and a draw for migrants from the rest of the country and the continent. The city houses the headquarters of more than 70% of companies doing business in South Africa; it generates 16.5% of the country's wealth; and at R161 656, in 2004 – the latest figures available – household income was nearly double the national average. Yet the city's unemployment rate in the same year was 32%. The population is growing faster than the job market; and nearly half the population is younger than 34. The traffic is horrific, the roads are potholed, much of the city is filthy, crime is rife. As in many major cities, great wealth sits uneasily beside great poverty.

Masondo presides over a mayoral committee of councillors with varying degrees of competence to tackle these problems, and an administration headed by a city manager whose predecessors spun off most essential services into companies wholly owned by the metro – everything from rubbish collection to the city's parks and the Johannesburg Zoo.

There have been some successes: decay in the CBD has been turned around by the establishment of the largest Urban Development Zone in the country. The city is trying its best to herd informal traders into formal markets. Derelict buildings have been renovated, and new, affordable – and award-winning – flats have made rental accommodation available. But as long as the population continues to swell – and it will – and officials in charge of essential services fall asleep at the switch, challenges will remain.

Masondo, now in his second term, has been mayor since 2000. It is an interesting role for a former trade unionist and community leader. Born in Soweto, he has a strong struggle history: the South African Students' Movement, which he joined in 1972; six years on Robben Island for establishing underground cells and networks; founding membership of the United Democratic Front; twice detained under emergency regulations.

On his release from prison, he joined the Soweto Civic Association and served on Soweto's Committee of Ten. At the same time, he signed on with the General and Allied Workers' Union, became a full-time organiser two years later and acting general secretary in 1985. In 1990 he was secretary of the Witwatersrand region for the trade union federation Cosatu, and served as the ANC's regional election coordinator for the first democratic elections in 1994. An ANC member of the provincial legislature, he was MEC for health, then served as political adviser to the premier before acceding to the mayoral seat.

He currently also serves as co-president of United Cities and Local Governments, an international organisation based in Barcelona, which was founded to increase the role and influence of local government in global governance.

Date of birth: April 21 1953

Masondo, David

David Masondo, chairperson of the Young Communist League (YCL), appears to be more of an academic than a politician. His comrades claim that he is an 'organic intellectual', whose leadership skills are the result of a long involvement in the student and mainstream politics of the country.

He has a charming demeanour, which seems to have won him many hearts and respect within the South African Communist Party (SACP), which he joined in 1993. He is a member of the party's politburo and its national executive committee, and is respected for his work in political education within the party.

It is probably his soft-spoken, down-to-earth and approachable nature that makes him a great teacher and credible leader. He has lectured in political studies at the University of the Witwatersrand and is completing his PhD at New York University. He has published and presented a number of academic and SACP papers.

Masondo is a low-profile politician. Even in the run-up to the 2009 general elections, he did not seem to involve himself in the electioneering campaigns. He is not media shy but is not the type of leader to bark empty rhetoric to hype up audiences. As leader of the YCL he is seldom quoted in the media, unlike his ANC Youth League counterpart. It is no wonder that people make the mistake of referring to the YCL's general secretary, Buti Manamela, as chairperson, instead of Masondo.

Masondo was a rural youth when he first became involved in politics. As a youngster in Mbokota village in Limpopo he was forced into the political struggles of the country. It was the conditions of rural poverty and apartheid as well as undemocratic traditional leadership and institutions led by tribal chiefs that sparked his political activism. He became a dissenter in his village, together with his young comrades, mobilising against corrupt chiefs who embezzled money meant for community projects. His work eventually led to the formation of the Mbokota Youth Congress in 1989. Since then, he has played a major role in re-establishing the ANC Youth League in villages in his area.

Masondo has made a name for himself in national student politics. During his studies at the Giyani College of Education, Masondo led the South African Students' Congress (Sasco) and was also elected president of the student representative council (SRC) at the college. In 1996 he became Northern Transvaal provincial chairperson of Sasco, and a year later its national deputy president. In 1998 he was elected SRC president at the University of the Witwatersrand, and in 1999 he was appointed a member of the National Youth Commission. When his term expired, he was named SACP national political education coordinator and youth desk coordinator. He served as chairperson of the ANC Youth League in Limpopo between 2003 and 2005.

Judging by his experience in political leadership, Masondo may be dubbed a political stalwart, especially in view of the many active years he seems to have ahead of him – if politics does not lose a place in his heart to the academy.

Date of birth: November 14 1974

Masualle, Phumulo

New Eastern Cape health MEC Phumulo Godfrey Masualle was a long-time MEC for finance, economic development and environmental affairs. He has a direct – often robust – way of dealing with problems. In 2000, after receiving complaints from community members that unauthorised people had invaded state-owned houses, he embarked on an aggressive campaign to evict them.

With strong support from the tripartite alliance, he was a front-runner to replace former premier Nosimo Balindlela, but lost the race by a sliver to colleague Mbulelo Sogoni.

A well-known Zuma loyalist, Masualle is a member of the ANC's national executive committee and national treasurer for the South African

Communist Party (SACP). He was in the spotlight for a controversial letter he wrote firing Wiseman Nkuhlu, economic adviser to former president Thabo Mbeki, as chairman of the Eastern Cape Development Corporation after Nkuhlu joined the breakaway Congress of the People.

He is known to have a keen interest in acquiring knowledge, obtaining, in succession, a national technical certificate at Mthatha Technical College, a national diploma in electrical engineering from the Peninsula Technikon, and a diploma in public service management and development from the Swedish Board for Investment and Technical Cooperation. He earned a postgraduate diploma in economic principles from the University of London in 2005.

Masualle started his working career as a trainee industrial technician in the Transkei post office and was industrial technician in the provincial department of commerce, industry and tourism from 1989 to 1994. In 1995 he moved to the office of the premier as administration secretary, a job he kept until 1999.

His political career started at the Peninsula Technikon where he served as a branch chairperson of the South African National Civic Organisation (Sanco) in 1988. Three years later he was elected chairperson of the Ikwezi township SACP branch, becoming deputy regional chairperson for the Transkei, then Eastern Cape provincial chairperson, and finally provincial secretary. He was MEC for public works and chairperson of the portfolio committee on finance and the standing committee on public accounts before moving to finance.

Date of birth: December 12 1965

Mathale, Cassel

If there is one thing that Limpopo ANC chairman and premier Cassel Mathale has achieved over the past few years, it has been to use his leadership position within the ANC to clinch multi-million-rand business deals. Unlike most politicians, who conduct their business in secrecy, Mathale's activities are an open secret. The companies' register shows that Mathale is a director of more than 10 companies, ranging from mining, construction and farming to the hospitality sectors. Some of these have benefited from lucrative government contracts in Limpopo. For instance, in 2007, while Mathale was the ANC's provincial secretary, he was among the beneficiaries of a R6.7-million black economic empowerment deal when his company acquired 43% of the shares in citrus enterprise Bosveld Sitrus. With former finance minister Thabadiawa Mufamadi, he is also a director of Manaka Property Investments.

Mathale told the *Mail & Guardian* in an interview that he sees no conflict between politics and business. 'This thing of conflict of interest is just a fabrication. As Africans we must not allow that. We should allow everyone to go into government. I have been involved in business all my life. The most important thing [as politicians] is to disclose our business interests to the public,' argues Mathale, who is also part of the provincial leadership of the South African Communist Party.

Those who know Mathale well say he leads a lavish lifestyle, with expensive cars and large houses. Every December he throws a huge party where he dishes out expensive bottles of whisky to his friends and comrades at one of his homes in Nkowankowa township near Tzaneen.

A staunch Zuma supporter, Mathale became ANC provincial chairperson after he defeated Limpopo premier Sello Moloto, who was regarded as a close ally of former president Thabo Mbeki. The ANC's Polokwane conference in December 2007 called on all provincial executive committees to list three candidates for consideration by the ANC's national executive committee. However, after Mathale won the ANC elections as the party's provincial chairman, his supporters, in defiance of ANC policy, resolved that he should be the only candidate for the Limpopo premiership.

Born in the dusty village of Dan near Tzaneen, Mathale was active in the liberation struggle while he was still in his early 20s. He was already involved in politics when he went to the University of the Western Cape, where he earned a BA in social science. He held leadership roles in a number of ANC structures from branch to provincial level. From 1986 to 1990, Mathale was a member of the regional executive committee of the United Democratic Front. He was also a national executive committee member of the ANC Youth League between 1996 and 1998.

Mathale served as the ANC's provincial secretary from 2002 until 2008, when he was elected chairman. One of his major achievements as

ANC provincial secretary was to deliver more than 70% of the province's vote to the ANC during the 2004 elections. Mathale also served as a member of the provincial legislature from 1994 to 2003. He was appointed to the provincial Cabinet as transport minister in 2008 to ensure a smooth transition.

Date of birth: January 23 1961

Matshiqi, Aubrey

As he was born in 1962, the same year that Nelson Mandela was sent to Robben Island, it is perhaps natural that Aubrey Mongameli Matshiqi has found his philosophy shaped in the ANC, its military wing Umkhonto weSizwe, the student movements and the South African Communist Party.

Matshiqi was born in Soweto and read English literature and history at Vista University. He has worked as an educator, teaching maths, science and English, and in the late 1990s was in the Gauteng province's strategy unit; he also had a stint as spokesperson for former Gauteng education MEC Mary Metcalfe. He works as a columnist for *Business Day* and as a political analyst at the Centre for Policy Studies.

Matshiqi was once the resident elections analyst for the SABC, ironically the same organisation that later blacklisted him alongside *Business Day*'s politics reporter Karima Brown, *Mail & Guardian* publisher Trevor Ncube, writer and journalist William Gumede, political analysts Sipho Seepe and Moeletsi Mbeki, and others.

He does consultancy work for government, political parties, policy institutes, academic institutions, foreign embassies and the corporate sector.

One of former president Thabo Mbeki's most forthright critics, Matshiqi is described by his peers as an organic intellectual with extensive contacts within the ruling ANC – hence his informed, incisive, at times humorous, commentary.

Date of birth: November 11 1962

Mayende-Sibiya, Noluthando

Noluthando Mayende-Sibiya, president of the National Education Health and Allied Workers' Union (Nehawu), is one of the few women leaders within Cosatu not afraid to speak their mind, even if her views differ from those of her chiefs. In 2007, when Cosatu leaders, including general secretary Zwelinzima Vavi, insisted that Cosatu members should actively participate in identifying ANC leaders sympathetic to the interests of the working class, Mayende-Sibiya came out strongly against the idea, saying the issue of ANC leadership should be left to ANC members. Equally, she publicly rebuked ANC leaders under Mbeki's presidency who questioned the integrity of the leadership of the South African Communist Party (SACP) for its 2007 critique of Mbeki's government.

Mayende-Sibiya's fearless and independent approach to issues has earned her respect among her colleagues. Her popularity within the ANC-led tripartite alliance was clear during the ANC's national conference in Polokwane in 2007, when she was elected to the party's national executive committee.

Nehawu spokesperson Sizwe Pamla describes Mayende-Sibiya as a calm but strong leader who has the interests of the workers at heart. 'She always provides good leadership, whether in meetings or rallies. She is also very passionate about women's issues and the fight against HIV/Aids. She makes sure that whenever she delivers a speech, she talks about issues that affect women,' says Palma. 'She is the kind of leader who would say if she is unhappy about something. She always looks forward, to find solutions to issues. Her quality leadership is the reason she is where she is today. You can understand why people have faith in her. She might not be the loudest person, but she always ensures that she makes her point. She is not for the spotlight, but a person for the moment.'

Mayende-Sibiya is one of the few unionists and women leaders in Cosatu who made it on to the ANC's 2009 candidate list for seats in the National Assembly. Her experience in the trade union movement and her popularity within the alliance put her in pole position to play a critical role in Jacob Zuma's new administration.

Born in Umlazi, KwaZulu-Natal, and a nurse by profession, Mayende-Sibiya was in 2004 elected Nehawu's first woman president in the organisation's 17-year history. Before that, she had served as the union's second deputy president. She joined Nehawu in 1988 while she was a trainee nurse at Prince Mashiyeni Hospital in KZN.

According to a Cosatu website, Mayende-Sibiya cut her teeth in politics during the turbulent years of student activism in the 1970s while in high school. She lived for a few years in Swaziland where her activist parents were forced into exile. She was also involved in the United Democratic Front in the mid-1980s.

Apart from her duties as Nehawu president, Mayende-Sibiya serves as a co-convener of the South African Progressive Women's Movement and an executive member of the SACP and the ANC. She heads the newly created ministry of women, youth, children and people with disabilities. **Date of birth:** July 7 1956

Mbalula, Fikile

Until 2004, Fikile Mbalula was a non-factor in the country's political landscape. The former ANC Youth League firebrand found himself in the limelight only in 2004 after he was elected Youth League president. His key task – albeit not as easy as he might have thought – was to make sure Jacob Zuma would become the next president of the ANC and the country. Mbalula's mission was accomplished in December 2007 during the ANC's watershed conference in Polokwane when his troops toppled former president Thabo Mbeki from the ANC's powerful position in favour of Zuma, a move that would result in the formation of a breakaway party, the Congress of the People.

Mbalula's position on who should lead the ANC to its centenary in 2012 earned him both enemies and friends within the liberation movement. His detractors accused him of being disrespectful after he referred to finance minister Trevor Manuel as a 'drama queen' and former defence minister Mluleki George as a 'comical Ali'. But supporters of Mbalula, who is affectionately known as Vutha within ANC circles, have praised him for his courage in taking on the intellectual Mbeki, when no one in the ANC dared to challenge the chief's authority. Mbalula was one of the few leaders within the ANC-led tripartite alliance who publicly berated Mbeki's centralist leadership style, arrogance and aloofness.

A larger-than-life character, Mbalula is today regarded as one of the most influential politicians in South Africa. After he stepped down as president of the Youth League in 2008, the ANC entrusted him with the responsibility for driving its election campaign. Mbalula is also a member of the ANC's national executive committee and sits on the party's powerful national working committee. His popularity within ANC structures was proved when he was nominated number 10 on the ANC's 777-strong candidate list for parliamentary positions for the 2009 elections, and he has been appointed deputy police minister. Insiders within the Youth League say that Mbalula will take over as ANC secretary-general in 2012. The Youth League wants him to serve as secretary-general for two terms and thereafter take over as ANC president and, ultimately, the country's president.

A father of two, Mbalula made headlines in 2008 when at the age of 37 he was forcibly taken to a circumcision school in Philippi, Cape Town, by his ANC comrades, including former ANC chief whip Tony Yengeni. After spending a month in the bush, Mbalula was flown back to Bloemfontein in businessman Tokyo Sexwale's private jet for a celebration at his mother's home in Bloemfontein. Among those at the celebration were Yengeni and ANC Free State chair Ace Magashule.

Born in a farming district in the Free State, Mbalula attended primary school in Botshabelo and completed his matric there in 1989. He became an active member of the ANC in 1990, beginning his leadership role in the Youth League as branch chairperson in Botshabelo. In 1997, he was elected secretary-general of the Youth League, a position he filled until 2004. He is studying for an economics degree part-time at the University of the Western Cape.

Date of birth: April 1 1971

Mbeki, Thabo

The turning point in Thabo Mbeki's presidency came a year into his second term, in 2005, when he sacked Jacob Zuma from the Cabinet and ran into an unexpected party backlash, which prevented him from axing his arch-rival from the party. It was the first time his many enemies in the ANC had coalesced into an active internal opposition. He described 2006 as his 'annus horribilis' – but much worse was to come.

Although some of his more fervent supporters proposed amending the Constitution to give him a third presidential term, Mbeki insisted that this was not his intention. His aim, typically, was to maintain remote control over government after his term ended in 2009 by holding on to the leadership of the ANC at its December 2007 party conference in Polokwane, Limpopo.

Exploiting widespread sympathy for Zuma and the perception that he was the victim of Mbeki's manipulation of the law enforcement apparatus, the anti-Mbeki lobby in the ANC and its communist and labour allies launched an intense organising drive in ANC branches, from which 90% of delegates to the Polokwane conference would come. As the conference approached, the two factions of the ruling party drew up separate lists for the party's 'top six' positions and its national executive committee (NEC).

Denialism – the refusal to face unpleasant facts – is fundamental to Mbeki's personality, and he was clearly astonished when provincial conferences nominated Zuma for the party presidency, ahead of him by a wide margin. The Polokwane conference itself delivered a humiliating public rebuke to the man who had held unchallenged sway over the ANC since the late 1990s. It was not just that he lost the party leadership to Zuma by a decisive poll of 1 505 to 2 329 votes. His supporters were hounded from every senior national position and from the top echelons of the NEC.

Close associates such as outgoing party chair Mosiuoa Lekota, who publicly attacked Zuma's political and personal morality before the conference, and Phumzile Mlambo-Ngcuka, who had replaced Zuma as South Africa's deputy president, did not even feature in the ANC's new NEC. The pattern was cemented in January 2008, when the newly elected national working committee, the ANC's inner leadership core, was packed with Zuma loyalists.

The Polokwane revolution involved a reassertion of party control over the government, which Mbeki had resisted throughout his presidency. He was expected to implement all conference resolutions, even those – including one mandating the dissolution of the Scorpions – he disapproved of. A tense stand-off ensued, while the Zuma faction continued to consolidate its grip on the ruling alliance by ousting Mbeki's supporters from the unions, the South African Communist Party (SACP), the ANC

Youth League and provincial ANC structures. His implacable foes in the Youth League and on the left continued to call for his removal as president.

In September 2008 they had their opportunity, after a ruling by Judge Chris Nicholson in the Pietermaritzburg High Court found that Mbeki's government probably abused the justice system in a bid to thwart Zuma's presidential ambitions. Exploiting the wave of anger which followed, members of the 'coalition of the wounded', including SACP boss Blade Nzimande and businessman Cyril Ramaphosa, whom Mbeki, through one of his ministers, had once publicly accused of plotting against him, convinced the NEC to ask him to step down. Within a week he had quit, half his Cabinet had resigned in protest and Kgalema Motlanthe replaced him.

Except as a symbol, Mbeki is politically a dead man. Now 67, he has no overt links with the newly formed Congress of the People and has made it clear that he 'refuses to rule from the grave'. He intends to continue serving South Africa through a planned leadership foundation.

His high-handed and centralising leadership style, his talent for making powerful enemies and his long-running ideological struggle with the left were his main undoing. But the irony is that on the policy front, he gave significant ground to his opponents in his last years as president. His administration effectively dropped privatisation and moved to more expansionary budgets, with significantly increased spending on welfare and infrastructure, as well as adopting the industrial policy so dear to the left. Although still an Aids dissident – he will doubtless go to his grave questioning whether HIV leads to Aids – he allowed the roll-out of antiretrovirals as part of a national treatment programme. Among his achievements, he can point to South Africa's macroeconomic stability over the nine years of his presidency and, in the latter years, impressive economic growth.

But on Aids, on his determined support of the increasingly repressive Zimbabwean president Robert Mugabe, on poverty and joblessness, he leaves a sense of squandered opportunities. The party he served for 50 years remains deeply split, its founding principles sullied by the greed and self-serving culture he did little to curb. Other than those who benefited from his policies, principally the black business elite, few will mourn his passing.

It didn't have to end that way. He was, in a sense, born to rule. The son of one of the country's most prominent ANC families, Mbeki holds an MA in economics from Sussex University and underwent military training in the Soviet Union before turning up in Lusaka, where the talents of this brilliant and urbane man were recognised. He held ANC ambassadorial posts throughout Africa and by the mid-1970s was chief adviser to ANC president Oliver Tambo. He then became ANC political secretary; later, director of information and publicity; and finally head of the ANC's international department.

It was Mbeki who charmed South African business leaders, editors and politicians in the late 1980s, acting as go-between during negotiations before political parties were unbanned in South Africa, and afterwards he was prominent in multi-party negotiations for a new, democratic South Africa. His appointment as first deputy president in 1994, instead of the hugely popular Ramaphosa, was not a popular move, but his power was unbreachable – until Polokwane.

Date of birth: June 18 1942

Mbete, Baleka

The second female deputy president of South Africa since democracy, Mbete has been described by her detractors as arrogant and autocratic. She is a tough politician, but those close to the former teacher say she is a good-natured person, friendly and easy to talk to. She lost her battle to continue as deputy president and left Parliament for Luthuli House.

Mbete joined the ANC in 1976 after fleeing apartheid South Africa to teach in Swaziland. She served the ANC in countries such as Tanzania, Kenya, Botswana and Zambia between 1977 and 1990. She returned to South Africa as secretary-general of the ANC Women's League and was active in the negotiations for the abolition of apartheid. Mbete participated in the transformation and reconciliation processes leading up to the first democratic elections in 1994, holding positions such as national spokesperson for the ANC election centre, member of the presidential panel on the Truth and Reconciliation Commission, and member of the Constitutional

Committee. Her name was one of the first 50 in the ANC's list of MPs in 1994, indicating the confidence the party had in her firm loyalty.

In 1996 she became the deputy speaker of Parliament, a post she held until she was appointed speaker in 2004 after Frene Ginwala. While in the National Assembly's second highest position, Mbete was found in 1997 to have received an improperly issued driver's licence; she claimed she was too busy to stand in queues. She was, however, not charged with any wrongdoing.

Her support for two controversial leaders of the ANC, former chief whip Tony Yengeni and current party president Jacob Zuma, has been too strident and vocal, attracting criticism from opposition parties for conflict of interest. Yengeni was found guilty of defrauding Parliament by not disclosing a massive discount on a luxury car in a scandal linked to the controversial arms deal. Zuma has for many years been facing charges of corruption, also linked to the arms deal. Under Mbete's leadership, Parliament has been involved in making decisions on reports of investigations undertaken by the auditor-general, the public protector and the Directorate of Public Prosecutions on the matter. She attracted controversy again in 2006 when she took a costly chartered flight to Liberia's capital Monrovia to attend the inauguration of President Ellen Johnson-Sirleaf, Africa's first elected female state president.

Mbete accepted a nomination from the Zuma camp just days after the ANC Women's League's decision to back Zuma for the presidency of the ANC at the Polokwane conference. Originally named as deputy secretary-general, she was then nominated from the floor for the post of ANC chairperson during the conference. She stood against ANC strategist and Mbeki loyalist Joel Netshitenzhe, but emerged victorious, largely because of the intense anti-Mbeki sentiment at the conference.

She must have suspected that a good understanding with the Zuma camp would bring some rich rewards, and she was soon occupying several powerful positions including chairing the ANC's political committee in Parliament, as well as continuing to be the speaker of Parliament. Her appointment to head the ANC's political committee in Parliament raised questions about how she was going to be both the parliamentary speaker and the ANC front person. Commentators described Mbete as both 'the referee and main goal-scorer'.

Those who have worked closely with her describe her as a 'political animal', a survivor and a go-getter who can dance to two tunes at the same time – that of her party and of Parliament. Her autocratic conduct kept National Assembly members in line though opposition party members concede that she did her best to afford all parties an opportunity to participate in Parliament. Her judgement was, however, questioned whenever she refused opposition party members a chance to ask what were seen as controversial questions.

On 25 September 2008 she became South African deputy president after the resignation of Phumzile Mlambo-Ngcuka in solidarity with Mbeki, when he was recalled from the presidency by the ANC.

Born in Clermont township in Durban, Mbete matriculated in 1968 and obtained a certificate in teaching from Lovedale College in 1973, working as a teacher in Durban before going into exile. She holds various postgraduate certificates in international law, governance and conflict resolution, and served as an adviser on these issues in the Burundi peace process.

Date of birth: September 24 1949

Mboweni, Tito

As South Africa's Reserve Bank governor, Tito Mboweni cuts a bold figure in South Africa's financial circles. He is respected for his independence and refusal to be swayed by popular demands, but he has also drawn criticism for his perceived arrogance and intolerance of criticism.

Credited with bringing South Africa's inflation rate into the targeted 3–6% range since his appointment as governor in August 1999, Mboweni was reappointed for a second term in 2004. Although the official inflation rate subsequently spiralled out of control, reaching as high as 13% in 2008, Mboweni's continued policy of high real interest rates was not always viewed positively from certain quarters in both business and labour, which argued that South Africa needed to target growth and job creation rather than inflation.

His current term will expire in August 2009 and Mboweni has made himself available for re-appointment, going so far as to decline an invitation to have his name put forward as an ANC MP for the April 2009 elections. Given his prominent standing in South Africa, he would undoubtedly have earned a position in the Cabinet if he had so desired.

Born in Tzaneen, Limpopo, in 1959, Mboweni went into exile in 1979 in Lesotho, where he completed a BA degree in economics and political science at the National University of Lesotho, joining the ANC in 1980. Mboweni went on to further his economic studies by completing an MA degree in development economics at the University of East Anglia in England in 1987.

In May 1994 he was appointed minister of labour as part of the first democratically elected government. Prior to this position he had served as deputy head of the ANC's department of economic policy. During his tenure as labour minister, Mboweni oversaw the passage of the Labour Relations Act of 1995, which entrenched the rights of workers. In his role as Reserve Bank governor, Mboweni has suggested that the laws introduced in the Labour Relations Act have become obstacles to economic growth.

In July 1998, Mboweni relinquished his Cabinet position when he was appointed as adviser to the Reserve Bank governor. At the time it was announced that he would succeed the then-governor, Dr C.L. Stals, when Stals's term came to an end in August 1999. This was initially not a popular choice, as Mboweni's labour credentials suggested that he would be a populist governor. However, Mboweni soon put paid to these concerns by adhering to the inflation-targeting mandate given to him by the government, despite intense criticism that inflation targeting was anti-growth and curtailed employment growth.

Although his mandate is set by government, Mboweni himself believes in inflation targeting as a model for long-term economic sustainability. The global banking crisis of 2008 has severely derailed South Africa's economic growth prospects and Mboweni, as Reserve Bank governor, faces one of his greatest challenges to date as other inflation-targeting central banks cut rates to stimulate growth.

Mboweni was appointed honorary professor in economics at a number of universities and has received a number of honorary doctorates; in a rare display of modesty, Mboweni does not elect to use his honorary titles. He was awarded the degree of doctor of economics by the University of

Natal, appointed professor extraordinary in economics by the University of Stellenbosch between 2002 and 2005, and installed as chancellor of the University of the North West in 2001 – and he serves as an honorary colonel in the 1st South African Tank Regiment.

He is known as a connoisseur of whisky and cigars as well as a keen fly-fisherman. He is also regarded as an indomitable force when it comes to critical journalists and economists and has been known to bring a knobkierie with him when addressing the press corps. Despite many heated exchanges, Mboweni has earned the respect of colleagues, journalists and economists for his fiercely held independence and conservative approach to monetary policy.

Date of birth: March 16 1959

Mkhize, Zweli

A close confidant of the man from Nkandla, KwaZulu-Natal's (KZN) new premier, Zweli Mkhize, has been instrumental in Jacob Zuma's accession to the presidency by organising the province's monolithic support for him.

A mixture of silk and steel, Mkhize fulfils a role on the cut-throat field of South African politics that would translate into the footballing equivalent of German midfielder Michael Ballack: influential at a national level, ruthlessly efficient and with a no-nonsense approach to the game of politics.

Mkhize has served on the party's national executive committee (NEC) since 1997 and chairs the NEC's education and health sub-committees. He was the perennial bridesmaid in the last decade, twice losing out narrowly to outgoing premier Sbu Ndebele – seen as close to Thabo Mbeki – for the position of provincial chair. After Zuma, a previous chairperson, left the province in 1998 for national office, Mkhize lost the leadership battle to Ndebele by 21 votes; in 2002 he lost by 17 votes.

A medical doctor, Mkhize graduated from the University of Natal and worked in hospitals in Zimbabwe and Swaziland after leaving South Africa in 1986 for political reasons. Born in Willowfontein outside Pietermaritzburg, Mkhize has been commended for his work as KZN health minister from 1994 to 2004; so successful was he that the

Treatment Action Campaign's Zackie Achmat reportedly suggested him as a replacement for national minister Manto Tshabalala-Msimang in 2004. He became MEC for finance and economic development after the ANC won an outright majority in the province in 2004.

During the corruption trial of Zuma's financial adviser Schabir Shaik, Mkhize was called to testify about Shaik's donations to the ANC during his time as provincial treasurer. And during Zuma's rape trial, the mother of Kwezi, his accuser, testified that Mkhize had met her to discuss her daughter's education and a fence for her home. It also emerged that Mkhize had paid the legal fees of Yusuf Dockrat, a lawyer Kwezi consulted after her alleged rape.

Following on the violent conflict in KZN in the 1990s, Mkhize emerged unscathed after a former bodyguard – standing trial for the murder of expelled ANC leader Sifiso Nkabinde – alleged that he was also implicated in Nkabinde's 1999 assassination. In March 2008 Mkhize won damages amounting to R150 000 from the *City Press* newspaper for defamation relating to the Nkabinde murder allegations.

With controversy around the loan arrears of government funding institution Ithala Bank, amounting to R321-million, and revelations that politicians, their wives and others connected to Ithala had benefited – some without due procedures being followed – Mkhize has been the only government official to reveal publicly that a R13-million loan was made to his wife for the purchase of a farm.

Date of birth: February 2 1956

Mlambo-Ngcuka, Phumzile

Phumzile Mlambo-Ngcuka, who was South Africa's first female deputy president, has a background very different from that of most of her colleagues, both the exiles and the inziles: she did not spend her formative years as an ANC politician-in-waiting but devoted her time to NGOs. Nonetheless, her rise in the party since 1994 has been rapid and, by and large, successful, with her occasional slips forgiven by the party and the public protector.

As an MP, she was given the public service committee chair and elevated to deputy trade and industry minister in 1996. Three years later she was named minister of minerals and energy; in that post, she popularised the notion of charters as the best way to measure progress in economic transformation.

An enduring image of Mlambo-Ngcuka was the brave, deeply hurt wife of Bulelani Ngcuka, national prosecutions head, who was accused by two prominent ANC politicians, Moe Shaik and Mac Maharaj, of having been an apartheid spy. Mlambo-Ngcuka attended hearings day after day in late 2003; when her husband was absolved of the charge, and her appointment to her Cabinet post was renewed, she greeted the news with humility and relief.

Mlambo-Ngcuka was born in Clermont, Durban, matriculated from Ohlange High School in Inanda, and enrolled with the University of Lesotho to study for a BA degree in social science and education. From 1981 to 1983 she taught in KwaZulu-Natal before moving to Geneva to join the Young Women's Christian Association as its youth director. She returned to South Africa in 1987 as a director of Team, an NGO based in Cape Town, working with squatters and African independent churches to promote self-reliance. She then went on to a post as director of World University Services, involved in the management of funds donated to development organisations by Swedish and Swiss government agencies.

In 1993, she set up a management consultancy company, Phumelela Services, to promote race- and gender-sensitive organisational development, general change management, restructuring of institutions and linking change with productivity, but moved on to Parliament a year later.

In June 2005, Mlambo-Ngcuka was appointed deputy president to replace Jacob Zuma, who had been fired for alleged corruption. She resigned in September 2008 after Thabo Mbeki was recalled by the ANC's national executive. And only weeks before the April 2009 election, she joined the Congress of the People.

Date of birth: November 3 1955

Modise, Thandi

The deputy secretary-general of the ANC, Thandi Modise is one of the politically tough, senior women in the party.

Her political activity began in 1976 when, as a student, she was jailed for her anti-apartheid activities. After her release, Modise slipped over the border into Botswana and was later transferred to Angola, where she received training with the ANC's military wing, Umkhonto weSizwe (MK). She said her reason for leaving the country was not so much about refusing to be taught half her subjects in Afrikaans, a big issue in 1976, but rather about the 'unprovoked' police harassment on school premises. When Modise was shot at by police one day as she was walking from school, she decided the next time she was shot at for no reason, she would have a gun to shoot back – and that influenced her decision to join MK. After her training she worked in the camps as a political commissar.

In 1978 Modise returned to South Africa to go underground as an MK operative. She was termed 'the knitting needles guerrilla' because while she operated underground as an MK cadre reconnoitring potential military targets, she tried to look like other ordinary women and carried a handbag from which a pair of knitting needles protruded. She was arrested in 1979 and jailed for eight years despite an advanced pregnancy – the first woman in the country to be jailed for MK activities. She served the sentence at Kroonstad Prison until she was released in 1988.

She has been a member of the national executive committee of the ANC Women's League since 1994 and held the position of deputy president until 2002. Modise chaired Parliament's portfolio committee on defence from 1998 until 2004, a period when Parliament had to start dealing with allegations of a corrupt arms deal. While speaker of the North West provincial legislature, she was elected deputy secretary-general of the ANC at the Polokwane conference in 2007.

Modise is seen as one of the most competent and principled members of the ANC, who has advocated a more moral policy on defence and believes strongly in asserting Parliament's oversight role. Her relationship with former president Thabo Mbeki's camp took a knock from the beginning of the arms deal investigation in the early 2000s when she chaired the defence portfolio committee. It is believed that Modise's independent spirit led to her being passed over for more senior positions befitting her talents and hard work. She was tipped to be appointed premier of the North West in 2004, but was overlooked in favour of Edna Molewa.

Modise controversially defended ANC Youth League president Julius Malema's assertion that the league was prepared to 'kill for Zuma'. She flanked ANC secretary-general Gwede Mantashe on the fateful Saturday when the two announced that Mbeki had been recalled as South African president. Though she made it to the nomination list for Parliament, the ANC preferred to keep Modise at Luthuli House to strengthen the team that will run the party from its headquarters.

Thandi Modise was born in Huhudi township near Vryburg in the Northern Cape, the youngest of six children. Her father, railworker Frans Modise, was an ANC activist. Modise completed her matric and a BComm degree while in jail.

Date of birth: December 25 1959

Mokgoro, Yvonne

Judge Yvonne Mokgoro is one of only three women on the Constitutional Court bench and one of two among the original members of the court appointed by former president Nelson Mandela in 1994.

Like justices Kate O'Regan, Albie Sachs and Pius Langa, she is set to retire from the court in October 2009. She will, however, continue to make an impact on the legal landscape through her work as chair of the Law Reform Commission, whose task it is to ensure that South African legislation remains relevant to changing times. Once retired she has indicated that apart from spending more time with her three grandchildren, she will continue to be involved in teaching here and abroad.

Mokgoro was born in Galeshewe township, Kimberley, and matriculated at the local St Boniface High School in 1970, studying while holding down a day job as a nursing assistant. She was encouraged to study law by an encounter with Pan Africanist Congress leader Robert Sobukwe, who was asked by her husband to act for her when she was arrested after a run-in with the security police. After a night in jail, she was impressed by the power of the law when Sobukwe helped secure her release on bail. He suggested she join the profession and use it as a tool against apartheid. Thus inspired, she went on to study law at the former homeland University of Bophuthatswana, obtaining BJuris, LLB and LLM degrees in the five years up to 1987. She completed a second LLM at the University of Pennsylvania.

Initially appointed as a clerk in the justice department of the homeland government, she was promoted to maintenance officer and public prosecutor in the Mmabatho Magistrate's Court upon completion of her LLB. She lectured at the University of Bophuthatswana throughout most of the 1980s, and in 1991 was appointed associate professor of law. After a year lecturing at the University of the Western Cape, she joined the Human Sciences Research Council's Centre for Constitutional Analysis as a specialist human rights researcher while lecturing part-time at the University of Pretoria.

Mokgoro serves on the committee of the Press Council, which selects the press ombudsman and members of the Press Appeal Board. Her particular fields of interest are human rights, customary law and the impact of law on society, especially on women and children. She is a member of the International Women's Association, the International Association of Women Judges, the International Federation of Women Lawyers, and the South African Women Lawyers' Association.

She is married to former North West director-general Job Mokgoro.
Date of birth: October 19 1950

Mokonyane, Nomvula

Nomvula Mokonyane's star has taken off since the lead-up to the 2007 ANC conference at Polokwane, when she stood up for Jacob Zuma in the ANC Women's League and secured its support for him instead of Thabo Mbeki, who had till then been a favourite of its leadership. She defended the league's choice of Zuma, even though he had come under heavy attack from women's rights organisations during his rape trial. Unlike Mbeki, who had expressed a desire that he be succeeded by a woman, Zuma had not been vocal in support of women's rights.

At Polokwane she helped the Zuma cause when she argued against those who said the top six of the ANC's officials should include three women in order to provide a true gender balance. The Zuma list had only two women, Baleka Mbete and Thandi Modise. Mokonyane and others successfully argued that the 50/50 balance should apply to the rest of the 80 members of the national executive committee (NEC), rather than the top six.

In the post-Polokwane period, Mokonyane became a national figure with her elevation to the party's NEC and prominent part in the 2009 election campaign. Until then Mokonyane had been a provincial player who served first as MEC for safety and liaison and then as housing MEC. Her performance in these posts was, at best, average. But her energy, vibrancy and streetwise manner have always been important to both ANC and provincial government officials in helping with their interaction with communities during local visits.

Appointed Gauteng premier in controversial circumstances in 2009, she has been a dependable member for the ANC. She was sent to lead the election campaign in the Western Cape, which had been identified as a problem area by the party. Whilst on this assignment she accused the office of the president of being dominated by the Congress of the People and of refusing to allow acting president Kgalema Motlanthe to campaign for the ANC.

One of 12 children and a practising Catholic, Mokonyane started her activism in the early 1980s as a founder member of the Congress of South African Students (Cosas) in Kagiso, Mogale City (formerly Krugersdorp). She later joined the Federation of Transvaal Women (Fedtraw) before being elected to the central committee of the South African Communist Party. She was sent by the party to coordinate its activities in the Western Cape after power was taken away from the provincial executive committee.

She has received training in local government and planning management and community development in Sweden. She completed a certificate course in emerging economics with the Wharton Business School at the University of Pennsylvania and studied leadership and governance at Harvard University.

Date of birth: June 26 1963

Molewa, Edna

The former premier of the North West, Bomo Edna Molewa, is a political survivor who was almost written off by other politicians, the media and commentators alike. She survived the axe when the newly elected provincial executive committee (PEC) of the ANC voiced dissatisfaction with her lack of consultation when taking decisions. In the corridors of

Mphekwa House, the ANC's North West provincial offices, Molewa was accused of failing to provide leadership as the province prepared for the ANC's national elective conference in Polokwane. Unlike other premiers she did not publicly declare support for either of the party's presidential candidates: former president Thabo Mbeki or his successor, Jacob Zuma. Her come-back to power politics as minister of social development surprised many and confirmed talk that behind the soft-spoken woman is an assertive and powerful politician.

Molewa started off as a teacher in the rural village of Makaunyane in the former Bophuthatswana homeland in 1976 and served in the ANC underground in the 1980s. She rose in the ranks of the trade union movement through the South African Commercial, Catering and Allied Workers' Union, which she chaired in Warmbaths before becoming its deputy president.

A gender activist who believes in increasing the influence of the women's movement in the country, Molewa was co-founder of the Federation of Transvaal Women. She is widely described as a self-made woman who came to the fore in various organisations that fought for the realisation of democracy in the country.

Sworn in as an MP in the first democratic National Assembly in 1994, Molewa was sent to the North West two years later. She served the province in three portfolios: first as MEC for tourism, environment and conservation, then as MEC for economic development and tourism, and finally as MEC for agriculture, conservation and environment. Thabo Mbeki appointed her premier of North West as part of his attempt to increase the representation of women in leadership positions in government.

The reaction to her appointment was cold; she was not considered prominent enough in the eyes of many in the ANC. She took over a province defined by large income disparities, where the levels of poverty were increasing fast enough to give any political leader a headache, a province which is still 70% rural and where poverty is still a challenge. One of her notable achievements was her ability to improve relations with traditional leaders, in particular the platinum-rich Royal Bafokeng Nation, which wields great economic and social influence in the province.

Progress was also made in economic development, although still centralised in big towns such as Rustenburg, Klerksdorp and Potchefstroom. Molewa's government failed, however, to bring sufficient change to the lives of poor people, a failure opposition parties in the province blame on the ANC PEC's efforts to control Molewa. The Democratic Alliance leader in the North West, Chris Hattingh, says that Molewa was always dancing to the music from the provincial ANC. 'She had no power to move or to do anything without the consent of this power that was sitting in a smoke-filled room and issuing instructions.' Hattingh described Molewa as having been 'a hostage in her own Cabinet ... If politics were set aside and we had to look at the strengths in the ANC, we would vote for Edna Molewa to return as the premier.'

The United Christian Democratic Party agreed, saying that the relationship between Molewa's government and the opposition was healthy. 'The approach was different; the premier is people-orientated,' said the UCDP's deputy leader, Kgomotso Ditshetelo.

The ANC Women's League – she is North West chairperson – was key to the resuscitation of Molewa's political career when it tasked her with leading the women's campaign to install Zuma in the Union Buildings.

Molewa has completed two leadership courses at prestigious US institutions: she studied economic leadership and administration management at the Wharton School of Business and leadership at Harvard University's Kennedy School of Governance.

Date of birth: March 23 1957

Moosa, Valli

Mohammed Valli Moosa has been in the headlines of late for all the wrong reasons. Although he left government in 2004 he is still a member of the ANC's national executive committee (NEC). It is the conflict of interest between his role on the NEC and its finance committee and his former role as Eskom chairperson that has landed him in hot water. In February 2008 it emerged that the Eskom board had awarded a R38-billion boiler contract to a consortium in which the ANC had an interest. A report by public protector Lawrence Mushwana criticised Moosa's handling of this situation.

Moosa's term as Eskom chairperson was not renewed in 2008 after a number of management blunders, including rolling power-cuts and massive coal shortages that cost the economy billions of rands. He is currently a businessman running his empowerment company, Lereko Investments, which he founded in 2004 along with long-time struggle comrade Popo Molefe and Lulu Gwagwa. Lereko has significant investments in the mining and hospitality sectors, amongst others.

Moosa rose to prominence when he became acting general secretary of the United Democratic Front (UDF) in 1985, following the arrest of the incumbent Molefe. In 1987 he was arrested and remained in prison for 14 months, until September 1988, when he escaped and took refuge with two other detainees in the US consulate in Johannesburg.

After the ANC was unbanned, he was seconded by the UDF to work for the party and assumed the position of secretary of its internal leadership corps under Walter Sisulu. When the UDF was dissolved he was elected to the ANC's NEC and the working committee in charge of negotiations. He was also part of the ANC's working group dealing with constitutional principles, where he played a major role in the drafting of the new South African Constitution. This would have prepared him well for his role as minister of provincial affairs and constitutional development, which he took over from the National Party's Roelf Meyer in 1996 after serving as his deputy during the short-lived Government of National Unity.

Moosa was appointed minister of environmental affairs and tourism in Thabo Mbeki's Cabinet from 1999 to 2004. Under his leadership the ministry moved towards a focus on sustainability, passing numerous pieces of legislation aimed at getting industries and individuals to clean up their act. Outdated legislation regulating pollution and waste was revised and new legislation regulating the use of plastic bags and driving vehicles on beaches was introduced. South Africa also hosted the World Summit on Sustainable Development in September 2002 – another high point of his tenure as minister.

Moosa matriculated in 1974 at Lenasia Indian High School and enrolled at the University of Durban-Westville for a BSc degree in mathematics and physics after he was refused government permission to enrol at the University of the Witwatersrand. At Durban-Westville he joined the

South African Students' Organisation (Saso) but eventually moved to the civic movement, becoming involved in the revitalisation of the Natal and Transvaal Indian congresses.

Moosa has also served on various boards and commissions; he was chairperson of the United Nations Commission on Sustainable Development from 2002 to 2003 and president of the World Conservation Union. He is a non-executive director of a number of boards of public and private companies, including Sanlam and Imperial Holdings.

Date of birth: February 8 1957

Moseneke, Dikgang

Deputy chief justice Dikgang Moseneke was the favourite to take over as chief justice from Pius Langa until he spoke his mind about the ANC at his 60th birthday party. Shortly after Thabo Mbeki's defeat at the ANC's Polokwane conference, Moseneke commented: 'I chose this job very carefully. I have another 10 to 12 years on the bench and I want to use my energy to help create an equal society. It's not what the ANC wants or what the delegates want; it is about what is good for our people.' His comments irked the new national executive committee of the ruling party and the ANC Youth League, who said he should apologise for 'showing disdain' for the Polokwane delegates. Made as they were before judgment was handed down in the Constitutional Court on the admissibility of search and seizure warrants in the Jacob Zuma case, Moseneke's comments gave the Youth League ammunition for its claim that Zuma would not get a fair trial. The matter was eventually resolved after acting president Kgalema Motlanthe, in his capacity as ANC deputy president, held talks with Moseneke.

Moseneke is still highly regarded by the legal profession and enjoys the support of friends such as former president Nelson Mandela, but his accession to the position of chief justice is not a fait accompli – although some prominent members of the legal profession believe he will be confirmed as the country's new chief justice when the incumbent retires. As deputy chief justice, Moseneke deputises for Langa as the presiding judge of the Constitutional Court and on the powerful Judicial Service Commission. He is also expected to step in should the chief justice be unable to fulfil any of his duties.

Moseneke has a long history of activism. He joined the Pan Africanist Congress in 1962, the same year he was incarcerated for 10 years on Robben Island as one of the jail's youngest political prisoners ever. While on the Island he studied by correspondence through Unisa, completing his junior certificate – for which he sat alongside ANC stalwart Walter Sisulu – and his BA and law degrees.

His legal career began in 1976 when he joined Klagbrun Inc in Pretoria as an articled clerk. Two years later he was admitted as an attorney and practised for five years as a partner in the law firm Maluleke, Seriti and Moseneke; his former partners are now High Court judges. In 1983 he was called to the Bar – the first black advocate to be admitted to the Pretoria Bar – and 10 years later attained senior counsel status.

Prior to the transition to democracy, Moseneke was involved in the drafting of the country's interim Constitution and in 1994 was appointed deputy chair of the Independent Electoral Commission. He served a term as an acting judge of the Pretoria High Court before being asked by Mandela to help 'modernise' Telkom and prepare it for listing, a request that resulted in five years spent in various corporate-sector leadership positions, including a position as CEO of the black economic empowerment company Nail. He rejoined the legal world in 2001 when Mbeki appointed him to the Pretoria High Court. The following year he replaced Judge Johann Kriegler at the Constitutional Court and after three years he was appointed deputy chief justice when Langa succeeded Arthur Chaskalson as chief justice.

Moseneke was a founding member of the Black Lawyers' Association and the National Association of Democratic Lawyers.

Date of birth: December 19 1947

Motlanthe, Kgalema

Kgalema Motlanthe took over as acting president after the ANC 'recalled' Thabo Mbeki as South African president in September 2008. Although he took a lot of flak when he continued with Mbeki's maligned mediation process in Zimbabwe, Motlanthe showed overall a steady hand in completing the process, leading to a government of national unity in that country. He also displayed good judgement in appointing a strong Cabinet and effecting changes where they were most needed. The appointment of Barbara Hogan to replace the recalcitrant and obstructive minister of health Manto Tshabalala-Msimang was a stroke of genius that inspired confidence. So was the removal of Charles Nqakula from safety and security and Brigitte Mabandla from justice, as the country's criminal justice system has been unable to respond effectively to a crime wave that makes South Africa one of the most dangerous countries in the world. He wisely kept intact his finance team led by Trevor Manuel.

Motlanthe's image was sullied, however, when he decided to sack suspended National Prosecuting Authority head Vusi Pikoli, even when the Ginwala inquiry had recommended that he stay. Motlanthe said he took the decision because the inquiry had found that Pikoli was not sensitive to national security matters, but he was unable to justify why this weakness overrode several strong points which Ginwala found in Pikoli's favour. The dismissal was seen as an ANC instruction to get rid of Pikoli, who had angered the ruling party by his dogged determination to prosecute Jacob Zuma.

Motlanthe also came under fire from his comrades for his refusal to sign into law some Bills, including one that gave Parliament the right to summarily dismiss members of the SABC board without due process. He insisted that the Bills could not pass constitutional muster, although at times it appeared that he wanted to show that he was not prepared merely to rubber-stamp ANC resolutions.

At the same time stories about Motlanthe's love life were leaked to the media in what appeared to be a strategy by his opponents within the ANC to deflate any ambitions he might harbour for high office.

Motlanthe was voted deputy president on a Zuma ticket at Polokwane in 2007. However, many in the Zuma camp still did not fully trust him and this distrust is likely to continue to haunt him in future. ANC branches voted him second after Zuma in their nomination lists before the 2009 elections, but he openly told the media that he did not want to be president again; however, he did not close the door on becoming deputy president again, a job he accepted after the April 2009 elections.

Motlanthe was born in Alexandra township, Johannesburg, to a working-class family. Most of his childhood was spent in Alexandra and much of his adult life was spent in Meadowlands, Soweto. In the 1970s, while working for the Johannesburg City Council, he was recruited into Umkhonto weSizwe. In 1977 he was found guilty of three charges under the Terrorism Act and sentenced to an effective 10 years' imprisonment on Robben Island. After his release in 1987, he was tasked with strengthening the union movement, joining the National Union of Mineworkers, where he first worked as an education officer; he was elected general secretary in 1992 when Cyril Ramaphosa left to lead the ANC. It was here, while engaged in bargaining with the Chamber of Mines, that he acquired his negotiation skills and his level-headedness, which were to be crucial when he later became ANC secretary-general.

Motlanthe became the voice of moderation and mediation during the intense leadership battle between Mbeki and Zuma. In comparison to Mbeki, who insisted that everything was fine under his leadership, Motlanthe acknowledged that the party was taking strain. He was sympathetic to Zuma, who had been fired as deputy president, but refused to condemn Mbeki. Both sides regarded him with suspicion, but at the decisive Polokwane conference he was elected deputy ANC president on the Zuma ticket.

Despite his protestations to the contrary, he is still regarded as a possible state president after Zuma's tenure.

Date of birth: July 19 1949

Motshekga, Angie

Angelina Matsie 'Angie' Motshekga has served Gauteng as a provincial minister for social development and education and is best remembered as a rival of Gauteng premier Paul Mashatile, against whom she fought for the leadership of the ANC in the province. In fact her elevation to national office will ease tensions and avoid a paralysing battle between their two camps. She has been appointed minister of basic education.

She was one of the first leaders in Gauteng to align herself with Jacob Zuma in the period leading up to the 2007 Polokwane conference, when most of the province was still entertaining the idea of Thabo Mbeki or Tokyo Sexwale as ANC president. Later the rest of the province threw its support behind Zuma and nominated him, rather than Mbeki, as president of the party. As a result of her stance she was elected to both the national executive committee and national working committee of the ANC at Polokwane.

Motshekga's career has had its controversies. In 2003 the ANC put her under pressure to explain why she had recommended that a female empowerment group, of which her husband was the director, be given a stake in a pension management deal a year earlier when she was MEC for social development. She had helped the Sediba sa Basadi group to land a stake in the Absa-owned Allpay Gauteng. Allpay is answerable to the social development department for its R170-million-a-year pensions contract. The *Mail & Guardian* revealed how her husband, former Gauteng premier Mathole Motshekga, had played a key role in registering and advising Sediba, creating an apparent conflict of interest for Angie Motshekga, but she survived the scandal without losing her seat.

When the ANC was facing defections to the newly formed Congress of the People (Cope), she called members who were leaving for Cope 'dogs', saying the party would work better now that the dogs were gone.

Motshekga was elected president of the ANC Women's League in 2008 in Bloemfontein after a bruising battle with her close friend Bathabile Dlamini. Her then fellow MEC Nomvula Mokonyane was at the forefront of what Motshekga called a painful campaign against her.

Motshekga was born in Pimville, Soweto, where she first became active in the struggle against apartheid. She holds a BEd from the University of the North and an MEd from the University of the Witwatersrand. She was an executive member of the National Education Union of South Africa in the 1980s and was elected convener of the teacher unity talks which led to the formation of the South African Democratic Teachers' Union (Sadtu). Her experience as an educator includes teaching at Soweto's Orlando High and lecturing at the Soweto College of Education and the University of the Witwatersrand.

She was a convener for gender in the office of the president, then proceeded to a post as a trainer in the department of public service and administration. She was elected a member of the Gauteng provincial legislature in 1999 and was appointed chairperson of the standing committee on education. She was appointed MEC for social development in 2000 and MEC for education in April 2004. In 2005 she was elected deputy chairperson of the ANC in Gauteng and a member of the ANC's provincial working committee.

Date of birth: June 19 1955

Motshekga, Mathole

A staunch supporter of Jacob Zuma, chief whip Mathole Motsekga is not without his fair share of controversy. His suggested means of dealing with criminals was to 'take them to the nearest empty building where we will find them guilty and beat them up'.

Motshekga was elected Gauteng ANC deputy chairman in 1991 and held this position until he was elected chairman when Tokyo Sexwale resigned. He lost the post when Luthuli House disbanded the party's provincial structure after hostile infighting while Motshekga was premier and ANC chairperson.

Motsekga is an ANC national executive committee member and the founding president of the Kara Heritage Institute as well as a member of the North West Commission on Religious Affairs. As president of Kara, he suggested renaming Christmas and other holidays to 'dechristianise' them, substituting the names of African holidays. This was very much in character, for African heritage, as much as the law, is what Motshekga is about.

He was born in the rural village of Bolobedu in what is now Limpopo province. He matriculated in 1969 and studied law at Unisa, where he obtained a BJuris and an LLB degree. He studied legal history, philosophy, constitutional and criminal law at Albert-Ludwigs University in Freiburg, Germany, and in June 1981 obtained a master's degree with distinction from Harvard Law School, which in 1994 awarded him a doctorate for his thesis on 'Concepts of Law and Justice and the Rule of Law in the African Context'.

He began his legal career as a candidate attorney with Savage, Jooste and Adams in Pretoria in 1977. He passed the attorney's admissions examination at the first sitting, a year ahead of the usual two years of articles of clerkship prescribed for candidate attorneys. Exactly a year later, he was admitted to the Bar. From June to December 1981, Motshekga was a visiting scholar at Harvard Law School, where he conducted research on African history, philosophy and culture at Harvard's Center for African Studies.

While he was in the US he participated in various anti-apartheid activities before going to West Germany, where he conducted further research at the Max Planck Institute for Foreign and International Law. He lectured at universities in Austria and Germany before returning to South Africa in 1984, when he was appointed senior lecturer in Unisa's department of criminal and procedural law. In July of the same year he was admitted as an advocate of the Supreme Court.

In 1985, Motshekga established the first community-based legal advice centre in Mamelodi, outside Pretoria, and in the years that followed he established a network of centres in various townships to support victims of apartheid, their families, political detainees and prisoners. These legal advice centres were later institutionalised as the National Institute for Public Interest Law and Research (Nipilar), co-funded by the European Community.

A long-time ANC activist, concentrating on legal matters, he was co-opted into the newly formed ANC department of legal and constitutional affairs in 1986. He played a role in the formation of the National Association of Democratic Lawyers. In preparation for constitutional negotiations and the establishment of a new order, he worked with the then-banned ANC in Lusaka to set up research teams on post-apartheid South Africa.

He was elected Gauteng premier in 1998, winning the race against Frank Chikane, the favourite of the ANC's national leadership. The ANC set up a commission of inquiry to probe allegations that Motshekga had abused donor funds while he was head of Nipilar and of mismanagement during his term of office. He was cleared, but Mbeki overlooked Motshekga when he was choosing a premier in 1999, preferring Mbhazima Shilowa.
Date of birth: April 2 1949

Motsoaledi, Aaron

New health minister Dr Pakishe Aaron Motsoaledi has a tough act to follow. There were groans of disbelief when his immediate predecessor, Barbara Hogan, was moved to the portfolio of public enterprises from health, where she had made a huge, welcome impact during only eight months in the post. Motsoaledi is, unlike Hogan, a medical doctor – he holds an MB BCh from the University of Natal. Health activists, although deeply disappointed that Hogan was not retained in the ministry, seemed willing to give him a chance when his surprise appointment was announced.

Few in the health sector are familiar with Motsoaledi – which is not surprising, as after a stint as chairperson of a health and nutrition education project in Jane Furse, he appears to have devoted his career to the ANC and a range of provincial posts in Limpopo, none of them in the health field.

In 1991 he became deputy chairperson of the ANC in what was then the Northern Transvaal. He headed the ANC's provincial election commission, the economics and infrastructure desk, and the research and briefing task team in 1994, the year he relinquished his position as chair of the Sekhukhune Advice Office, where he had served for eight years. Elected to the provincial legislature, he held successive posts as MEC for education, for agriculture, land and environment, and for transport, returning to agriculture in 2004. He was elected to the ANC's national executive committee in 2007 at the Polokwane conference.

Motsoaledi has an enormous pile of problems on his desk: a collapsing public health system, the tricky implementation of a national health insurance scheme, HIV/Aids, a burgeoning TB pandemic, and demoralised health workers – at the time of his appointment, doctors in the public health sector were picketing over poor salaries and some had gone on an illegal strike. The challenges mount up.

Dr Eddie Mhlanga, director of hospital services, has studied and worked with Motsoaledi and is sure he can handle it. 'He's a superb implementer,' he says, 'speaks his mind and listens to what people have to say.'

Date of birth: August 7 1958

Mphahlele, Letlapa

Letlapa Mphahlele is best known as the Azanian People's Liberation Army (Apla) commander who authorised the 1993 St James Church and

Heidelberg Tavern massacres in Cape Town. He is also the very serious president of one of two Pan Africanist Congress (PAC) factions. Crack a joke and he erupts in wild laughter, but a mention of the PAC is treated with absolute seriousness – jokes aside.

Mphahlele became party president during the fiercely contested national party congress held in QwaQwa in September 2006. His victory was believed to be due to his success in charming party youth structures, the Pan Africanist Youth Congress and the Pan Africanist Student Movement of Azania, which also harboured aspirations of ousting then-party president Motsoko Pheko.

Mphahlele is known within PAC circles as a robust leader who will not take no for an answer. Those who have crossed his path bear the psychological scars that tell the tale of his silent wrath. His strong will is probably a characteristic honed by many years spent as a foot soldier in exile.

When he became president many party stalwarts, out of fear for his reputed autocratic nature, resigned from their duties. Among these influential party front-men were national organiser Mofihli Likotsi and party deputy president Themba Godi. Godi later became founder and president of the breakaway party, the African People's Convention, with Likotsi as his deputy.

Critics are quick to point out that Mphahlele's struggle to rejuvenate a once powerful and influential political organisation is a vain attempt. Asked how he planned to increase the party's electoral support from a low 0.73% in the 2004 general elections to 10% in 2009, Mphahlele said: 'We are aiming far beyond 10% and our approach starts with the revitalisation of the PAC: strengthening branches, rebuilding party infrastructure, engagement with all stakeholders and partnerships with civic organisations, youth movements and women's organisations. We won't run a race where we don't set winning as our goal.' He did shake things up, all right. First, he cancelled all members' membership status and asked them to re-apply. He was accused of meddling with the party's constitution and the result was the formation of a breakaway camp, led by firebrand and former party secretary-general Thami ka Plaatjie.

Two years after the QwaQwa national congress, Mphahlele lived up to his reputation by convening an 'emergency national congress' at Fort Hare University. He succeeded in extending his term of office from three to five years and usurping the powers of the national organiser, the deputy president and the national chairperson.

Mphahlele was born in Rosenkrantz in Limpopo, where he started his schooling in Seleteng, Ga-Mphahlele. In 1978, when he was in standard eight, Mphahlele was forced into exile. His first stopover was in Botswana, where he joined the Soweto SRC. Two years later, he joined the PAC.

In January 1981 he left Botswana for Tanzania and did basic military training in Bagamoyo. In mid-1981 he went to Guinea-Conakry for advanced military training, including specialisation in anti-aircraft artillery, then returned to Tanzania and was based at Itumbi military camp, where he became commissar and editor of the camp newsletter, the *Mgagao People's Daily*. He rose through Apla ranks until he became the army's operations director.

He was arrested in Botswana in 1987 for possession of arms of war and was released in February 1990. In the wake of the new dispensation, with no general amnesty in sight, he left for a second spell in exile in April 1994. He was abducted from Lesotho in December 1995 and charged with terrorism. Charges against him were only withdrawn in September 2002.

Mphahlele has authored two books, *Child of This Soil: My life as a Freedom Fighter* and *Matlalela: The Flood Is Coming*. There is an ascetic side to his nature: he is a strict vegetarian and is not interested in a cup of tea either, adding, 'I'd rather have water.'
Date of birth: December 8 1960

Msimang, Mavuso

As the director-general of the most maligned department in government, Mavuso Msimang joined home affairs in May 2007 to implement the department's umpteenth turn-around strategy. Despite various attempts to bring in new leaders and new technology, the problems remained the same: corruption in the creation and distribution of identity documents and fraudulent passports that are sold on the black market for non-South Africans to gain access to other countries – especially Britain, for entry to which South Africans until recently did not need a visa.

Msimang had his work cut out for him. The bad publicity that the department received had finally hit home and morale in the department was at an all-time low. Even the we–never–fire–people–for–incompetence ANC was starting to get impatient and looked to the former chief executive of the State Information Technology Agency (Sita) to make miracles happen. By the time of publication they had started happening, albeit at a painfully slow pace.

In the department Msimang has a large following, with senior managers feeling they finally have a competent leader to steer them through a difficult course. The first item on his to-do list was to fire key personnel who had been involved in corrupt practices and financial mismanagement. There were some early visible successes. It had been taking up to six months to receive an identity document; now it would take three weeks. And the late registration of births, a loophole used to obtain identity documents fraudulently, was stopped.

Msimang, however, has remained in the firing line and the Polokwane battle also took its toll. The public spat between Msimang and home affairs portfolio committee chairperson Patrick Chauke won him few friends. There was an undercurrent to the battle, with Msimang being seen as a supporter of Thabo Mbeki while Chauke was trying to reposition himself as a Jacob Zuma man in order to continue in Parliament after the elections. The fight began when Msimang refused to let provincial managers appear in front of the committee, insisting he would answer any questions relating to provincial home affairs offices. He had the support of the minister, Nosiviwe Mapisa-Nqakula, but she was of little help, as she was an Mbeki supporter herself.

Msimang earned a BSc at the University of Zambia and completed an MBA at the United States International University in Nairobi. He spent time in the NGO sector, living in Ottawa and working for the development agency World University Service, before moving to Ethiopia and Kenya for the World Food Programme and, later, Unicef. Before he joined Sita, Msimang was CEO of South African National Parks and served at the helm of South African Tourism.

Date of birth: October 19 1941

Mthethwa, Nathi

Should the left get its way, Nathi Mthethwa will emerge as a major beneficiary for his unflinching support for ANC president Jacob Zuma. With the ANC keen to show the electorate its determination in crime-fighting, his police portfolio is likely to be at the centre of the criminal justice system.

Mthethwa's rise from chair of the parliamentary portfolio committee on energy and mineral affairs to minister in charge of one of the most important portfolios in government has its roots in his support for Zuma. Mthethwa, who like Zuma hails from KwaZulu-Natal, stood firmly behind Zuma and was one of his vocal supporters in the National Assembly in the lead-up to the 2007 ANC conference at Polokwane. When Zuma supporters made a clean sweep at the conference, Mthethwa slotted in at number 48 on the newly elected national executive committee, ranking higher for instance than key Zuma backer Angie Motshekga and finance minister Trevor Manuel. He also made it on to the party's powerful national working committee, which is tasked with running the day-to-day operations of the party.

Although it was suggested that Zuma wanted Mthethwa sent to Luthuli House as head of the presidency, he soon landed the senior parliamentary post of chief whip. When Mbeki was recalled, Mthethwa was appointed to his current position of minister of safety and security, where he said all the right things – although not before tripping up a bit. In total disregard for South Africa's human rights-based legal system, Mthethwa declared that criminals should not enjoy the same rights as ordinary citizens and also repeated his deputy's controversial statement that police officers should shoot to kill when faced with gun-wielding criminals.

He returned to a more acceptable line when he promised to root out corruption among the police and made a strong call for the appointment of a permanent national commissioner to replace incumbent Jackie Selebi, on leave pending his appearance in court on charges of corruption and defeating the ends of justice. Mthethwa also gave offence to the ANC's new opposition, the Congress of the People, when he took away VIP protection from one of its leaders, Mosiuoa Lekota.

Mthethwa was born in KwaZulu-Natal. He holds a diploma in

community development from the University of Natal, a mining engineering certificate from Rand Afrikaans University, and a certificate in communications and leadership from Rhodes University. He has previously served as regional secretary of the ANC Youth League and for a decade after 1994 was a member of the Youth League's national executive committee and national working committee. He was detained in 1989 under the state of emergency after joining the ANC underground the year before.

Date of birth: January 23 1967

Mushwana, Lawrence

Public protector Mabedle Lawrence Mushwana has earned himself a reputation for sweeping high-profile politicians' dirt under the carpet. Events in the past six years have confirmed that Mushwana has failed to live up to the name of his office. Since his appointment in 2002 he has succeeded in protecting only ANC heavyweights. His track record of investigations, which have been labelled in many cases as jokes, has left many people wondering whether the office was created to protect the public or the state.

Whenever cases of abuse involving ANC members emerge, Mushwana is quick to use his bag of tricks to make their problems vanish. On several occasions he has rebuffed opposition party complaints about his performance, claiming that the majority of his findings deal with poor service delivery. 'South Africa is effectively a one-party state. This is not of our making,' he says.

Among the most unusual decisions Mushwana made was the dismissal of allegations against former deputy president Phumzile Mlambo-Ngcuka regarding a holiday trip she made to the United Arab Emirates with family and friends in December 2005 at taxpayers' expense. Mushwana found Mlambo-Ngcuka not guilty of any wrongdoing and declared she had not contravened the executive code of ethics: as the country's number two, she was entitled to go on holiday at the state's expense.

Significantly, in 2003 Mushwana ruled in favour of president Thabo Mbeki's wife Zanele after she was accused of buying a house from the department of public works in Port Elizabeth below market price. She then attempted to sell it for double the price a few months later. Mushwana found that Zanele Mbeki was within her rights to sell the property at whatever price she desired.

Among those who have escaped sanctions are former defence minister Mosiuoa Lekota, Ekurhuleni Metro police chief Robert McBride, and home affairs minister Nosiviwe Mapisa-Nqakula.

When ruling in favour of senior ANC leaders, Mushwana said he could only make findings based on the information available to him. He emphasised that there were no high-profile Democratic Alliance leaders to talk about. However, in a surprising twist of events, in February 2009 Mushwana chastised former Eskom chairperson Valli Moosa for improper conduct in the awarding of a multi-billion-rand contract to an ANC-linked company, the Hitachi Consortium, in 2007. At the time the contract was awarded, Moosa was a member of the ANC's national executive committee. His rebuke appeared to be a first sign of independence – rather late in his tenure.

Born in 1948 in Limpopo province, Mushwana – who speaks 10 of South Africa's 11 official languages – studied at Unisa, where he obtained a BJuris degree. He also attended the University of Zululand where he obtained an LLB, and was later admitted to the Bar. He started his career in 1972 as an interpreter at the magistrate's court in Mhlala, Bushbuckridge, and became a public prosecutor there three years later. By 1977, he had risen to the position of magistrate and served in various districts. He was twice detained under state of emergency regulations.

In 1992 he set up his own firm of attorneys in Pretoria and Bush-buckridge. From 1994, he served on several parliamentary committees and co-chaired the joint parliamentary budget committee, and the code of conduct and ethics committees. He has also served on the Judicial Service Commission.

Mushwana participated in the drawing up of the South African Constitution. He is well known for his role as deputy chairperson of the National Council of Provinces. In 2002 he resigned from this position to take up office as the country's second public protector. The National Assembly voted overwhelmingly in favour of his appointment. Mushwana, whose contract expires in October 2009, has asked his staff to prepare for his departure.

Rumours are circulating that he has been tipped for a position within the criminal justice system, perhaps as the national director of public prosecutions.

Date of birth: March 31 1948

Naidoo, Kumi

Kumi Naidoo is a man who lives his principles. He has gone hungry, gone underground and gone into exile for his beliefs. He has worked as a journalist, youth counsellor and lecturer at the M.L. Sultan Technikon in Durban. He is honorary president of Civicus: Worldwide Alliance for Citizen Participation, an international alliance that aims to 'nurture the foundation, growth and protection of citizen action throughout the world'.

He grew up in Chatsworth and became involved in the anti-apartheid struggle at 15 as part of the leadership in organising student uprisings and boycotts, and grassroots youth organisations. Around the same time, his mother committed suicide. As well as meeting women struggling for gender equity, this had a major impact on him and he became a prominent spokesperson on issues of gender violence and equity.

His activism resulted in his expulsion from high school and he completed matric through a self-study course. He studied for a BA in law at the University of Durban-Westville (UDW), followed by an honours degree in political science. As a young man wanted by the police for his anti-government work, part of his studies were done in hiding, but he remained involved in underground movements and mass mobilisation against the government through his role as vice-president of the SRC at UDW.

Following his arrest for violating state of emergency regulations when he was 21, he spent four days in jail and then fled the country in the middle of his trial and went into exile in England. He earned a doctorate in political sociology at Oxford University, where he was a Rhodes Scholar.

Naidoo returned to South Africa in 1990 to work with the ANC. He was the official spokesperson for the Independent Electoral Commission during the national elections in 1994, when he also directed training for more than 300 000 electoral staff nationally. He was founding executive director of the South African National NGO Coalition.

He has worked hard on gender issues, organising the first National Men's March Against Violence on Women and Children in 1996. He was also a board member of the Association for Women's Rights in Development and is an adviser to the United Nations Development Fund for Women. He believes that in order to support the notion of democracy, one must also support gender equity, and he spends at least a quarter of his time talking on gender equity on any platform he is given.

In 2005, he co-founded and is the co-chair of Global Call to Action Against Poverty, a global coalition of anti-poverty campaigners who are trying to pressure world leaders to fulfil their promises on poverty and in particular pushing for cancellation of poor countries' debt, a fair and just global trading system, and more and better aid, amongst other issues.

Naidoo's skills and passion stretch to many areas. He serves as a board member of the Global Coalition for Climate Action, Food and Trees for Africa, and is chair of the board of the Partnership for Transparency Fund, which finances civil society organisations that fight corruption. He has also edited two books, *Putting Young People at the Centre,* and *Civil Society at the Millennium.* He has written opinion pieces for publications including the *Mail & Guardian, Sowetan* and *The Guardian.* With so many issues to deal with, he lists his priorities as gender equity, poverty eradication, and environmental justice and sustainability.

Naidoo made headlines early in 2009 when he engaged for 21 days in a solidarity fast for Zimbabwe. His appeal received pledges from almost 40 000 people who fasted with him for a day. A week after his fast ended, he had his first solid meal – egg curry and rice, which he cooked himself. **Date of birth:** January 8 1965

Ndebele, Sbu

Sibusiso Joel Ndebele ended his premiership of KwaZulu-Natal (KZN) in 2009 and, with it, his participation in provincial politics. He has moved into the Zuma Cabinet as minister of transport.

Ndebele's tenure as provincial premier, which began in 2004 when the

ANC won an outright majority in KZN for the first time, was marked by the debilitating effects of the ANC's internal leadership battle between Thabo Mbeki and Jacob Zuma. A pro-Mbeki supporter, who had initially called for a third term for Mbeki as state president, Ndebele found both himself and other 'third-termers' increasingly isolated and vilified in a province which has provided the fulcrum of support for Zuma. His Canute-like attempts to keep the 'Zunami' at bay both within the ANC (of which he was provincial chairperson) and within government played themselves out in his leadership of KZN.

In an attempt to inveigle himself into the ANC's ascendant Zuma faction, Ndebele has been reticent to act against ministerial failings in the province. The R2-billion overspend by the provincial health department in the 2007/8 financial year received no condemnation or action from the premier's office, for example.

A librarian by training, Ndebele has also shown a predilection for intellectualism: his office hosts the annual African Renaissance Conference and talk shops have been a feature of the ANC's five years in power in KZN.

In his inaugural address as premier, Ndebele talked of providing a new financial impetus to the province. According to Stats SA, KZN experienced 4.1% economic growth in the first four years of his tenure. Government's infrastructure investment has centred on big-money projects like the R7-billion Dube Trade Port and the R2.2-billion Moses Mabhida stadium. Ndebele's vision appears to have centred on rampant development.

He was to come under criticism after unveiling a planned Zulu theme park development in eMacambini on the KZN north coast in 2008. Around 10 000 families are expected to be relocated for the development and the local community has protested against the proposed removal and the lack of consultation about the development.

Born in Rorke's Drift, near Eshowe, in northern KZN, Ndebele matriculated from Eshowe High School in 1968, before studying for a diploma in library science at the University of Zululand. The son of a Lutheran priest, his early political involvement included participating in the University Christian Movement (UCM) at the university and acting as publications director of the South African Students' Organisation

(Saso) in 1972.

He worked as an assistant librarian at the University of Swaziland between 1974 and 1976. Together with the likes of Jacob Zuma, he helped set up ANC structures in Swaziland. He was arrested for ANC activities in South Africa in 1976 and sentenced to 10 years on Robben Island.

An ANC national executive committee member since 1994, Ndebele was the KZN south coast regional secretary from 1990 to 1998. He became the provincial chair in 1998 and held this position for a decade. Ndebele served two terms as a reasonably successful MEC for transport, kick-starting initiatives like the Zimbambele project, which involves rural households in the maintenance of strips of public road and employs around 37 500 people.

Date of birth: October 7 1948

Ndungane, Njongonkulu

Njongonkulu Winston Hugh Ndungane, the former Anglican Archbishop of Cape Town, believes that one of the greatest issues facing South Africans in the post-apartheid era is the struggle against poverty and inequality.

Born in Kokstad to an unemployed teacher and a poor Anglican priest, he graduated from Lovedale High School in Alice, where his schoolmates included Chris Hani and Thabo Mbeki. In his book *A World with a Human Face*, Ndungane recalls how as a young man, he stopped on his way to a soccer match to listen to Pan Africanist Congress founder Robert Sobukwe speak out against the pass laws. Following this chance encounter, he turned to political activism, for which he was later arrested and convicted by the apartheid government. In August 1963 he was sentenced to a three-year jail term and imprisoned on Robben Island. There he struggled with religious questions, and it was in a prison cell, he says, that he found God.

Ndungane was ordained a priest in July 1974 in the diocese of Cape Town. The next year, he left South Africa to attend King's College London, where he completed a bachelor's degree in divinity and then a master's in theology. On his return to South Africa he first took up the post of principal of St Bede's Theological College in Umtata, then worked as a liaison officer and, later, executive officer in the Anglican Church. He was consecrated Bishop of Kuruman and Kimberley in 1991 and five years later succeeded Nobel laureate Desmond Tutu as the Archbishop of Cape Town.

The Archbishop is unfazed by the inclusion of women in the church. When his African counterparts threatened to boycott a sitting of the primates of the Anglican Communion because of the inclusion of Bishop Katharine Jefferts Schori, presiding bishop and primate of the Episcopal Church in the US, Ndungane said that boycotting the event because of the presence of a woman who had been legitimately elected by the church in her country was like fiddling while Rome burns. He earned notoriety among conservative Anglicans for his liberal approach to homosexuality when he spoke out in support of the consecration of the first openly gay Episcopalian bishop in the US, Gene Robertson.

Ndungane serves as the executive director of the Historic Schools Restoration Project, which aims to revive historically important but under-resourced schools that played an important part in black education before the era of Bantu education. The project, he says, represents both the tragedy and hope of education in South Africa.

Deeply invested in alleviating poverty and unemployment in Africa, he is also a strong proponent of trade justice and debt cancellation. In 2006, he set up African Monitor, an independent, non-profit organisation that tracks the allocation of development funding from Western countries and its delivery in Africa in order to meet the Millennium Development Goals.

Ndungane retired from his position as Archbishop of Cape Town at the end of 2007 and was succeeded by Thabo Makgoba. In April 2008, then-president Thabo Mbeki awarded him the Order of the Baobab in recognition of his contribution to the struggle for liberation and his dedication to ending inequality and poverty.

Date of birth: April 2 1941

Netshitenzhe, Joel

Long regarded as one of the ANC's best brains, Joel Netshitenzhe rose through ANC ranks when he was in exile, working under Thabo Mbeki in the party's department of information and publicity.

After receiving basic military training in Angola, and using the nom de guerre Peter Mayibuye, he was a radio journalist for the ANC station Radio Freedom and edited the ANC publication *Mayibuye*.

As head of the policy unit in the presidency under Mbeki, he oversaw and monitored the implementation of government policy in all departments and was Mbeki's sounding board in all policy matters. During Mbeki's presidency he authored some of the party's strategic documents and was at the centre of how the party sought to position itself. Several times he was touted as a future ANC president or deputy president but is believed to have turned down several nominations.

Because he was closely linked politically to Mbeki, he was defeated during the fateful ANC conference at Polokwane in 2007, when he competed for the position of national chairperson, losing out to Baleka Mbete, who obtained 2 326 votes to Netshitenzhe's 1 475. He was, however, returned to the ANC's national executive committee and told colleagues that he wished to serve out his contract as head of policy in government.

Netshitenzhe was born in Sibasa in Limpopo and attended Mphephu High School and, later, the University of Natal, leaving after his first year for exile to join the ANC. From 1982 to 1984 he studied for a diploma at the Institute of Social Sciences in Moscow, and in the mid-1990s he obtained a postgraduate diploma in economic principles from the University of London.

He was part of the ANC's negotiation team at the Codesa talks from 1992 to 1994 and became head of communication in president Nelson Mandela's office before joining the Government Communication and Information System as CEO in 1998. In 2001 he was made head of policy coordination and advisory services in the presidency.

Date of birth: December 21 1956

Ngcobo, Sandile

When the Supreme Court of Appeal in Bloemfontein delivered a majority judgment rendering legal the search and seizure warrants issued against lawyers acting for ANC president Jacob Zuma in his long-standing battle with the National Prosecuting Authority, it was left to the

Constitutional Court to settle the matter. The highest court in the land delivered a majority judgment against Zuma. Judge Sandile Ngcobo was the only justice to issue a dissenting judgment.

Ngcobo was appointed to the Constitutional Court in 1999, reportedly after the intervention of then-deputy president Thabo Mbeki; the Judicial Service Commission had recommended Johannesburg High Court judge Edwin Cameron, who had to wait another nine years before his own appointment to the Constitutional Court.

Ngcobo's law career has followed a successful trajectory, in South Africa and the United States. Born in Durban, he completed his undergraduate BProc studies at the University of Zululand in 1975 and obtained distinctions in constitutional law, mercantile law and accounting. The following year was spent in detention; upon his release, he worked in the Maphumulo magistrate's office, joined the Durban firm of K.K. Mthiyane, then moved on to the Legal Resources Centre in Durban while studying for his LLB at the University of Natal in Durban. A Fulbright Scholar, he studied at both the Georgetown University Law Center in Washington and at Harvard Law School, where he obtained an LLM.

He was admitted as an advocate in 1988 and practised both in South Africa and the United States until 1996, when he was made a Supreme Court judge in the Cape provincial division. A year later he moved on to the Labour Appeal Court, and in 1999 he was named acting judge president of both the Labour Court and the Labour Appeal Court. He also lectured part-time at the University of Natal.

At the advent of South Africa's democracy, Ngcobo served on the newly constituted Independent Electoral Commission as presiding officer of the electoral tribunal; he also served on the Truth and Reconciliation Commission's amnesty committee.

Date of birth: March 1 1953

Nkabinde, Bess

After just three years at the highest court in the land, Constitutional Court judge Bess Nkabinde was at the centre of South Africa's most prominent case involving alleged judicial misconduct and increasing attacks on the judiciary. Nkabinde is one of the judges that Cape judge president John Hlophe visited on a supposed 'mandate' to intervene on behalf of ANC president Jacob Zuma in his search and seizure case, part of his long-running battle with the National Prosecuting Authority. Hlophe is reported to have told Nkabinde, whom he mistook as a Zulu speaker, that people would lose their positions after the 2009 elections and nudged her to look favourably at the case against Zuma.

Nkabinde approached colleague Yvonne Mokgoro to state her concern over Hlophe's visit. This was later reported to the leadership of the court and a complaint was laid against Hlophe who, in retaliation, laid a counter-complaint against Nkabinde and the rest of her colleagues. Hlophe also instituted a damages claim against 13 judges for R10-million. He won the first round when the majority of an unprecedented five-person Bench of the Johannesburg High Court found that Hlophe's rights had been violated when Nkabinde and her colleagues sent a press statement to the media before hearing Hlophe's side of the issue. This decision was, however, reversed by a nine-person Bench of the Supreme Court of Appeal. It was suggested by Hlophe's lawyers that Nkabinde and acting judge Chris Jafta had been coerced into laying their complaint against Hlophe.

The situation has threatened the independence of the judiciary, as it provoked repeated attacks on the judiciary from some political parties. In the search and seizure case, the Constitutional Court ruled for the National Prosecuting Authority, declaring that attempts to influence the court had not succeeded.

Nkabinde was born a Batlokwa princess in Silwerkrans in the North West. She completed her matric at Mariasdal High School in the Free State in 1979 and obtained a BProc degree in 1983. Three years later she received her LLB degree from the University of Bophuthatswana. She also holds an industrial relations diploma from Damelin.

She commenced her career in 1984 as a state law adviser for the former homeland government of Bophuthatswana. She enrolled as an advocate in 1988 and did her pupillage at the Johannesburg Bar, being admitted in 1989. For the next 10 years she practised as an advocate until she was appointed a High Court judge. She continued to serve as an acting judge in the labour courts and was appointed to the Supreme Court of Appeal in Bloemfontein in 2005. She replaced retiring chief justice Arthur Chaskalson in the same year on the Constitutional Court.

Date of birth: May 15 1959

Nkoana-Mashabane, Maite

The new international relations minister is relatively unknown in foreign affairs circles, although Maite Nkoana-Mashabane has served as high commissioner to Malaysia and India. Her appointment was seen by some in the ANC as an indication that the position has been downgraded in the government hierarchy, with foreign affairs – close to the top under former president Thabo Mbeki – slipping far below domestic concerns in Jacob Zuma's government.

Nkoana-Mashabane, who has never served as an official in the department though she accompanied Zuma to China in 2008, is best known for an issue not of her making. During her stint in India, her fellow diplomat-husband Norman Mashabane – who died in a car crash in October 2007 – was accused of sexual harassment in his posting in Indonesia.

They both returned to Limpopo in 2005, Mashabane as a member of the Limpopo legislature, and Nkoana-Mashabane as MEC for local government and housing as well as deputy secretary-general of the provincial ANC. In the early 1990s she had been chairperson of the provincial ANC Women's League and a member of its working committee, and had spent a year as an ANC MP before her first foreign posting in 1995.

Born in Ga-Makanyane village, she became politically active in the 1980s, being involved in the United Democratic Front, the Mass Democratic Movement and ANC underground structures. She is a member of the ANC's powerful national working committee, and after the Polokwane conference she served on the ANC subcommittee that deals with international relations, perhaps a harbinger of her current post.

Her reviews as provincial minister were mixed. Her department won the national Govan Mbeki Housing Award in 2008 for best provincial housing minister, despite the poor quality of the houses that were delivered. As local government minister, she was tasked with overseeing the province's municipalities, which were racked with instability, but she was not particularly successful. According to the Limpopo Democratic Alliance leader, Desiree van der Walt, 'She failed to rise above factional politics when municipalities were engaged in after-Polokwane squabbles. Political purge was her practice.' At the same time, she won praise for leading the provincial task team that brought a cholera outbreak under control in 2008.

Date of birth: September 30 1963

Nogxina, Sandile

Sandile Nogxina has been head of the economically vital department of minerals and energy affairs for a decade. An advocate by training, he has been instrumental in putting in place a range of policies geared towards transforming the mineral and energy sectors, from new-order mining rights to amendments to electricity regulations and cleaner liquid fuels.

Critics would argue, however, that the department has dragged its heels in implementing policy in many critical areas, not least in addressing the ongoing energy crisis, especially electricity generation from renewable resources, and has paid scant attention to carbon taxes. In the mining sector, local beneficiation of minerals has seen little investment, mining safety continues to cause grave concern and, in the face of a looming worldwide recession, widescale retrenchments are adding to the country's unemployment woes.

Nogxina began his legal career as a public prosecutor in 1982 at the magistrate's court in Umzimkhulu in the former Transkei, qualifying for a bachelor of law degree at the University of Fort Hare, followed by a master's in law development at the University of Warwick in the UK, as well as a higher diploma in tax law from the University of the Witwatersrand, after which he was admitted as an advocate.

After joining the ANC in 1977 and Umkhonto weSizwe three years later, his political career began in earnest. He went into exile in 1987, serving as legal adviser and researcher in the ANC's department of legal and constitutional affairs at its headquarters in Lusaka, Zambia. During this time, he received specialised training in military intelligence in Moscow.

From 1991 to 1994, he was seconded to the ANC's constitutional committee while taking up a position as senior researcher at the Centre for Development Studies at the University of the Western Cape. In 1994, he spent time on special assignment in the legal department of the World Bank and a year later was appointed special adviser to the minister of public service and administration before becoming deputy director-general, moving to the department of minerals and energy affairs in 2008. During the mid-1990s, he also attended courses on civil service reform, policy formulation and public-sector labour relations in the Netherlands, Italy and Switzerland.

Despite his impressive credentials, the department has made uneven progress under his leadership. It is good at trotting through the policy (often with little consultation and in the face of opposition from stakeholders) but it is weak at implementation – and there is also the shadow of political interference.

Date of birth: June 26 1958

Nombembe, Terence

The office of the auditor-general could be described as a combination of Sherlock Holmes and the Lone Ranger. It not only has to sniff out concealed financial crimes, whether committed with intent or out of ignorance, but it also rides forth as an independent protector of citizens' interests against the iniquities of bureaucracy at every level of government and all its agencies.

Terence Nombembe is just two years into his seven-year term and, given that auditing is a slow, painstaking and nitpicking job, he seems to be shaping up admirably in his dual role. So far, he has pronounced on the shocking state of affairs within 60% of South Africa's 283 municipalities and the station-level performance of the South African Police Service, both areas of real and immediate concern to the average citizen.

After studying for a BComm degree at the University of Transkei in 1982, Nombembe was accepted as a trainee accountant by KPMG in Umtata. This was followed by the award of a BCompt degree from Unisa and a position as internal auditor for Unilever in Durban, which included a stint as accountant for the Lipton tea and soup factory in

Pietermaritzburg. After qualifying in 1990 as a chartered accountant, he took up positions of senior internal auditor for BP South Africa, finance manager for BP Botswana in Gaborone from 1994, and market research manager for BP South Africa in Cape Town from 1996.

He was a founding partner in 1997 of the auditing firm Gobodo Incorporated – one of the best-known forensic auditors in the country. In June 2000, he was appointed deputy auditor-general and CEO in the office of the auditor-general. In December 2006, taking over from Shauket Fakie, he was the first person of African ancestry to become auditor-general in the institution's 95-year history.

Described as 'bursting with enthusiasm' at the time of his appointment, Nombembe has ambitious plans for his office, including developing much closer relationships with its stakeholders, from ministers and MPs to accounting officers in all three tiers of government, other auditors both local and international, the media and ordinary citizens.

To him, it is vital that his office constantly makes clear to the public the risk and prevalence of corruption and fraud, and the need to prevent it. The rot at the root of local government stems from a failure to comply with established policy, he says, which in turn stems from a general lack of capacity, a shortage of experienced staff and inadequate management systems. To begin to address this, he has promised to focus on the quality of his office's reports by striving for credibility, independence and transparency in the face of political interference and manipulation. Basically, the responsibility of his office is to report back to taxpayers on what government at every level does with their hard-earned contributions. To this end, his office is playing a direct role in the recruitment and training of young auditors.

Date of birth: September 30 1961

Nongxa, Loyiso

Professor Loyiso Nongxa made history when, in 2003, he became the first black vice-chancellor of the University of the Witwatersrand. His herdboy-to-Oxford tale endeared him to many South Africans. Nongxa grew up in the former Transkei as the youngest of five children. When he was not in school, he was tending his father's sheep, and ploughing and harvesting the fields. But following his exposure to mathematics in his teens, first at Freemantle High and later at Healdtown High in the Eastern Cape, he shone academically. After completing undergraduate and postgraduate qualifications cum laude at Fort Hare University, he became the first African Rhodes Scholar from South Africa to go to Oxford University, where he obtained a doctorate in mathematics.

Thereafter, he climbed the academic ladder in the conventional way. He taught at the University of Lesotho and the University of Natal, then moved into management as the dean of the faculty of natural science at the University of the Western Cape. From there, he went to Wits as deputy vice-chancellor in charge of research.

Wits's recent history of searching for a vice-chancellor had been extremely rocky, and when Nongxa was named vice-chancellor in 2003, his first task was to project an image of stability. This was not easy to do in the university's generally volatile atmosphere. 'I can appreciate why Wits is perceived to be ungovernable and a difficult place to survive at,' he said shortly after his appointment. 'But my message is: governance and leadership problems are not unique to Wits.' He made it clear that the primacy of academic values would be central to his vision; 'the first law of academic leadership', he said, 'is that "thou shalt not attempt to exercise authority or influence over academics".'

He has had to put fires out since his arrival – student riots over fee increases, the departure of a number of high-profile academics to the University of Johannesburg, a crisis at Wits Business School, which was also having problems finding a leader, financial woes, poor management of student aid, and a higher-than-acceptable drop-out rate. And Wits has been accused publicly, by former president Thabo Mbeki among others, of a lack of transformation.

One of Nongxa's projects is rural outreach. The university has identified rural schools in Gauteng, Limpopo and Mpumalanga that produce good results and has invited top students entering grade 10 in those schools to come to the university to see what student life involves and to meet professionals in a range of fields to talk about careers and opportunities for financial assistance. He has also promoted the university through the rest of Africa.

However, Wits faces growing competition as the result of an aggressive repositioning strategy by the University of Johannesburg, and there are fears it is relying on its past reputation – as the 'jewel in the crown' of South African higher education – instead of producing a fight-back plan. These realities could impact on Nongxa's vision, captured in the Wits 2010 strategic plan, that the university become one of the top 100 universities in the world by 2022.

Date of birth: October 22 1953

Ntsaluba, Ayanda

Ayanda Ntsaluba is director-general of the department of foreign affairs, but it was his stint as director-general of the department of health that brought him to the attention of the public.

He was part of the team that produced the ANC's health plan for the party's 1994 election manifesto. He is also often praised as the best foreign affairs director-general the country has had.

He hails from the Eastern Cape. A qualified doctor, he had an excellent education and graduated from the University of Natal in 1982. He did his internship at Umtata General Hospital and continued to work there as medical officer until September 1985, when a period of detention and solitary confinement interrupted his work. On his release he went into exile, but returned after six years to specialise in obstetrics and gynaecology.

During his years abroad in the 1980s he studied international relations, political economy and philosophy at the Moscow Institute of Social Science. But most of his exile years were spent in southern and East Africa – in Zambia, Angola, Tanzania and Uganda – working in numerous health facilities. He also studied at the University of London and was admitted as a fellow of the College of Obstetricians and Gynaecologists of South Africa.

In June 1995 Ntsaluba was appointed deputy director-general for policy and planning in the national department of health and in 1998 he became the acting director-general of health before the position was made permanent three months later. He chaired the steering committee of the South African Aids Vaccine Initiative and served as a member of one of the working groups of the World Health Organization commission on macroeconomics and health.

But his time as director-general coincided with some of the most turbulent years in the department, with the debate about Aids denialism raging heatedly, and it was probably with a feeling of relief that he moved to the department of foreign affairs.

He immediately identified seven key areas in his efforts to build the country's foreign policy: consolidation of the African agenda; building South-South cooperation; strengthening North-South cooperation; participation in global governance; strengthening political and economic relations; organisational strengthening; and provision of support services. And for the most part, his efforts at achieving these objectives have been impressive, especially seen against the backdrop of former president Thabo Mbeki's not-so-silent hand in the department.

North-South cooperation has had mixed results. While relations with Nordic states, the Netherlands and the United Kingdom have remained amicable and mutually supportive, political differences with southern European states such as France and Italy have resulted in relations taking a turn for the worse.

Sympathetic observers have pointed out that foreign affairs blunders, such as voting against the abuse of human rights in Burma and siding with despotic leaders in Zimbabwe and Iran, cannot always be laid at Ntsaluba's door. They claim that South Africa's position on Zimbabwe and its submissions to the United Nations Security Council have been presidency initiatives.

Ntsaluba has emerged as a respected and efficient administrator, though critics say communicating to the nation on critical foreign policy issues would be welcome, even once in a blue moon.

Date of birth: 31 May 1960

Ntshalintshali, Bheki

From taxi driver to deputy general secretary of the influential trade union federation Cosatu, Bheki Ntshalintshali has become one of the driving forces within the federation. Although Ntshalintshali has kept a low profile for most of his career as a unionist, he is one of the brains behind Cosatu's success.

Born in the rural town of Piet Retief in Mpumalanga, Ntshalintshali began his trade union career as chairperson of the Chemical Workers' Industrial Union's shop steward committee in Secunda, where he worked for Sasol as an artisan. He was among 6 000 workers who were dismissed by the petrochemical giant for participating in a political strike in 1984. Although the company later took back most of his colleagues, he was left out in the cold, as he was seen as the strike's chief instigator.

The Chemical Workers' Industrial Union recruited him in 1985 as a national organiser, tasked with recruiting Sasol plant workers. While working for the union he was asked by Cosatu in 1986 to facilitate the establishment of the federation's Highveld Ridge region. As a result of his hard work, Ntshalintshali was elevated to the position of national deputy general secretary for the chemical union in 1994. The union sent Ntshalintshali to study industrial relations for a year at Ruskin College in Oxford. On his return to South Africa, he was appointed its collective bargaining coordinator, and played a major role in establishing the bargaining council for the industry.

Ntshalintshali, whose parents were from Mozambique, first joined Cosatu as a full-time employee in 1999 as its organising secretary. A year later he was elected to his current position as Cosatu's deputy general secretary.

Ntshalintshali's colleagues in the federation describe him as a humble but hard worker who articulates Cosatu's position with ease. Said Cosatu president Sdumo Dlamini: 'I always say, unlike some of us who shout louder, Bheki works hard in the background. He is a very good administrator and a critical thinker. He is a social activist. He is one guy who is able to follow socio-economic debates around the world.'

Apart from his internal work at Cosatu, Ntshalintshali represents the federation on the World Social Forum's International Council, the United Nations Commission on Sustainable Development and the United Nations' climate forum. He is also a commissioner with the Employment Conditions Commission, which deals with the minimum conditions of employment of vulnerable workers, such as domestic and farm workers. In 2007, Ntshalintshali was appointed chairperson of the technical task

team of the Joint Initiative for Priority Skills Acquisition (Jipsa), a position vacated by ANC secretary-general Gwede Mantashe. He is tipped to take over from Zwelinzima Vavi as Cosatu general secretary in 2009.
Date of birth: February 14 1954

Nxesi, Thulas

Tembelani 'Thulas' Nxesi has become a respected voice, synonymous with the struggles and plight of teachers. He also commands huge political clout, making him one of the young emerging politicians within the tripartite alliance. As chief administrative officer of the South African Democratic Teachers' Union (Sadtu), he is responsible for the union's operations and for shaping its strategic vision. Such is his stature that when speculation arose some time ago that the minister of education, Naledi Pandor, would not retain her post, Nxesi was among those touted as her successor. He has since become an ANC MP.

Respected education commentators reacted positively to the rumours suggesting that he would be suitable for the job. Russell Wildman, an education researcher at the Institute for Democracy in South Africa, said Nxesi has been in the sector long enough and is aware of the plight of teachers and the effects of poor school funding. But 'how successful he [would] be to operate in a constraining environment would be a challenge. He has the ability to function with flexibility,' Wildman said.

In some quarters, Nxesi is seen as an inflexible populist, a radical leader and someone too militant to lead a professional body like a teachers' union, which deals with issues that require tact and patience. Some also argue that he uses Sadtu as a convenient tool to advance clearly political issues at the expense of shop-floor struggles. With a membership of 220 000, Sadtu wields enormous power to influence issues both within the tripartite alliance and in the labour bargaining chambers. During the gruelling leadership tussle within the ANC in 2008, Sadtu was among those that played a decisive kingmaker's role, nailing its colours to Jacob Zuma's mast.

Nxesi has been general secretary of Sadtu since 1994, which makes him one of the longest-serving officials within the sector; cynics say he is the union's 'secretary for life'. Before he joined Sadtu he belonged to the National Education Union of South Africa (Neusa), the first formal body to unionise teachers. In 1990 Neusa merged with other progressive teacher unions to form the current Sadtu.

From 1979 to 1983, Nxesi enrolled for a BA in education at the University of Fort Hare. He was expelled a number of times for his political activities while a student leader but completed his degree in 1985. In the same year he began teaching at Ukusasa Senior Secondary School in Tembisa on the Witwatersrand, where he became head of the social science department. But he was fired two years later for being a 'disruptive element'.

Nxesi's wealth of experience in education has attracted the attention of the world's largest teachers' union, Education International; he is its current president.

Date of birth: June 9 1959

Nyanda, Siphiwe

General Siphiwe Nyanda, the new minister of communications, became the first black leader of the South African National Defence Force (SANDF) after replacing General George Meiring in 1998, following disclosure of Meiring's links to a discredited intelligence report. A former leader of Umkhonto weSizwe (MK), the ANC's military wing, Nyanda retired as head of the defence force in May 2005 and joined the private sector as chief executive of the Ngwane Defence Group. Ngwane positioned itself as South Africa's first black-owned defence company. Nyanda's partners included former MK soldier Damian de Lange and former defence minister Joe Modise's adviser Fana Hlongwane.

Nyanda publicly announced his support for ANC president Jacob Zuma in September 2006 with a hard-hitting column published in the *Sunday Times*, accusing the media of launching 'vitriolic attacks against Zuma and those who supported him'. He subsequently became an integral part of the Zuma camp fighting for control of the ANC. Their campaign culminated in Zuma's victory over Thabo Mbeki at the ANC's 2007 Polokwane conference. Nyanda was voted on to the ANC's national executive committee and was elected chair of the party's subcommittee on peace and stability.

His was a prominent voice in the ANC's attack on the Scorpions investigating unit; he accused the unit of being infiltrated by foreign spies and apartheid agents. The party ultimately succeeded in disbanding the Scorpions in 2009. Nyanda conceded during a public debate on the matter that the ANC's attack on the Scorpions wasn't completely unrelated to Zuma's pending criminal case.

The ANC placed Nyanda at number 33 on its list for the 2009 parliamentary elections and it was widely expected that he would become a minister in Zuma's Cabinet after the elections.

Schooled in Soweto and expelled from the University of Zululand for his political activities, Nyanda became active in the ANC underground in the 1970s. He also had a short stint as sportswriter for the *World* newspaper.

He rose through MK's ranks during the 1970s and 1980s and served as chief of staff of MK from 1992. He received military training in the former East Germany and Soviet Union. In the late 1980s and early 1990s Nyanda played a part in the ANC's Operation Vula, the party's effort to strengthen links between activists inside the country and officials in exile.

After the 1994 elections he became chief of staff of the SANDF, where his main task was the integration of the old South African army and MK. In 1997 he was appointed deputy chief of the SANDF, and a year later he secured the top job.

Date of birth: May 22 1950

Nzimande, Blade

Bonginkosi Emmanuel 'Blade' Nzimande is the general secretary of the South African Communist Party (SACP). He is regarded as the architect of former president Thabo Mbeki's removal and central to the elevation of Jacob Zuma as head of the ANC. Like Cosatu general secretary Zwelinzima Vavi, who has consistently supported him, Nzimande believed that Mbeki was responsible for the breakdown in relations between the ANC and its alliance partners. He blamed Mbeki for a lack of consultation and a divisive style of governing, prompting Mbeki at one point to call him extraordinarily arrogant. Nzimande and the SACP aligned themselves with Zuma and invested heavily in his victory at the Polokwane conference.

The rise of Nzimande in the party coincided with the declining influence of former heavyweights Charles Nqakula, Sydney Mufamadi, Geraldine Fraser-Moleketi, Essop Pahad and a host of others who had led the SACP since the early 1990s but who disapproved of where Nzimande was taking it. He is set to play a prominent role in Zuma's new government, with the SACP seeking to maximise its gains from Polokwane, in his new role as minister of higher education and training.

Nzimande was born in Edendale in Pietermaritzburg. The eldest of three children, he comes from humble beginnings. His mother, Nozipho, was a primary school teacher and his father, Thambano, a domestic worker. Nzimande has honours and master's degrees from the University of Natal, Pietermaritzburg, and a doctorate in sociology from the same university. He has lectured in industrial psychology at the University of Zululand and the University of Natal, where he was director of the education policy unit. He left the unit in 1994 to take up a seat in Parliament, where he became chairperson of the parliamentary committee on education.

Nzimande was groomed in the political school of KwaZulu-Natal Midlands militant Harry Gwala, who brooked no independence and was branded a warlord for his refusal to countenance any negotiation with the Inkatha Freedom Party. The two were close during the early 1990s when the province was mired in political violence but later had a fall-out. Gwala was suspended from the SACP.

Nzimande was elected SACP general secretary in July 1998, a key moment that cleared the way for the radicalisation of the party, which then embarked on a collision path with government. He has been labelled a Stalinist by party members who left the SACP after bitter battles. He was accused of purging anyone who differed with his ideas, but the 2007 SACP congress reaffirmed support for his leadership. An attempt by the Gauteng provincial branch to put up a candidate to challenge his position faltered when they could not even secure a second province to back them. His critics were mainly incensed with his decision to line up the party behind Zuma, who had never before demonstrated or articulated any progressive left policies. But with those voices rendered barely a whisper, Nzimande went on to join Zuma's campaign, with expectations high that

the new government would not only preach left but would also act left.
Date of birth: April 4 1958

O'Regan, Kate

At just 37 years old, Kate O'Regan was the youngest judge and one of only two women to be appointed to the Constitutional Court in 1994. She was, at the time, an associate professor of law at the University of Cape Town (UCT), with limited practical experience. Along with three other judges, including chief justice Pius Langa, she will retire in October.

O'Regan was born in Liverpool and moved to South Africa with her parents as a seven-year-old. She obtained a BA and an LLB (cum laude) from UCT, an LLM from the University of Sydney with first class honours, and a PhD from the London School of Economics in 1988.

During the first half of the 1980s O'Regan worked as an attorney in Johannesburg, dealing mainly with labour and land rights cases, representing trade unions, anti-apartheid organisations and communities facing the threat of eviction in terms of apartheid land policies. In 1988 she joined UCT's labour law unit as a researcher and two years later became a senior lecturer in the university's faculty of law, where she was a founder member of both the Law, Race and Gender Research Project and the Institute for Development Law. She has also been an adviser to the ANC on land claims legislation and to the National Manpower Commission on gender equality law, and served as a trustee of the Legal Resources Trust.

In 2008 she was appointed by the United Nations secretary-general to chair the UN's internal justice council, established to help ensure independence, professionalism and accountability in the internal administration of justice within the UN. One of the primary responsibilities of the council is to identify suitable candidates for appointment as judges of the UN Dispute Tribunal and Appeals Tribunal and to make recommendations to the General Assembly on the appointment of such judges.

Unusually for a judge, in March 2009 she spoke out publicly against the government's decision to refuse the Dalai Lama a visa.

O'Regan has been an honorary consulting editor of *South African*

Law Reports since 1997 and serves on the editorial board of many of the country's legal publications. She has maintained her interest in teaching during her tenure as a judge and has not ruled out the possibility of returning to the academic world after October 2009.

Date of birth: September 17 1957

Pandor, Naledi

Political activism runs deep in the veins of science and technology minister Naledi Pandor, whose grandfather, the famed Professor Z.K. Matthews, was an ANC leader in the 1940s and 1950s, and first proposed the writing of the Freedom Charter. Pandor's father, Joe Matthews, served as ANC representative in London and much later joined the Inkatha Freedom Party. After the April 1994 general elections, he was appointed deputy minister of safety and security in the Government of National Unity.

Pandor received most of her education in exile and matriculated from Gaborone Secondary School in Botswana. She holds master's degrees from the universities of London and Stellenbosch and has lectured at the universities of Cape Town, Botswana and London.

Elected to Parliament, Pandor became the ANC's deputy chief whip but moved on to the National Council of Provinces, of which she was chairperson. Coming as she does from a family of intellectuals who could also be described as 'political royalty', it was fitting that the highly educated Pandor would be named education minister in 2004. Since then, she has had the backing of a group of long-serving senior bureaucrats in the national department. Add to the mix her reputation as an independent thinker, as well as her decisiveness (which is earning her respect internationally) and her intolerance for slackness, and she appeared to be in a position to turn around a system that has failed to deliver any significant return on investment in the last decade.

The past three years have centred on action, in line with Pandor's mantra: quality improvements in education. A good starting point has been a renewed political commitment to early childhood development, to ensure that all children who enter grade one by 2010 have passed through grade R (the reception year). The education budget has provided for an increase in the number of sites for grade R, benefiting 600 000 more children. In the critical foundation phase, grades R to three, Pandor's Foundations for Learning campaign got off the ground with focused support for the poorest schools in the areas of literacy and numeracy.

Pandor had to face up to the fact that 10 years of outcomes-based education provided no cause for celebration. She understood that if she had scrapped it, it could have meant a system collapse under the mere suggestion of another major policy change. She acted by announcing that she had put together a team to try to fix shortcomings in areas such as teacher training.

The year 2008 saw the introduction of the national senior certificate, the new school-leaving qualification. As the first-ever national exam, it was pulled off without major hiccups, though the release of the results turned into a nightmare for some learners who had to wait months to hear whether they had passed. This was attributed to the introduction of a new computer system, as well as a failure by some provinces to submit marks earned from the continuous assessment system. While the overall pass rate was 62.5%, there were 22 000 more matriculants than in 2007 who qualified to go to university. Some alleged that the mathematics pass marks had been 'inflated'.

A significant achievement was the multi-billion-rand Kha ri Gude mass literacy campaign, which took off in April 2008. By all accounts Pandor has personally driven this campaign, which last year reached 360 000 people, oversubscribed by 60 000.

By 2010 public universities will have received R5.9-billion in infrastructure development funds, targeted specifically at refurbishing buildings, erecting new ones and improving graduate outputs in science, engineering and technology. This is the biggest capital injection in higher education for 20 years. Pandor has earmarked these funds for spending in line with the needs of the country. A quiet infrastructure renaissance is occurring at many universities.

She is the first to concede there are problems at schools and within the department and does not sweep issues under the carpet but tackles things head on. Accessible to the media, Pandor is diplomatic in the way she handles various situations.

Date of birth: December 7 1953

Patel, Ebrahim

Although the new minister of economic development does not share the views of some of his colleagues – particularly Trevor Manuel – on inflation targeting and the government's macroeconomic Gear policy, Ebrahim Patel has not been called to a Cabinet post to be a rubber stamp. He was not on the ANC's parliamentary list but was included after a last-minute request from Cosatu, which wanted a workers' voice in the inner circle.

A long-time general secretary of the Southern African Clothing and Textile Workers' Union (Sactwu), Patel has chalked up numerous successes, from involvement in South Africa's attempt to restrict the flood of cheap Chinese clothing and textiles that was destroying Cape Town's garment industry, to hammering out policies at the International Labour Organisation (ILO), on whose governing body he served, in such areas as decent work in the context of globalisation, a global wage report, and human resource development.

Born in District Six, Cape Town, to a garment worker mother, he was one of the top ten matriculants nationally, winning a scholarship to the University of the Western Cape (UWC). His university career began in 1980 but was frequently interrupted by detentions occasioned by his involvement in anti-apartheid activities, struggles over broadening access to housing and electricity, campaigns against the 1983 tricameral parliament, and support for workers on strike at Leyland Motors and Wilson-Rowntree in the Eastern Cape. He left UWC in 1982 to work at the University of Cape Town's Southern Africa Labour and Development Research Unit, and finished his degree at UCT, where he unionised his colleagues and other workers – an early indication of the direction his life would take.

In 1986 he joined a textile union as a full-time organiser; it eventually became part of Sactwu. Over more than two decades, says Cosatu, he has 'concluded hundreds of recognition, wage and other collective agreements'. From 1993, when he was part of the team that drafted the ANC's Reconstruction and Development Programme in which the plight of the poor was prioritised, to February 2009, when he and other labour leaders negotiated a framework for the country's response to the global economic meltdown, he was at the forefront of labour policy both nationally and internationally.

He was chief negotiator at the Presidential Jobs Summit in 1998 and led organised labour's negotiations over the final form of the controversial Labour Relations Act and Basic Conditions of Employment Act. He has served on the Financial and Fiscal Commission and the Council for Higher Education, and when the National Economic Development and Labour Council (Nedlac) was formed, he led the country's labour federations as overall convener and continued serving on the Nedlac executive council. He represented labour on the Presidential Working Group and the Millennium Labour Council.

In his new post, Patel will focus on 'economic policy making'. As others contributing to the subject include the more conservative Manuel and new finance minister Pravin Gordhan, robust debate in Cabinet is a distinct possibility.

Date of birth: January 10 1962

Phosa, Mathews

When Nakedi Mathews Phosa was sacked as Mpumalanga premier in 1997, he decided to hang up his gloves and officially announced his retirement from politics, intending to devote his time to making money.

Born in Nelspruit, Phosa earned the BProc and LLB degrees at the University of the North and served his legal articles of clerkship at the well-known law firm Godfrey Rabin Attorneys from 1979 to 1981. In 1995 he was awarded an honorary doctorate in law by Boston University. After his retirement in 1997, he put his experience in law and politics to good use and made his mark in the business world. Phosa accepted directorships in a variety of companies and propped up his public image by playing leadership roles in NGOs, shaking off the suspicion of corruption that had cost him the premiership.

It all lasted only a decade. In 2007 he re-emerged in one of the most powerful positions in the ANC, that of treasurer-general. Suddenly the poet-turned-politician-turned-businessman was back in the fray, ready to climb the political ladder all the way to the top, just as he always thought he should.

Phosa joined up with the walking wounded in the Zuma camp, all in some way unfairly treated (mostly dismissed) by former president Thabo Mbeki. In 1997 Mbeki fired Phosa as premier during an investigation for fraud and corruption. Mbeki said Phosa was tainted and therefore could not continue in his position. Then in 2001, using safety and security minister Steve Tshwete as the messenger, Mbkei accused Phosa of being part of a plot, with Cyril Ramaphosa and Tokyo Sexwale, to overthrow him, an allegation Tshwete had later to retract.

A few years later, as the highest-ranking law professional in the ANC, Phosa made his law skills available for use by the Zuma faction. During Zuma's corruption trial he helped the ANC put together a legal team which weighed in as a friend of the court and argued that the trial would have a direct impact on the party.

Although the job of treasurer-general is not a full-time one and Phosa spends more time in his private office than at Luthuli House, he has managed to occupy the media spotlight much more prominently than his predecessor, Mendi Msimang. During the ANC's most difficult period, after the sacking of Mbeki as national president, it was Phosa who faced the barrage of questions from the media and the rest of the world. He was seen by his colleagues as the most reasonable voice in the top leadership at a time when the party needed to tread more carefully than ever to convince Mbeki supporters as well as the public that the decision had not been taken out of vengeance. However, even his best efforts did not hold water; within two months a breakaway party was born.

Phosa's new-found popularity and his raised profile in the media have come at a price. His detractors see him as ambitious and willing to do anything to fulfil his dream of becoming the president of South Africa, not in 2009 but definitely in 2014. To do this he will have to become ANC president at the party's 2012 conference, a position that he is said to be canvassing for already.

As a businessman Phosa has won various honours since 2006, including an award for being the 'most admired business person in Mpumalanga' and the PMR Africa Diamond Arrow award for 'outstanding service and contribution to the economic growth and development in Mpumalanga'.

Phosa is also a key player in the Afrikaner community, serving on the board of the Afrikaanse Handelsinstituut and the Innibos Arts Festival. He is a professor extraordinary at the University of the Free State and an honourary trustee of Die Woordeboek van die Afrikaanse Taal Trust, which is responsible for producing the definitive dictionary for the Afrikaans language.

Date of birth: September 1 1952

Pityana, Barney

As vice-chancellor of the University of South Africa, Nyameko Barney Pityana is one of only a handful of intellectuals who have dared to publicly challenge some of the highest-ranking politicians in the country, including former president Thabo Mbeki and ANC president Jacob Zuma. In 2005 he attacked Mbeki for the underfunding of South African higher education and in 2008 it was Zuma's turn, when Pityana decried his lack of moral character.

His outspokenness has been a hallmark of his public life, first as chairperson of the South African Human Rights Commission from 1995 to 2001 and subsequently as the leader of Unisa, one of the world's few mega-universities. But this has alienated him from the ruling elite, an estrangement that was confirmed by his association with the ANC's breakaway group, the Congress of the People, whose election commission he headed for the 2009 poll.

Despite the ANC's verbal retaliations when Pityana attacks its front men, he is something of an untouchable. Arguably, this is related to his political DNA as an Africanist whose thinking has been shaped in the presence of and by working together with black consciousness leader Steve Biko.

But as vice-chancellor, Pityana has had a bumpy ride from time to time. His appointment itself and the subsequent merger between Unisa, Technikon Southern Africa and some of the campuses of Vista University were a source of conflict between Pityana and Kader Asmal, then minister of education. Unisa went against Asmal's wishes by appointing Pityana for five years in 2001 and the university initially fought the merger. Pityana also came under fire for his apparently insensitive handling of a highly publicised sexual harassment case between the chair of the university council and a senior academic, and for giving academic refuge to ousted Haitian president Jean-Bertrand Aristide. He was also accused of a lack of understanding of the academic environment.

Despite criticisms of Pityana's running of Unisa, his international profile has enhanced that of the university and he has been described as the force behind Unisa's aggressive exploration of new frontiers, in particular in the rest of Africa. He has also been a prominent player in enhancing distance learning on the continent, and as the former chairman of Higher Education South Africa he has tried to strengthen this sector.

But many commentators believe that Pityana's aspirations go beyond Unisa, given his influence in areas such as law and theology, in both of which fields he holds degrees. He has, for instance, been in the running for the position of Anglican Archbishop of Cape Town.

Pityana credits his family for his love for learning. His mother, in particular, was a force to be reckoned with. She was one of only a handful of black women who matriculated in 1942.

Pityana attended Lovedale College in the Eastern Cape, a mission school which educated many of South Africa's leaders, including Thabo Mbeki. It was here that he joined the ANC Youth League. Expelled from the University of Fort Hare for his student activism, Pityana met up with Biko, sharing ideologies and a room. Pityana later became president of the South African Students' Organisation (Saso), which led to his year-long incarceration. Armed with BA and BProc degrees from Unisa, he left the country, returning to South Africa only in 1993. Two years later he earned a PhD in religious studies from the University of Cape Town.

While in exile he obtained an honours degree at King's College in London. After training at Ripon College, Cuddesdon, in Oxford, he was ordained as an Anglican priest, serving as parish priest in Milton Keynes and Birmingham. For four years, from 1988, he was director of the World Council of Churches' programme to combat racism.

Date of birth: August 7 1945

Price, Max

Max Price, who succeeded Njabulo Ndebele as the University of Cape Town's vice-chancellor in July 2008, is known in academic medical circles as a 'creative visionary' who has the flair and determination to implement his ideas.

A medical doctor who was dean of health sciences at the University of the Witwatersrand for 10 years, he won the support of the UCT senate and council with his intellect and vision – despite his status as a white male at a time when most universities in South Africa are struggling to transform the racial dynamics of their staff.

While it is too early to judge his achievements at UCT, transformation is high on his agenda. He has indicated that more needs to be done to ensure the success of historically disadvantaged students, and he wants to change an alienating institutional culture that leaves black staff and students feeling marginalised.

He has made it clear that while he believes that UCT is the academic hub of the South, it can compete on an equal footing with ivy league institutions in the North without trying to be a clone of them. And he argues that universities should protect the space for debate and value diverse views, particularly if they are controversial views, and that these institutions should nurture and promote public intellectuals and policies for national debate.

In this vein, he refused to discipline students involved in the production of UCT's Rag magazine *Sax Appeal*, whose content was regarded as blasphemous by many Christians. While he apologised to the aggrieved parties, he said the university would not censor the magazine but would give more backing to the academic input into the publication's editorial advisory board.

He stood by his principles in another case when in August 2001, while dean of health sciences at Wits, he appeared as a friend of the court and expert witness in support of three applicants challenging the then minister of health in the High Court for refusing to make the antiretroviral drug nevirapine available to HIV-positive pregnant women. He acted at a time when academics were perceived to be nervous about criticising the ANC government.

His former colleagues at Wits speak about this Rhodes Scholar's boldness in establishing and implementing the graduate entry medical programme (GEMP), which aims to change the demography of medical

147

doctors. Not many black African students had previously been gaining admission to the Wits medical school. The faculty initially took in a small number of students but the numbers have grown over the years, despite a few hiccups in the beginning; the first intake of newly qualified doctors graduated in 2006.

Price was also involved in setting up the first university-owned private teaching hospital – the Donald Gordon Medical Centre in Johannesburg. The hospital suffered funding problems as potential donors felt that their contributions would feature as a footnote to the R100-million that Donald Gordon, founder of the Liberty Life Group, had donated. After two years of unsustainable loss-making, the hospital group Medi-Clinic joined the venture and the situation was turned around. The hospital provides highly specialised training to doctors who want to become 'super-specialists'.

Price was also instrumental in establishing the Wits Health Consortium in 1998, to regulate private contract research. Private contract research undertaken by Wits's medical academics had brought little benefit to the institution, and his initiative was informed by the need to develop a more commercial approach to contract research and other income-generating opportunities.

Price earned his MB BCh from Wits, an honours degree in philosophy, politics and economics from Oxford University, and an MSc in community health in developing countries from the London School of Hygiene and Tropical Medicine. He was a member of the ANC commission on health service financing in 1993–4 and has consulted locally and internationally on health issues.

Date of birth: October 6 1955

Radebe, Jeff

The former Robben Island detainee has enjoyed many highs and lows in the past 15 years of South Africa's democracy, but in his former role as the minister of transport Jeff Thamsanqa Radebe was viewed as a relative success. He takes on a new challenge as minister of justice and constitutional development.

Politically he has managed to integrate himself with the Jacob Zuma-led faction of the ANC, becoming their public bullyboy with his attacks on defecting ANC cadres, such as Mosiuoa Lekota, who left to form the Congress of the People.

As the ANC's head of policy, Radebe found himself in a very senior position going into the 2009 election. This is quite a different situation from when he was at the helm of public enterprises and was dubbed by critics as 'Mr Privatisation'.

If everything goes according to Radebe's plan, public transport will become the 2010 Soccer World Cup's legacy in South Africa. Some R13.6-billion has been allocated to public transport projects in the host cities and the ministry insists that most are on track for completion before 2010.

However, there have been other massive failings, particularly Radebe's inability to get the taxi industry on board with the taxi recapitalisation programme and the various rapid bus transport systems that are planned for South Africa's major cities. Another recent problem was the R1.2-billion shortfall in bus subsidies, which saw Radebe rebuked by the Treasury, following legal action taken by the bus companies.

Radebe is regarded as an astute strategist. Imprisoned on Robben Island during the 1980s, he was head of the ANC's political education department.

He was born in Cato Manor, in Durban, KwaZulu-Natal (KZN), and lived there until 1958, when his family was relocated under the Group Areas Act to KwaMashu. He cut his political teeth by helping form youth organisations in KZN while studying law at the University of Zululand before heading into exile, where he served the ANC in several fields, including the information and international departments.

A master's degree in international law from Leipzig University followed. He returned to South Africa in 1986 on an ANC mission and was arrested and sentenced to 10 years on terrorism charges, reduced to six years on appeal. He was finally released in June 1990. During the 1990s, as the ANC's Southern Natal chairperson, he was actively involved in peace talks with the Inkatha Freedom Party, which won him favour with Nelson Mandela.

In 1994 he was appointed minister of public works and assumed the unenviable task of creating a national asset register. Radebe's time at the helm of public works was viewed as quite a success, as the department expanded its core functions to include the establishment of public works programmes to alleviate poverty, a policy that is still important for the ANC in 2009.

In 1999 Radebe was appointed minister of public enterprises by then-president Thabo Mbeki. Once regarded as a champion of the poor, Radebe was dubbed a sell-out by leftists in the tripartite alliance when in 2000 he announced plans to restructure South Africa's major state-owned assets, such as Eskom, Transnet and Telkom. In 2002 he was voted off the central committee of the South African Communist Party because of his commitment to privatisation.

In 1997 he married Bridgette Motsepe, a former beauty queen, now businesswoman and mining magnate. This makes Radebe and businessman Cyril Ramaphosa brothers-in-law – Ramaphosa is married to Motsepe's sister.

Date of birth: August 6 1953

Ramaphosa, Cyril

Cyril Ramaphosa will be remembered for three things: driving the multi-party negotiations that led to the first democratic elections; chairing the Constitutional Assembly, which wrote the Constitution; and overseeing the Black Economic Empowerment (BEE) Commission. History will also recall his being shouldered aside by Thabo Mbeki as first deputy president of the country. For some admirers Ramaphosa's accession to the presidency would have been a happier outcome than the ultimately divisive reign of Mbeki.

At the time his role in achieving a peaceful political transition seemed to open the door for bigger things. But piqued at not becoming Mandela's deputy in the Government of National Unity that took office in 1994, Ramaphosa refused a proffered post of foreign affairs and ultimately opted for 'redeployment' in racially transforming business. It must have been satisfying for him to see his one-time rival ousted in favour of Jacob Zuma as ANC president at the Polokwane conference of the ANC in December 2007. In 2001 Ramaphosa as well as fellow black BEE entrepreneur Tokyo Sexwale and former Mpumalanga premier Mathews Phosa had been named by the Mbeki loyalist and safety and security minister, Steve Tshwete, as under suspicion for plotting against the president, an outrageously intimidatory move.

Ramaphosa's early experiences in business were mixed. He joined the ill-fated New Africa Investments Limited (Nail) after quitting politics in 1996 but left before a boardroom scandal marked the start of that company's slow unravelling. And as chairman of industrial holding company Johnnic, formed as a result of one of the first big BEE 'deals', he presided over a disappointing evolution of the company from big fish to minnow. At Nail Ramaphosa failed to arrange the acquisition of JCI, the mining company that was also on offer.

Yet while Ramaphosa has not scaled the same heights as a player in business as he did in politics, he has had a significant impact on BEE, firstly as a pioneer in this area, and secondly as chairman of the BEE Commission, whose recommendations to the government in 1999 formed the basis for the present legislation.

At times his heart does not seem to have been in business at all, and this may have led to his being named time and again as a presidential contender, though he has always denied the ambition. It is true he would be more than merely acceptable to the still largely white business community as well as the growing black middle class. However, left-wing elements in the alliance movement would be uncomfortable with the elevation of a single-malt and fly-fishing-loving BEE mogul to a party trying to appeal to the black poor and working class, whatever his political pedigree.

That pedigree was formed early on, though Ramaphosa, unlike Mbeki, did not hail from a political background. The son of a police sergeant from Venda who quit the force after his son was detained in 1976, Ramaphosa became involved while he was studying at the University of the North with the radical South African Students' Organisation (Saso) and the Black People's Convention. His political activities brought him to the attention of the apartheid regime, and led to his detention on two occasions.

He earned his BProc degree from Unisa while working as a law clerk for a Johannesburg firm, then joined the Council of Unions of South Africa (Cusa) as legal adviser. He attracted attention when he organised the nascent National Union of Mineworkers (NUM) into a formidable force, in the process building a reputation as a shrewd but personable negotiator. After leading the NUM into the ANC-aligned Cosatu federation, he played an important role in strengthening the union movement as an anti-apartheid political force, ensuring that he became ANC secretary-general in 1991. He was at the side of Nelson Mandela at the great man's first public speech after his release from jail.

Hence the persistent idea that Ramaphosa will one day return more strongly to politics – he has retained a seat on the ANC's national executive committee – from a sojourn in business. However, he has stayed in business long enough to amass a sizeable though unknown fortune, housed in the family trust that together with his long-term friend James Motlatsi and others owns the Shanduka Group, an unlisted investment holding company. At the same time he has the reputation of a man who sits on too many boards to be of much use to any of them. This was particularly so in the years when the names of Ramaphosa, Tokyo Sexwale, Saki Macozoma or Patrice Motsepe cropped up in every BEE deal, earning them the title of 'the usual suspects'.

The investments that Shanduka has made in financial services, particularly in Standard Bank and Alexander Forbes, have been astute and testimony to his legendary negotiating skills. Yet Shanduka's investments are so wide-ranging one can almost ask, 'What does it not have investments in?' In its holding of minority, passive stakes that have influence perhaps but no real power, Shanduka is also typical of the BEE firms that have been created through 'narrow-based' empowerment. It is this narrow-based BEE that Ramaphosa is associated with, though he himself is avowedly in favour of broad-based empowerment, and has set up a Shanduka Foundation to help educate and give business skills to the previously disadvantaged.

Ramaphosa's political mastery in helping achieve a peaceful transition has been recognised outside the country. He has been party to various attempts to bring peace to troubled regions, and most recently was appointed one of a group of global leaders to advise the United Nations on business and human rights. One can only wonder what South Africa might have been like now had he indeed become president after Mandela.

Date of birth: November 17 1952

Ramatlhodi, Ngoako

Ngoako Abel Ramatlhodi is something of a political chameleon and could at some stage fall victim to the climate of mistrust and factional struggles that pervade the ANC.

During the first decade of post-1994 democracy, he appeared to be solidly in the Thabo Mbeki fold. Indeed, before the unbanning of the ANC in 1990, Ramatlhodi, like Mbeki, had been quite close to ANC president Oliver Tambo, serving time as his speechwriter. In 1994 Ramatlhodi was appointed premier of the Northern Province (now Limpopo) and served two full terms, before stepping down in 2004. When Mbeki, as president, became embroiled in controversy when he voiced his scepticism about the conventional scientific view of HIV/Aids, Ramatlhodi was one of his staunchest defenders, launching propaganda attacks on the president's critics, such as the then-head of the Medical Research Council, Professor Malegapuru Makgoba. Thus when Bulelani Ngcuka – perceived as an ally of Mbeki – was due to step down as national director of public prosecutions, there was widespread speculation that Ramatlhodi might be appointed by Mbeki in his stead.

Two factors combined to dash that hope and turn Ramatlhodi into one of Jacob Zuma's most ardent supporters. The first was a corruption probe into Ramatlhodi started by the Scorpions in March 2004, following an exposé in the investigative magazine *Noseweek*, which linked him to allegations of kickbacks for a large Limpopo tender. When Ramatlhodi applied for admission as an advocate in mid-2004 – a qualification he would have needed to occupy the position of director of public prosecutions – the criminal investigation emerged from the woodwork and the court ruled that his application should stand down until the Scorpions' investigation was finalised one way or another – thereby effectively disqualifying him for the post.

There were also suggestions of suspicion in the Mbeki camp that Ramatlhodi had already been 'captured' by the Zuma camp and could not be trusted. Either way, Ramatlhodi increasingly came out in support of Zuma's claim that he was the victim of a political investigation by the Scorpions – even as he parried efforts by the unit to investigate the Limpopo matter. Eventually Ramatlhodi became one of the most consistent attendees at Zuma's numerous appearances in court and also succeeded in obtaining the 20th spot on the ANC's 77-member national executive committee (NEC).

Apparently Ramatlhodi began to contemplate once again the prospect of high legal office when he reapplied for admission as an advocate in 2008, at a time when it was clear the ANC was determined to replace Vusi Pikoli as director of public prosecutions. The matter was again postponed because of the unfinished Scorpions investigation, but at the end of 2008, following representations from Ramatlhodi's lawyers, the National Prosecuting Authority announced that it was reversing the decision to charge him and was closing the Limpopo case.

Ramatlhodi's path to high office now appears clear – he was 23rd on the ANC's provisional list for the national Parliament for the 2009 elections – but doubts about his reliability may remain. Despite his high ranking on the NEC, Ramatlhodi is not part of the ANC's national working committee, which controls the day-to-day affairs of the party and is dominated by Zuma's inner circle.

Ramatlhodi has deep roots in Limpopo. He was born in Tauyatswala, a small village near Potgietersrus in what was then the Northern Transvaal. His father was a mineworker, his mother a housewife. As a child his nickname was 'Montsho' because he was the darkest-skinned kid in the family. He matriculated at Tembisa High, achieving rather poor marks though sufficient to enable him to attend university.

According to his official ANC biography, Ramatlhodi decided to become a lawyer after seeing his jailed brother humiliated by prison warders. He enrolled for a BJuris at the University of the North in 1976, but his introduction to politics came mainly through Marimba Artists, a poetry and drama society that focused on writing political poetry.

Ramatlhodi was expelled from university in 1977 for political reasons, but allowed back in 1978 to repeat his second year. Meanwhile he had joined the ANC after a trip to Botswana. In 1979 he was again expelled and took the university to court. Readmitted, he failed at the end of the year and was refused readmission. He then worked for six months for a Johannesburg lawyer until he went into exile in July 1980. He studied law at the University of Lesotho and graduated with a bachelor of laws degree in 1986.

Between 1986 and 1988 Ramatlhodi was sent by the ANC to Zimbabwe, where he obtained his master's in international relations at the University of Zimbabwe. In Zimbabwe he was appointed head of the ANC's regional politico-military committee. He was subsequently recalled by the ANC leadership to Zambia, where he became a speechwriter for Tambo.

Date of birth: August 25 1955

Ramphele, Mamphela

Mamphela Ramphele has had multiple careers – as a doctor, an activist whose name is notable in the struggle for liberation, an academic, a university administrator, a World Bank managing director and, now, a businesswoman. Her status as one of South Africa's leading intellectuals is unchallenged, as is her style – as unusual in South Africa at the beginning of the 21st century as it was in the 20th – of speaking truth to power.

Born and schooled in Kranspoort in what was then the Northern Transvaal (and is now Limpopo) to primary school teachers, she enrolled for pre-med at the University of the North at Turfloop and in 1968 was accepted by the University of Natal Medical School. It was here that she met Steve Biko and through him became involved in the South African Students' Organisation (Saso); with Biko, she was a founder of the Black Consciousness Movement (BCM). After qualifying as a doctor she set up a BCM clinic near King William's Town, where she and Biko were then based.

In 1977, she was banished to Lenyenye township near Tzaneen, where she founded the Ithuseng Community Health Programme. When the banishment was lifted seven years later, she enrolled at the University of Cape Town, completed a BCom in administration and started a PhD in social anthropology; she also earned diplomas in tropical health and hygiene and in public health from the University of the Witwatersrand. With UCT economics professor Francis Wilson, she co-authored *Uprooting Poverty,* based on the research they undertook for the second Carnegie Inquiry into Poverty and Development in South Africa; it won the prestigious Noma Award for publishing in Africa.

She was appointed deputy vice-chancellor at UCT in 1991, and vice-chancellor five years later. And in 2000, she became the first African to serve as a managing director of the World Bank. Her brief was to manage the World Bank's human development activities in health, education, nutrition, and social protection. The World Bank Institute, providing training for staff and clients, was part of her remit, as was oversight and guidance of the group's information and communication technologies.

She served for a year as co-chair of the Global Commission on International Migration, then returned to South Africa to form a financial services company, Circle Capital Ventures, with her son Hlumelo Biko, born a few weeks after the death of his father in detention.

Ramphele is a trustee of the Nelson Mandela Children's Fund and a director of Idasa. She has published widely on a variety of topics, including the status of indigenous languages, migrant labour, and transformation in South Africa.

Date of birth: December 28 1947

Ramulifho, Khume

As the Democratic Alliance's national youth spokesperson and Gauteng Youth leader, Khume Ramulifho cannot be more different from his counterpart in the ANC Youth League, Julius Malema. Unlike Malema, he doesn't seek the headlines; a keen debater, he has a somewhat cleverer turn of phrase than his opposite. When Malema refused to debate with him, referring to him as 'Helen Zille's garden boy', he replied, 'What's wrong with garden boys? It is also a profession,' and predicted that Malema 'would do no better than a garden gnome were he to engage in a debate with the DA youth ... because he has no substantive views on how to tackle the critical issues of youth unemployment, crime and the state of the education system'. Calling Malema 'a one-trick pony', he said Malema could learn a lot from DA youth.

Born in the rural area of Lomondo in Limpopo, he was educated there, gaining his matric in 1997. A debater and top student, he wanted to study law, but was discouraged by his family. His older brother and sole support advised him to go for a career in a different field as he had seen too many of his peers studying law for years on end. So in 1998 Ramulifho entered the Vaal University of Technology (VUT), where he earned a national diploma and then a BTech in human resource management.

In his first year at VUT, he developed an interest in politics and was particularly attracted to the Democratic Party. He ran for the student representative council, and lost. A year later, the Democratic Alliance Students' Organisation (Daso), which he founded, put up eight candidates, and lost again, to the South African Students' Congress (Sasco), the largest national organisation for students in the country. But in 2000, Ramulifho's Daso won all but one seat.

For several years he worked on surveys and analyses for banks and other corporates, and as a personnel officer for the South African Police Service, before focusing entirely on politics after his election as Johannesburg Metro councillor. At 30 he is fast approaching the cut-off age for DA Youth, but he also serves as the DA's deputy chairperson for Gauteng South and is on the DA's 2009 list for the provincial legislature.
Date of birth: February 27 1979

Sachs, Albie

'Let us have one good amandla. This is my last amandla – where I am going there will not be many amandlas,' said Albie Sachs at his last political meeting in 1994.

Albert Louis Sachs was described as the most 'politically high profile' of the candidates for a place on the Constitutional Court when they were interviewed by the Judicial Service Commission (JSC). He had been a member of the ANC for decades and in exile since 1966. He had lost an arm, and sight in one eye, in Mozambique from a bomb planted by apartheid security agents in 1988.

He was also highly qualified for a seat on the court: he had taught constitutional law in the UK and in Mozambique, where he had conducted research into a new constitution.

The JSC did not give Sachs a warm reception, putting it to him that he had been promised a position on the court, an assertion he denied. The JSC also questioned Sachs about his involvement in a commission of inquiry into the death in ANC detention of an Umkhonto weSizwe commander codenamed Thami Zulu. Zulu had been held in solitary confinement in an ANC camp for a year; he died shortly after his release. The internal inquiry cleared the movement of blame, putting Zulu's death down to 'South African security'. Despite heavy grilling by some members of the JSC, Sachs was appointed to the Constitutional Court. He went on to author landmark judgments, such as the one recognising same-sex marriages.

Sachs studied law at the University of Cape Town and became politically active there, regularly joining anti-apartheid protests. He was in Kliptown when the basis for South Africa's Constitution – the Freedom Charter – was signed in 1955.

Sachs joined the Bar at the age of 21 and defended victims of apartheid's unjust laws. He was also detained more than once and spent time in solitary confinement; in one instance he credits his survival to a court order that allowed him to have books in his jail cell.

He spent 11 years studying and teaching law in England – earning a PhD at the University of Sussex and teaching law at the University of Southampton – and worked for a further 11 years in Mozambique as a law professor and legal researcher at Eduardo Mondlane University in Maputo. It was here that he was injured by the car bomb.

During the 1980s, working closely with Oliver Tambo, leader of the ANC in exile, he helped draft the organisation's code of conduct as well as its statutes. After recovering from his injuries, he devoted himself fulltime to preparations for a new democratic constitution for South Africa. In 1990 he returned home and, as a member of the constitutional committee and the national executive committee of the ANC, took an active part in the negotiations which led to South Africa's constitutional democracy.

In addition to his work on the Constitutional Court, he has travelled to many countries, sharing the South African experience in healing divided societies. He has also been engaged in the sphere of art and architecture, and played an active role in the development of the Constitutional Court building and its art collection on the site of the Old Fort prison in Johannesburg. He is a recipient of the Alan Paton literary award for his book titled *The Soft Vengeance of a Freedom Fighter,* one of three autobiographical works.

Sachs will be saying his last 'amandla' to the Constitutional Court in October 2009.

Date of birth: January 30 1935

Sexwale, Tokyo

The apparent return of Mosima Gabriel 'Tokyo' Sexwale to the mainstream of political life received a setback when he failed to win any high position in the ANC at the Polokwane national conference in December 2007. Sexwale was a candidate for the position of national chairperson, but withdrew in favour of the Zuma camp's nominee, Baleka Mbete, to great applause from delegates. Mathews Phosa, who with Cyril Ramaphosa and Sexwale had been accused several years earlier of conspiring to oust then-president Thabo Mbeki, was made national treasurer. In any event, the charismatic Sexwale threw in his lot with the ultimate winner of the presidency, Jacob Zuma. They are both veterans of the ANC's armed wing, Umkhonto weSizwe.

Aided by his charm and commanding presence, Sexwale has done well in taking advantage of South Africa's version of all-encompassing affirmative action, known as black economic empowerment. He has built up a considerable empire, with the help of white wheeler-dealer Mark Wilcox, who as CEO of Mvelaphanda Holdings actually runs the show. Sexwale left the Gauteng premiership in 1998 after only four years to go into business. That he left politics so suddenly in the first place has led to all sorts of unsubstantiated rumours, fuelled by the kind of smears that became commonplace in the Mbeki era.

Certainly it seemed he had no future in the ANC while Mbeki was president. Once Mbeki's power was waning, Sexwale might have considered a run for the ANC presidency, and hence the country's presidency. His newly acquired wealth would probably have put him out of the running, since the preference was clearly for a president with a common touch, and one who would receive the blessing of the South African Communist Party and trade union federation Cosatu.

Also, it has long been gossiped that Tokyo's choice of a white wife made him unpopular with the black majority, who supposedly frown on this kind of arrangement. Sexwale met Judy Moon, who worked for a Cape Town legal firm, while she was visiting prisoners on Robben Island, where he was incarcerated. He was serving an 18-year sentence for terrorism. They married three years after he was released from prison, in 1993, and the next year he was made premier of Gauteng.

The story of Sexwale's early years that led to that prison sentence is by now well known. He was attracted to black consciousness as a youth growing up in Soweto, where he earned the nickname 'Tokyo' because of his fondness for karate. He joined the ANC underground and went into exile in 1975, undergoing officer's military training specialising in army engineering in the USSR before returning to South Africa as a guerrilla fighter.

In 2005 he played another role, as South Africa's homegrown Donald Trump in the country's local version of *The Apprentice*. He was criticised for being indecisive when announcing that he would employ both of the two finalists. Sexwale's own wealth is tied up in Mvelaphanda Holdings, which owns more than 51% of the shares in the Mvelaphanda Group. Mvelaphanda Holdings claims to be 90% black-owned.

Yet while being identified as a businessman, his role has taken him into controversial areas, particularly in relation to the recent race for the ANC presidency. As the lead partner and adviser in Absa's Batho Bonke deal, he was in a position to hand out largesse to many black people throughout the country, including, it is alleged, journalists, a judge (who got R6.9-million-worth of shares) and political commentators. It was also reported in 2007 that he bought a R715 000 7-series BMW for the controversial former wife of Nelson Mandela, Winnie Madikizela-Mandela; this was interpreted as buying her vote in the ANC leadership race.

When he was Gauteng premier, the Sexwales were a celebrity couple and media darlings, but he is currently less in the news than previously. Now he owns a chunk of the print media. Commentators were alarmed when the pragmatic but intensely political Sexwale's Mvelaphanda Group bought, at the end of 2007, 25.5% of Avusa, which publishes the influential mass-circulation *Sunday Times*. There has, however, been no sign so far of Sexwale trying to use this stake to shape editorial coverage.

As well as serving on a number of boards, he is a trustee of a range of charitable organisations, such as the Nelson Mandela Foundation. He has received various awards, including the French Legion of Honour and several honorary doctorates, as well as the freedom of Havana, and he is an honorary colonel in the South African National Defence Force. His charisma is undoubted, and it has often been recorded that he was voted 'the sexiest politician in South Africa' by white women 'from Pretoria to Sandton' in a phone-in survey on the John Berks Radio 702 show. Sexwale is now minister of human settlements – formerly called housing.

Date of birth: March 5 1953

Shabangu, Susan

Susan Shabangu's appointment as deputy minister of safety and security in 2004 was a surprise. Nothing in her life had prepared her for the task. Coming from a background in the women's and trade union movements, she seemed an odd choice for the post. On the other hand, nothing in her background had prepared her for her previous job as deputy minister of minerals and energy, but she'd made a great success of it after her appointment in 1996. She chalked up a number of accomplishments, among them encouraging mining companies to come up with a comprehensive Aids policy, promoting small-scale mining and devising nuclear energy strategies.

It was hoped her enthusiasm and creativity would produce innovative ways to deal with crime. But the shockingly high levels of crime in South Africa have not abated and she has gained notoriety – and considerable support from a crime-weary population – for telling the police to 'kill the bastards' (read: 'shoot to kill'). Newspaper headlines since have demonstrated almost daily the extent to which the South African Police Service has taken this injunction to heart. Some commentators reckon Shabangu's statement to be good personal PR for someone trapped within a lame-duck administration; certainly it shows she is good at recognising, and tapping into, public concerns and attitudes. But many have pointed out that, among other problems, her injunction does not fall within the ambit of the Constitution.

Born and educated in Soweto, Shabangu became assistant Transvaal secretary for the Federation of South African Women in 1980, the year she entered politics. A year later she joined the Anti-Republic Campaign committee and in 1982 was a founder member of the Release Mandela Campaign; she stayed active in that organisation until Madiba's release in 1990.

In the mid-1980s she moved into the labour field as organiser and administrator for the Amalgamated Black Workers' Project. In the early 1990s, she was a member of Cosatu's national task team aimed at educating workers during the run-up to the first democratic elections, and she was on Cosatu's list for Parliament in 1994. Once an MP, she was active in committees dealing with transport, trade and industry and, naturally, labour. Shabangu is now minister of mining.

Date of birth: 28 February 1956

Shaik, Moe

Loyalist and strategist, Moe Shaik has been key to shaping ANC president Jacob Zuma's journey to the Union Buildings. The two men are comrades who worked together in the underground and security structures of the movement, in exile and internally.

Shaik's brother Schabir is the businessman at the centre of the corruption, fraud and racketeering charges facing Zuma. Another brother, Shamin 'Chippy' Shaik, was chief procurement officer for the defence department during the arms deal – which lies at the heart of the charges – and left the country for Australia in 2007. Moe Shaik has publicly acknowledged his brother Schabir's lapse of judgement and appears to have stewarded Zuma's fight-back campaign as a way of making up. Shaik was instrumental in ensuring that the Hefer Commission probed allegations that the former national director of public prosecutions, Bulelani Ngcuka, was an apartheid-era spy. The commission disavowed the allegation but the damage had been done and Ngcuka left office a short while later. Shaik then continued to mobilise behind the scenes for Zuma's later political victory.

For a strategic thinker he is surprisingly mouthy, which may curtail his political career. Shaik incurred the wrath of finance minister Trevor Manuel before the Polokwane conference when he speculated on Manuel's chances of getting into the next government. And ahead of the election, he declared to a public meeting that the following day's newspapers would lead with a story stating that Zuma's charges would be dropped. He was right, but had clearly spoken out of turn. Shaik was upbraided by ANC Youth League president Julius Malema and other ANC leaders who wanted to be seen to be doing the right thing.

Shaik's ANC roots are deep; he spent years as an underground cadre and was a leading operative, in KwaZulu-Natal, of Operation Vula, an ANC campaign to link ANC officials in exile with activists inside the country. After 1990, he was involved in negotiations over integrating the military and intelligence services. Meanwhile, he earned a master's degree in optometry at the University of Durban-Westville and lectured there, but was drawn back into government. In 1997 he was named consul-general in Hamburg, Germany, and shortly afterwards ambassador to Algeria. After the Hefer Commission fiasco, he resigned from the department of foreign affairs, and little more was heard of him – until Polokwane.

Shaik did not make it on to the 2009 lists for Parliament, but he is an important political activist and backroom player in the new presidency. **Date of birth:** August 26 1959

Shiceka, Sicelo

Sicelo Shiceka marked his return to national politics in 2008 by taking over the poisoned chalice that is the local government and provincial affairs portfolio, now called cooperative governance and traditional affairs. He had been on the margins since he was removed as Gauteng local government minister in 1999. At that time, Shiceka was part of a group, including then-premier Mathole Motshekga, who ran the Gauteng provincial government but were in conflict with the national leadership of the party. Luthuli House removed them from power.

In his new portfolio Shiceka immediately set about working on the return of Khutsong to Gauteng, a crucial move in restoring stability to an area characterised by violence, election boycotts and ungovernability since then-president Thabo Mbeki placed the town in North West province. The move was important as it returned to the fold a community who had, by and large, boycotted the 2004 elections in protest against the demarcation. Shiceka also started consultations with residents of Moutse and Matatiele, who had also been unhappy about their relocation to Limpopo and Eastern Cape respectively.

Shiceka first returned to the national stage when he was elected to the ANC's national executive committee at Polokwane at the end of 2007. He took over the local government ministry in September 2008 after his predecessor, Sydney Mufamadi, resigned when Mbeki was recalled as president

Shiceka spent his initial months in the ministry consulting widely. He embarked on a tour of the provinces – the Intergovernmental and Community Dialogue – meeting with premiers, MECs, traditional leaders, ward and municipal councillors, mayors and organisations like the South African Local Government Association (Salga). The intention of these engagements, which started in the Eastern Cape, was to understand the impact of government's service delivery machinery on the ground and to come up with better ways of fast-tracking it.

Shiceka was born in Johannesburg and started his activism in the Soweto Youth Congress in the 1980s. He joined the trade union movement later and became an organiser for the Paper Printing Wood and Allied Workers' Union in 1989. He was elected on to the provincial executive committee of the South African Communist Party in 1991 and the following year he became provincial secretary for the trade union federation Cosatu. He was appointed Gauteng MEC for development and planning and local government in 1994 and served until 1999, but was not returned to office by the new premier, Mbhazima Shilowa. He was, however, sent to Parliament by the ANC in 2004 and became minister in September 2008.

Date of birth: June 8 1966

Shilowa, Mbhazima

The deputy president of the Congress of the People (Cope) will best be remembered as the radical Cosatu general secretary who dropped all his worker rhetoric and turned into a suave, capital-embracing, urbane Gauteng premier.

Shilowa was brought into Gauteng as premier and as ANC provincial chairperson at a time when the province was paralysed by ANC infighting and desperately in need of a neutral figurehead. He was relatively successful in this and avoided personal involvement in corruption or scandals. But he still came under criticism for failing to act against his ministers Paul Mashatile and Angie Motshekga when they were implicated in dealings that showed conflicts of interest.

Shilowa is one of the politicians known to be close to former president Thabo Mbeki. He was the first to warn the ANC that should they fire Mbeki as president, there would be a split in the ANC. After Mbeki's recall he joined the breakaway party, Cope, which consisted mainly of ANC members unhappy with the leadership of ANC president Jacob Zuma and those around him.

Shilowa will also be remembered as the security guard who rose from the trade union ranks to be premier of South Africa's richest province. He made good work of it, running a stable and relatively clean government. He introduced Gauteng Online so that every school would have access to a computer and email; he stopped the taxi violence when he first came into office; he embraced the concept of the Gautrain and spent much time as premier working towards its completion; and under his watch, Gauteng was the first ANC-run province to roll out antiretrovirals to prevent mother-to-child transmission of HIV, when it was national policy to withhold ARVs from pregnant women.

When many provincial structures of Cope nominated Shilowa as the party's presidential candidate, he declined and instead went along with the suggestion that an outsider, the Rev. Mvume Dandala, be the face of the party in the elections.

Shilowa was born at Olifantshoek in Limpopo and completed his secondary education at Akani High School in 1978. The following year he moved to Johannesburg to seek employment and started working at a hardware store in Germiston. He then moved to Anglo Alpha Cement in Roodepoort and was later employed by PSG Services in Johannesburg.

In 1981, Shilowa joined the trade union movement and became a shop steward fighting for better working conditions and defending the rights of his fellow workers. He was elected vice-president and later president of the South African Transport and Allied Workers' Union. Shilowa played a prominent role in the formation of Cosatu in 1985 and was elected deputy chairperson of Cosatu's Gauteng region. In 1991, he became deputy general secretary of Cosatu and, in 1993, general secretary. On June 15 1999 he was elected premier of Gauteng and had to give up his Cosatu post.

He is married to Wendy Luhabe, chairperson of the Industrial

Development Corporation and chancellor of the University of Johannesburg.
Date of birth: April 30 1958

Shope-Mafole, Lyndall

Lyndall Shope-Mafole was the princess-in-waiting. She had it all: a prominent family name; a powerful ANC matriarch in her mother, Gertrude Shope, chief ANC representative in Zambia during the days of exile; and an equally respected father, Mark Shope, former general secretary of the South African Congress of Trade Unions (Sactu) and an early MK member. She had her own impeccable struggle credentials, gained from years of representing the ANC on the international stage during the apartheid era. She was also a popular director-general in the department of communications, where she was involved in various initiatives to drive the development of broadband communications in South Africa. A glittering future awaited her as part of the younger, hot-and-happening ANC generation.

She was set to become a leader in the ANC in her own right. At the ANC's 2007 conference in Polokwane she was elected through the youth structures of the party to the national executive committee (NEC), which meant that she was on her way to becoming a key role-player in South African politics, even though she was not a vocal supporter of Jacob Zuma and was known to be close to the Mbeki family. While she grew uneasy with Zuma's supporters and the embarrassing outbursts of people like ANC Youth League president Julius Malema, she maintained that the ANC was her political home and that change would come from inside. Then came the sacking of former president Thabo Mbeki. For Shope, this was the breaking point where everything changed.

She used the weeks that followed the NEC decision that Mbeki must leave the Union Buildings to draft her resignation letter to the ANC. Once the deed was done and she explained to her family the reason for her decision, she called the leaders of the Congress of the People (Cope) and applied for membership. Her resignation from the ANC sent shockwaves through the party and her family. She became the second NEC member to pack her bags and move to Cope. Hopes that the ANC might face a real split started to gain ground. Shope-Mafole was welcomed with open arms by the Cope leaders and was asked to chair the first session at the national convention in Sandton in November 2008, out of which the party was born.

She was chosen as a member of Cope's leadership and given the responsibility of managing international relations for the party. Her role grew to such an extent that she had to quit her million-rand-a-year job as director-general in the department of communications to devote herself full-time to Cope.

Shope-Mafole holds a master's degree in telecommunications engineering from the José Antonio Echeverria Higher Institute of Technology in Cuba and was a commissioner with the Independent Broadcasting Authority, the forerunner of the Independent Communications Authority of South Africa.

She was married to the late Tebogo Mafole, deputy director-general of the department of foreign affairs.

Date of birth: January 1 1958

Sisulu, Elinor

An academic, human rights activist and prize-winning author, Elinor Batezat Sisulu has combined studies in history, development studies, English literature and feminist theory into a formidable package.

She was born in Harare and educated first at the University of Zimbabwe, where she earned BA and honours degrees; she moved on to the United Nations Institute of Economic Development and Planning in Dakar, Senegal, and then to the Institute of Social Studies in The Hague, where she obtained an MA.

In between, she worked as a research officer in the ministry of labour in Zimbabwe, researching and writing about employment trends, including women's work, and publishing a number of books and papers on female labour in Zimbabwe. In Lusaka, Zambia, she was an associate expert for the International Labour Organisation, looking at cooperation between the ILO and southern African liberation movements.

She came to South Africa in 1990 and worked as a freelance writer and editor while researching a biography of her famous in-laws, Walter and Albertina Sisulu; she had married Max Sisulu in the mid-1980s. The work, entitled *In Our Lifetime*, won the prestigious Noma Award for writing in Africa.

It was not her first writing prize: a best-selling children's book about the first democratic elections, *The Day Gogo Went to Vote*, first published in the United States, won several awards, and was named a notable book by the Smithsonian Institution and the American Library Association.

Sisulu has been engaged for more than a decade in two compelling projects: children's literature, and justice in Zimbabwe. In 2004 she established the South African office for the Crisis in Zimbabwe Coalition, a major umbrella body of Zimbabwe NGOs, and has spoken out strongly and often about human rights abuses in that failed state.

She has also been a prime mover in the establishment of a children's literature network in South Africa. She serves as judge in a number of literary competitions and is a member of the advisory committee of the Centre for the Book in Cape Town.

Date of birth: March 9 1958

Sisulu, Lindiwe

The gaze of Lindiwe Nonceba Sisulu is set firmly on the highest office in the land.

Definitely the best-dressed and healthiest-looking minister, she is also one of the most competent in the Cabinet. Her department of housing was efficient and, although millions of South Africans are still homeless, people don't feel completely forsaken and at a loss as they would if they had to deal with, say, home affairs or public enterprise.

Sisulu has a lot going for her. Since the takeover at Polekwane she has been catapulted into the inner circle surrounding Jacob Zuma, and has played a vital role in ensuring he becomes the country's president. In between all her electioneering, however, Sisulu also managed to run the housing department expertly, building houses and upgrading shack settlements. She was not big on traipsing through townships, dodging rubbish and shouting 'Viva delivery!' For starters she doesn't do sensible shoes, but has a preference for their rather more elegant and pointy high-heeled sisters.

But Sisulu brought something more than elegance to the housing department, and she will be sorely missed when she goes to the sexier ministry of defence and military veterans. She has brought insight, forward planning and top strategy to this department and to government. Sisulu these days can talk on any international stage about housing delivery, slum elimination and poverty.

As minister, Sisulu piloted the Housing Development Agency (HDA) Bill – for an agency designed to identify well-located state-owned land where housing can be built and to fast-track its development – through both houses of Parliament, creating a sharp and effective tool to remove bottlenecks from crippling the rate of houses delivered to the homeless. At least that's in theory. And theory is something Sisulu's very good at. Another of Sisulu's strengths is her ability to surround herself with competent, independent-thinking people. This showed in her appointment of the highly competent housing director-general, Itumeleng Kotsoane.

Between 1994 and 2000, government implemented a one-size-fits-all housing policy, providing RDP houses in grid-system settlements for the poor and the unemployed, far away from the urban centres, where the land was cheap and plentiful and thousands of people could be crammed together in poorly serviced suburbs. When Sisulu became housing minister in April 2004, sustainable human settlement plans and housing developments for the poor were taken seriously for the first time. She drafted policy changes that made a priority of the needs of the poor and homeless and gathered some of the best brains in the business to develop the Breaking New Ground (BNG) approach to housing, designing human settlements in an interpretation of the state's response to people's constitutional right to housing. The BNG policy articulates the 'need to shift the official response to informal settlements from one of conflict and neglect to one of integration and cooperation'.

Since 1994, according to the department, 2.6-million houses have been built, one million of them erected or currently in construction during Sisulu's term in office over the past four years. The last two years have seen plenty of ribbon-cutting and keys handed over to grateful, crying women. But it is simply not enough. In Cape Town alone there is a backlog of over 400 000 houses and yet only 20 000 are being built in the entire province. Only about one-tenth of the required dwelling units are built each year.

This was not Sisulu's fault. She was responsible for policy and direction only. But she did have the power to hold provinces and municipalities accountable for service delivery and at least cajole them to implement her policies – something she did not do.

The decomposing albatross around her neck was the N2 Gateway housing project, supposedly her flagship. In 2008 residents of the site where the project is supposed to be built refused to move without guarantees that they could come back once the area was developed. The Cape High Court ruled in the department's favour, and the case is now going to the Constitutional Court. The community, who lived in shacks, argue that they will be unable to afford the bonded houses to be built on the land. Government has fought this community tooth and nail, exposing a serious faultline still present in the department's policies: Sisulu and her team still don't have a plan that doesn't include forced removals of poor people to the periphery of cities.

The daughter of struggle stalwarts Walter and Albertina Sisulu, Lindiwe left South Africa and joined Umkhonto weSizwe in 1977 after her release from detention under the Terrorism Act. She earned a bachelor's degree in education and history at the University of Swaziland in 1980, lectured at the university, at a teacher training college and at a high school, and worked as a journalist on *The Times of Swaziland*. In 1989 she earned a master's in history at the University of York, returning to South Africa the following year as personal assistant to Jacob Zuma, who was then the ANC's head of intelligence.

In 1996 she was appointed deputy minister of home affairs, and five years later minister of intelligence, leaving that post to assume the ministry of housing in 2004.

Date of birth: May 10 1954

Sisulu, Max

Max Vuyisile Sisulu, who has been appointed speaker in the National Assembly, is about as close as it comes to struggle royalty. Eldest son of Walter and Albertina Sisulu, he had a front-row seat in his family's battles with the apartheid regime: his father was jailed for 26 years on Robben Island, while his mother lived under house arrest and constant threat of imprisonment for well over a decade.

It was not surprising that he would quickly follow in his parents' footsteps, becoming the youngest political detainee in South Africa in the early 1960s. He went into exile at the tender age of 17 after his release from solitary confinement.

Once outside the country he joined the ANC's military wing, Umkhonto weSizwe, in 1964, travelling to Odessa in the Soviet Union to undergo military training. It was in the USSR that Sisulu began his tertiary education, studying economics and earning a master's degree at the Plekhanov Economic Institute in Moscow. His studies in Russia gave him the grounding that he would need to become a major force in shaping the ANC's thoughts on economic planning and strategy, but he continued to study elsewhere over the years: he undertook research on transnational corporations and the microelectronics industry in South Africa at the University of Amsterdam and a course in new technology and work methods at the University of Sussex's Institute for Development Studies. In the 1990s he obtained a second master's degree, in public administration, from the Kennedy School of Government at Harvard University.

His time in exile included two major streams, youth and economics; he was constantly being deployed from one to the other. He worked first as a youth leader in the ANC's youth and students' movement in Tanzania. In 1982 he was named deputy head of the ANC youth movement, and head of the movement a few years later.

In the mid-1970s, he moved to ANC headquarters in Lusaka as part of its politico–military council. He narrowly escaped death at one point when a parcel bomb mailed to headquarters exploded, killing his colleague, the ANC's deputy chief representative, John Dube. Sisulu also spent some time as ANC representative in Hungary. On his return to Lusaka he was appointed head of the ANC's department of economic planning in 1986.

In 1991, with the thawing of relations between the apartheid government and the ANC, the economic planning department relocated to South Africa. Sisulu established the National Institute of Economic

Policies and became its first director. Following the 1994 elections he went to Parliament, serving in the National Assembly as chairperson of the reconstruction and development programme portfolio committee as well as the finance committee. In 1997 he was appointed chief whip.

His stint in government ended with his appointment in 1998 as deputy CEO of Denel, the country's defence industry parastatal. When he left Denel in 2003, he took up a post as group general manager at petrochemicals giant Sasol.

Despite his long track record in politics and business, Sisulu is very much a behind-the-scenes player. He does not often step into the limelight, but he fills important roles for the party, such as membership of the ANC's finance committee. In addition, he has, for a decade, served as chair of the ANC's economic transformation committee, which brings together the economic minds of the tripartite alliance, as well as business people, to debate and give direction to economic policy. Sisulu has returned to Parliament as National Assembly speaker.

Sisulu is married to author and human rights activist Elinor Batezat Sisulu.

Date of birth: August 23 1945

Skweyiya, Thembile

Constitutional Court judge Thembile Skweyiya was the first African to acquire senior counsel status. He was schooled in Cape Town before moving to the Eastern Cape's Healdtown Institution for his matric. In 1963 the University of Natal awarded him a BA degree in social science; this was followed by a bachelor of laws degree in 1967. He was actively involved in student politics as a member of the student representative council and joined a committee for clemency for political prisoners.

Skweyiya served as a legal adviser and member of the panel of advisers for the South African Students' Organisation (Saso), which was later banned by the apartheid government. He served his articles from 1968 until 1970 and was admitted as an advocate the same year, joining the Natal Bar. He was also admitted, four years later, as an advocate of the High Court in Lesotho.

He practised as an advocate for 25 years, initially handling commercial and civil cases but from the early 1980s he spent more and more time representing political prisoners throughout the country. He also participated in inquests into the deaths of political prisoners in detention. The focus of his work, however, shifted back to commercial and civil cases when he acquired senior counsel status in 1989.

In 1994, after the first democratic elections, he was scheduled to take up the post of inspector-general for intelligence services but ended up in business instead, as chairperson of empowerment company Worldwide African Investment Holdings, Cape-based radio station KFM and Zenex Oil. He also served as the deputy chairperson of Coca-Cola bottler Fortune Beverages and the South African Tourism Board.

Between 1995 and 2001 Skweyiya spent time on the bench in KwaZulu-Natal and the Eastern Cape as an acting judge for brief terms. In 2001 he finally accepted a permanent position on the Bench. He spent several months as an acting Constitutional Court justice before the position was made permanent in February 2004.

He is the brother of the former minister of social development, Zola Skweyiya.

Date of birth: June 17 1939

Skweyiya, Zola

At the end of his decade-long tenure as minister of social development, Zola Sidney Themba Skweyiya has emerged as the knight-champion of South Africa's aged, the orphaned and the economically marginalised. The multi-headed dragon of poverty, domestic and substance abuse, and societal breakdown is far from being slain. But as a result of tireless efforts to provide government-funded succour, a clampdown on graft in grant dispensation and the passage of progressive legislation like the Children's Act, it is taking a beating. Over 12-million South Africans are currently receiving state welfare grants, the phased equalisation of state pensions has already begun, and government is gradually increasing the child-support-grant age limit to 18 years. The last two are in no small part due to Skweyiya's advocacy in Cabinet and within the ANC. He has also been a vociferous supporter of the basic income grant.

Born into poverty in Simon's Town in the Western Cape, Skweyiya's empathy for the poor is palpable: whether calling on South Africans to adopt more orphans or proclaiming how alcoholism is destroying communities, he has consistently outlined a moral, holistic vision for South Africa.

Considered a free-thinking maverick within the party, Skweyiya has also proved to be the ANC's conscience, especially during its more tumultuous moments. Rising above the Jacob Zuma–Thabo Mbeki factionalism that infected the party prior to its 2007 conference in Polokwane, he urged circumspection and more comradely behaviour amongst members. When Mbeki was recalled as state president by the ANC in September 2008, Skweyiya broke ranks with silent party members on the behaviour of ANC Youth League president Julius Malema, criticising him for 'shocking disrespect' towards Mbeki and calling him an 'embarrassment' to the ANC. A party elder – he joined the ANC as a 14-year-old – Skweyiya has also warned of some of the failings of the ANC as a political party and in government. He has raised concerns about the dangerous increase of ethnicisation in South Africa and the lack of attention government has paid to social cohesion.

After matriculating from Lovedale College in the Eastern Cape, Skweyiya enrolled at the University of Fort Hare, where he met and worked with ANC and South African Communist Party stalwart Govan Mbeki. He fled South Africa in 1963 and graduated with a doctorate in law from the University of Leipzig, in East Germany, in 1972. His work in exile included setting up an ANC branch in Addis Ababa in Ethiopia in 1985 and acting as head of the ANC's legal and constitutional affairs department in Lusaka, Zambia. A constitutional law specialist, Skweyiya also helped set up the Centre for Development Studies and the South African Legal Defence Fund at the University of the Western Cape.

After the first democratic elections in 1994, he served as minister of public service and administration. Skweyiya found the amalgamation of the various administrations inherited from apartheid a tough task, and the Presidential Review Commission, investigating problems in the public service, suggested his ministry be scrapped and the functions brought under the control of the presidency. According to reports, Skweyiya agreed. Social development appears to have fitted Skweyiya much better.

He has left a once-sickly department well on the road to recovery and he is now based at Luthuli House.

Skweyiya is married to controversial businesswoman Thuthukile Mazibuko-Skweyiya. She was cleared by the public protector for accepting an interest-free home-improvement loan from Sandi Majali, whose Imvume management company had diverted R11-million of public money into the ANC's 2004 election war-chest. Her Fikza Investment Holdings also owes money to the late Brett Kebble's estate.

Date of birth: April 14 1942

Surty, Enver

Enver Surty suddenly found himself thrust from a low-key position as deputy minister of education to the justice hot seat in September 2008 when the ANC fired Thabo Mbeki and, as a consequence, a host of other ministers resigned in solidarity with him. Surty took it in his stride and walked straight into what he described as a storm amidst public outcries about the disbanding of the Scorpions and attacks on the judiciary over the prosecution of ANC president Jacob Zuma.

The judiciary was divided over the handling of a complaint by Constitutional Court judges that Cape judge president John Hlophe had tried to influence their decision on Zuma's political fate. Hlophe's counter-complaint and subsequent court action in the Johannesburg High Court did not make things any easier for the incoming minister, a lawyer himself.

Surty, however, walked a fine line and appeased all groups when the need arose. He did his duty like a good cadre of the movement in Parliament when the time came for the memorial service for the Scorpions. In a masterly way he discouraged litigation by judges against one another but in the same breath held that he respected their right to do so. He deferred to Luthuli House by repeating their mantra that claims that the judiciary was under attack were 'exaggerated' but also quickly took issue with those who attacked the judiciary for threatening the integrity of the institution. He tiptoed gently around the legal world in which he had spent close to 20 years and consulted widely on issues such as proposed legislation to transform the structure of the courts and bring the administration of the courts under the control of his department.

When Hlophe removed himself from special leave and arrived at his High Court chambers in February 2009, Surty read him the riot act, reminding him that the Judicial Service Commission had not yet resolved the complaint against him. When Hlophe, in his now familiar militant style, called the minister's bluff, Surty retreated but called for a meeting to resolve the issues, while still eyeing mediation efforts on the resolution of Hlophe's fight with the Constitutional Court judges.

Surty attended school first in Rustenburg and later south of Johannesburg at Lenasia High School. He studied at the University of Durban-Westville and completed a BA degree and honours in philosophy, then studied towards his BProc with Unisa. He also holds a master of laws degree, which was awarded in 1996 by the University of the Western Cape. He practised as an attorney for 17 years and represented the ANC after its unbanning. He held observer status on the ANC's national executive committee, was elected to Parliament in 1994 and rose to the position of chief whip in the National Council of Provinces. He was appointed deputy minister of education in 2004 and held that post until he was elevated to the justice ministry in late 2008. Zuma has demoted Surty back to his former post as deputy minister of basic education.

Date of birth: August 15 1953

Taljaard, Raenette

Raenette Taljaard made waves in 1999 when, at the age of 25, she became the youngest woman to join Parliament. The rise of the Democratic Alliance (DA) MP to political stardom was quick, successful and short-lived. She went from being DA leader Tony Leon's speechwriter in 1999 to shadow minister of finance and member of the portfolio committee on finance in 2002. Three years later she resigned from Parliament.

She is renowned for her determination to get to the bottom of the arms deal scandal. Since 1999, Taljaard has been the ANC's nemesis, pushing relentlessly for an investigation into allegations that the party benefited from the deal in the run-up to the 1999 elections. Since claims emerged that the 2003 report on the arms deal probe was heavily edited before being presented to Parliament, Taljaard has tirelessly called for the cover-up to be investigated, and for ruling party members, including former president Thabo Mbeki, to clarify their role in the deal.

The tough and feisty Taljaard was no pushover in Parliament or among her peers. She stuck to her principles, often arguing with Leon over party policies. Even finance minister Trevor Manuel wasn't immune from her frank and penetrating criticism. In 2004 in the National Assembly, she made him hot under the collar when she asked for clarity on the ANC's relationship with Saddam Hussein. This was at the time the Oilgate scandal exploded, revealing that the ousted dictator's oil may have funded the ANC's 2004 election campaign.

Manuel retaliated angrily, saying Taljaard's 'links with the mafia' should be investigated too. This was a personal jab at her then-relationship with Mario Ambrosini, IFP leader Mangosuthu Buthelezi's controversial special adviser. Manuel later withdrew his remarks and sent her a handwritten note of apology. When she resigned from Parliament, he paid tribute to her for the role she played while on the finance committee, saying: 'I think that, either notwithstanding or because of her youth, she demonstrated both the curiosity and the confidence that she drew from Bertrand Russell, this afternoon. I think that it's very important; notwithstanding the disagreements we've had on issues. They've been on issues and have never been on personalities. I think that her role in the committee and in this House has defined what I would consider responsible opposition. This House will be poorer for your absence, Raenette; thank you very much for the role that you've played here.'

Taljaard's decision to quit Parliament was unexpected, given the efficient job she had done for the DA. She said she resigned for personal reasons; the emotional strain and stress of the job had taken its toll. However, her personal clashes with Tony Leon contributed to her decision. More importantly, she wanted her 'intellectual independence' back. Taljaard is passionate about education. She holds a BA in law and an MA in political science from Rand Afrikaans University and an MSc in public administration and public policy from the London School of Economics and Political Science.

After stepping out of the political spotlight, she turned her focus to advocacy work. In 2006 Taljaard assumed directorship of the Helen

Suzman Foundation, a political think-tank aimed at strengthening democracy in South Africa. She also lectures on economics, public financial management and utility regulation at the University of the Witwatersrand's School of Public and Development Management.

While she has no plans to return to politics, the arms deal probe and the regulation of military security remain a priority for Taljaard. She has lectured extensively on the dangers of the private sector's role in the privatisation of the military and appeared before Parliament's defence committee as an expert witness in this field.

Date of birth: July 4 1972

Tlhagale, Buti

Described as a 'private man', Catholic archbishop Buti Joseph Tlhagale, much like his Anglican counterpart, the Archbishop of Cape Town, is unafraid to stand firm for what he believes in, regardless of whether it is in the religious or the political arena.

Father Chris Townsend of the Southern African Catholic Bishops' Conference describes him as 'an uncompromising person with a strong sense of social justice'. Tlhagale has denounced Zimbabwean president Robert Mugabe for having done his country 'incalculable harm' and has expressed regret at South Africa's role in Zimbabwe as mediator.

He continues to criticise the legalisation of abortion and homosexuality, and in January 2009 warned of legislation that would allow the harvesting of eggs from African women for investigation in other countries, likening the legislation to 'biological colonialism'.

In 2005, on the death of Pope John Paul II, Tlhagale did not hold out much hope that his successor would come from Africa. 'In Rome the cardinals enjoy a huge number of Africans becoming Christians but they don't think we are ready [for high positions] . . . They fear paganism might come through the back door.' In this respect, the Archbishop added, the Catholic Church was 'like a train that will not take a sharp turn'.

Sharp turns or not, Tlhagale remains an important figure in the Catholic Church. In 1999 he was ordained Archbishop of Bloemfontein and in 2003 was appointed Bishop of Johannesburg. In 2007, Pope Benedict XVI raised the diocese of Johannesburg to the status of a metropolitan archdiocese and appointed the Most Rev. Buti Joseph Tlhagale, OMI, as its first Metropolitan Archbishop.

Tlhagale was born in Randfontein. In 1967 he entered the novitiate of the Oblates of Mary Immaculate (OMI) at Quthing, Lesotho, and the Mater Jesu Scholasticate in Roma the following year. In 1976 Tlhagale was ordained to the priesthood by the now deceased Archbishop Fanyana Butelezi. After ordination he worked extensively in the Soweto community, serving at Our Lady of Fatima in Dube, Our Lady of Mercy in Emdeni and Christ the King in Orlando East. Tlhagale has been a visiting lecturer at St Joseph's Scholasticate in Cedara, KwaZulu-Natal, and has taught philosophy at St Peter's Major Seminary in Hammanskraal, writing on theology, inculturation and labour matters.

Date of birth: December 26 1947

Trikamjee, Ashwin

Pundit Ashwin Trikamjee knows a thing or two about juggling roles. This Hindu priest and attorney also sits on the SABC board, is chairperson of the KwaZulu-Natal Gambling Board and is a well-respected sports executive. 'I do my best at all times to serve the people and not myself,' he says, 'and remain positive with our country despite the present controversies.'

During his days as chairperson of the South African Soccer Federation's Professional League (FPL), Trikamjee played an important role in the merging of the FPL with the National Soccer League, helping to bring unity to the soccer fraternity in the country. 'In 1991 Madiba was released and there were the Kempton Park negotiations. There was a level of urgency for sports bodies to get together and form one organisation in order to get world recognition,' he recalls.

Born in the Grey Street area of Durban, Trikamjee says that growing up in a primarily Indian area limited his life to going to school – and sport. As the second child among four other siblings, Trikamjee played cricket and soccer as a teenager with friends in the streets. It was perhaps here that his defiance towards the apartheid government began. Trikamjee clearly recalls his anger when a dog, set loose by the police, bit his friend, after a game of soccer on the tar.

He holds a BJuris from Unisa, his areas of specialisation being tax law, commercial law and litigation. In the 1980s Trikamjee remembers taking on cases he treasures most in his memory. There was the time, for example, when security police raided the Azanian People's Organisation's KwaZulu-Natal office, but Trikamjee made an urgent application and managed to have what had been taken away returned. 'Those were the days when acting against the security police was mad. This was the time when black consciousness was in my blood.'

Trikamjee is deputy chairperson of the Lion Match Company, chairperson of Fasic Investment Corporation, a black economic empowerment company formed to pursue BEE deals, and chairperson of Garlicke and Bousfield, one of South Africa's leading law firms.

He isn't a stranger to controversy. Trikamjee admits he was 'somewhat upset' by the cloud of discontent that arose after his appointment to the SABC board. One of the many objections was that no one on the board was or had been a practising journalist, and he agreed with the complaints made by labour and civil society to then-president Thabo Mbeki.

Trikamjee is chairperson of the South African Hindu Maha Sabha, co-chairperson of the National Religious Leaders' Forum and commissioner of Interfaith Action for Peace in Africa, an interfaith religious leaders' initiative.

Date of birth: November 29 1944

Trollip, Athol

The Democratic Alliance's Athol Trollip was born in Bedford, Eastern Cape, and educated at Woodridge College in Thornhill. He pursued his studies in agricultural management at the University of Natal, Pietermaritzburg, before travelling and working in Australia, New Zealand, Scotland and England.

Trollip follows in a family lineage of politicians. His grandfather, also Athol Trollip, was a United Party MP representing the Port Elizabeth Central constituency, and his father served on the Smaldeel Divisional Council in the Eastern Cape.

Trollip prides himself on creating unity within the DA in the Eastern Cape. Under his watch the province received the internal DA's award for

Province of the Year in 2004. Trollip speaks, reads and writes English, Xhosa and Afrikaans fluently. This enables him to communicate with a broad spectrum of people in the Eastern Cape.

He has worked for 20 years on his family farm in Bedford. As an activist farmer he has held various leadership positions in the community: these include chairmanship of the Farmers' Association and of the Bedford Club. He also served as a committee member of various sporting associations and on the Smaldeel Soil Conservation Committee.

His experience as a farmer explains why his main area of concern and expertise is agriculture. Trollip serves on the Eastern Cape provincial agricultural portfolio committee. However, he is also interested in health and public accounts, with which portfolios the DA has entrusted him for when he enters the National Assembly after the elections. Here he plans to help shape the debate on land redistribution.

Trollip entered politics when he was elected executive councillor of the Amathole District Municipality. He joined the Eastern Province legislature in 1999 and was re-elected in 2004. Trollip is the leader of the DA caucus and the leader of the official opposition in the Eastern Cape.

Within his party Trollip has held various positions, including that of Democratic Party provincial chairperson in 1998; he has been DA provincial leader since 2002. He has served on the DA federal council and federal executive. He is the leader of the DA parliamentary caucus.

Trollip ran for the position of DA national leader when Tony Leon retired in 2007. He and Joe Seremane were, however, defeated by Helen Zille at the polls.

Date of birth: March 12 1964

Tshabalala-Msimang, Manto

Dr Mantombazana 'Manto' Edmie Tshabalala-Msimang was appointed minister in the presidency on September 25 2008, a post she lost after the April 2009 elections. She had been the country's minister for health since June 1999, and during her tenure she gained notoriety for her pronouncements on HIV and Aids. She is a member of the ANC national executive committee and has been an MP since 1994.

Tshabalala-Msimang was born in Durban and matriculated from

Inanda Seminary in 1959. She studied for a BA at the University of Fort Hare and in 1962 went into exile, studying medicine at the First Leningrad Medical Institute in the USSR, where she graduated in 1969. She then worked in Tanzania, where she obtained a diploma in obstetrics and gynaecology from the University of Dar es Salaam. In 1980 she received a master's degree in public health from the University of Antwerp.

Tshabalala-Msimang's appointment as minister in the presidency was seen as a way of tactfully removing her as minister of health, in which position she earned international notoriety for herself and the South African government. Her inaction on measures to counter the impact of the HIV epidemic led the government into repeated humiliations in court. Among her many pronouncements and actions that were seen as damaging to treatment, care and support initiatives in South Africa, and to the country's international reputation, were her questioning of the link between HIV and Aids; her repeated dismissal of 'Western' medicine; her support for unproven and untested anti-HIV concoctions; her suggestion that healthy diets including beetroot, lemon juice and olive oil alone were enough to hold back the ravages of HIV; and her support for questionable figures such as vitamin pedlar Matthias Rath.

While the incredible strains put on public health care by the HIV epidemic may not have been within her control, slow and inefficient responses were. The South African National Aids Council, which is supposed to spearhead the country's response to HIV, was neutered for much of her rule, the roll-out of antiretrovirals appeared to take place slowly and grudgingly, and much of its success was due to foreign donors and support. The accompanying TB epidemic has also not been addressed urgently or effectively; South Africa has some of the highest levels of the disease in the world.

More generally, Tshabalala-Msimang has presided over the steady erosion of South Africa's healthcare indicators and increasing collapse of the healthcare system. South Africa will almost certainly miss the health-related Millennium Development Goals it committed to, as maternal and infant mortality rates increase while life expectancy falls. Outbreaks of diseases in healthcare facilities have signalled the failure of basic infection control and management.

Under her reign the department of health at both national and provincial levels slipped into a state of unskilled disorganisation, with lack of accountability apparently running rampant and more attention being paid to form and plans than to implementation. Research has indicated that up to one in five deaths among newborns could have been prevented. One of her few successes was the passage of legislation to control smoking.

In 2007 Tshabalala-Msimang received a liver transplant, according to her doctors because of autoimmune hepatitis. However, the *Sunday Times* gave voice to persistent rumours about her heavy drinking, by alleging in a front-page article that she needed the new liver because of alcoholism. Other damaging exposés included allegations of theft (in one case from a patient) while she worked in Botswana. Tshabalala-Msimang threatened legal action for the *Sunday Times*'s use of her medical records, but threats to sue for libel have failed to result in a court case.

While the minister was on sick leave, her deputy, Nozizwe Madlala-Routledge, stepped into the breach with outspoken pronouncements on a number of issues, including the HIV/Aids epidemic and high mortality among children at an Eastern Cape hospital. The power struggle between the minister and her deputy resulted in the latter being fired.

From 1994 to June 1999 Tshabalala-Msimang was chair of the parliamentary portfolio committee on health, and from July 1996 till June 1999 she was deputy minister of justice. According to her CV, she is a former board member of the Global Fund to Fight Aids, Tuberculosis and Malaria, and former chair of the Non-Aligned Movement of Health Ministers, the SADC Health Sectoral Committee of Ministers, and the WHO Africa Regional Committee of Health Ministers.

She is married to Mendi Themba Msimang, former South African high commissioner in London and the ANC treasurer-general until 2007.

Date of birth: October 9 1940

Tulelo, Vuyiswa

In the midst of the furore surrounding ANC youth leader Julius Malema's 'kill for Zuma' statements in 2008, an explanation was left begging and when free-to-air channel etv took it upon itself to get answers, the hard task of accounting was given to Vuyiswa Tulelo. As the newly elected secretary-general of the ANC Youth League (ANCYL), it was Tulelo who faced up to tenacious television anchor Debora Patta.

At the end of the interview, after Tulelo had sparred with Patta and in the process told South Africans that Malema was merely using metaphorical language, the news bull terrier simply got up and walked off with a stern face. One blogger, after watching Tulelo suddenly thrust into the spotlight, summed up the interview as follows: 'After watching the interview [Tulelo] had with Debora Patta on *3rd Degree*, I am in awe of her. She is smart, she is strong, she stands her ground, she knows what she's about and she articulates it well.'

Then in July 2008, after eight years of waiting in the wings as deputy secretary, Tulelo got her chance to show her mettle by organising a largely event-free ANCYL conference. The disastrous Mangaung conference three months earlier had resembled more of a brawling match than a congress as delegates threw bottles at one another and exposed their bottoms.

Tulelo, who hails from Galeshewe township in Kimberley, is a future ANC star and potential Cabinet material. She is the daughter of highly devout parents, and her younger sister is also in public service as a staff sergeant in the South African National Defence Force.

At just 13 years Tulelo became an activist after joining a group who were protesting against school fees. Despite her young age, the Galeshewe Young Students' Organisation made an exception and allowed her to join. The following year, she spearheaded efforts to start her school's first-ever student representative council and she eventually served two years as SRC chairperson. At the age of 15, she was provincial secretary of the Congress of South African Students (Cosas).

She joined the regional branch of the ANCYL in her home province of the Northern Cape in 1995 and two years later became the first female deputy chair of any of its provincial structures. Tulelo resigned from this position in 1998 when she packed her bags and made her way to the University of the Witwatersrand, where she studied towards a BA in politics. At Wits, she continued where she left off, becoming SRC president in 1999 and being co-opted on to the national executive committee of the

ANCYL. She then served two terms as deputy secretary-general of the Youth League before being elected to her present position. In 2008 she was elected vice-president of the International Union of Young Communists and she sits on the boards of the National Youth Commission and Umsombomvu Youth Fund.

Date of birth: July 17 1975

Tutu, Desmond

Archbishop Emeritus Desmond Mpilo Tutu is a much-loved and -respected figure, mainly for his vocal stance as an opponent of South Africa's apartheid government but also for his wicked sense of humour and his remarkable inability to tire. In his current position as chairperson of The Elders, the retired Anglican Archbishop and elder statesman remains irrepressible and is showing no signs of slowing down.

In 2007, with Nelson Mandela, Graça Machel and others, Tutu convened The Elders, a group of world leaders available to contribute their wisdom, leadership and integrity to tackle some of the world's toughest problems. Other founding members of the group include former United Nations secretary-general Kofi Annan; Gro Harlem Brundtland, former director-general of the World Health Organisation; former US president Jimmy Carter; former Chinese foreign minister Li Zhao-xing; and Aung San Suu Kyi, whose chair is left symbolically empty because of her confinement as a political prisoner in Burma.

In the late 1980s, as South Africa's townships exploded under the pressure of states of emergency and heightened oppression, Tutu famously threatened to leave the country if black South Africans continued killing one another. An iconic photograph shows Tutu having waded into a mob to rescue a man accused of being an *impimpi*, or government informer. Another, from the same era, shows Tutu, arms outstretched, facing down the government's armoured vehicles. In still another, he is in the front row, with other clerics, marching through the streets of Cape Town in 1989, calling for the release of Nelson Mandela.

When inclusive democracy came to South Africa in 1994, Tutu continued his independent, critical commentary. He objected to pay rises for MPs, saying that parliamentarians had missed a golden opportunity to demonstrate they were serious about stopping the gravy train: 'They stopped the gravy train', he said, 'only long enough to get on it.' He spoke out strongly against the controversial arms deal and lent his considerable prestige to the anti-Aids campaign at a time when government was ignoring the pandemic.

Nor has he slowed down. In 2008, Tutu expressed his deep disappointment with the divisions that had opened up in the ANC after the sacking of its former president Thabo Mbeki; in the same year he labelled Zimbabwean president Robert Mugabe 'Frankenstein' and called for other countries to intervene in that troubled country's political, economic and humanitarian crisis. He has repeatedly criticised Jacob Zuma, saying that he does not look forward to a Zuma presidency and does not want a president he would be ashamed of.

Desmond Tutu was educated at Johannesburg Bantu High School before training as a teacher at Pretoria Bantu Normal College, followed by a BA from Unisa. After three years as a high school teacher, he entered St Peter's Theological College in Rosettenville and was ordained as a priest in 1960. He spent three years at King's College, London, obtaining honours and master's degrees in theology, and returned to South Africa in 1967 to preach and to teach. He served as chaplain at the University of Fort Hare and lectured in theology at the National University of Lesotho. In 1972 he was named assistant director of the Theological Education Fund of the World Council of Churches in the UK, and three years later he was appointed dean of St Mary's Cathedral in Johannesburg.

From there he rose rapidly in the church: Bishop of Lesotho, general secretary of the South African Council of Churches and, in 1986, two years after being awarded the Nobel Peace Prize, Archbishop of Cape Town and Primate of the Church of the Province of Southern Africa (now the Anglican Church of Southern Africa).

In 1995, 'the Arch', as he is known, was chosen by then-president Nelson Mandela to chair the Truth and Reconciliation Commission and offer recommendations of amnesty to those who made a full confession of apartheid-era crimes.

He battled on, despite a cancer diagnosis – successfully treated – and went on to take up visiting professorships at Emory University in the

United States and to accept a great number of international awards: the freedom of several cities around the world, the French Legion of Honour, Germany's Order of Merit, the Indian government's Gandhi Peace Prize, and others. The author of the description of South Africans as 'the rainbow people of God' has never stopped urging his countrymen to rise to that description.

The Archbishop's pleas for justice and reconciliation in South Africa have drawn him into the political arena for most of his life – but he has always insisted that his motivation is religious, not political.

Date of birth: 7 October 1931

Van der Westhuizen, Johann

Judge Johann van der Westhuizen, who was appointed to the Constitutional Court in 2004, wrote the landmark judgment in the 2008 *Nwamitwa* case that allowed a Limpopo princess to accede to the chieftaincy of her people. The case was a significant contribution in the area of customary law as it declared that this branch of the law was not static and could be developed by indigenous groups in South Africa in line with the Constitution. It also scored a major victory for women's emancipation and struck a major blow to the primogeniture system whereby only males can be appointed as chiefs.

A prominent human rights figure during apartheid, Van der Westhuizen was the founding director of the University of Pretoria's Centre for Human Rights in 1986 and was heavily involved in human rights litigation. He participated extensively in the drafting of South Africa's Constitution as a member of the Independent Panel of Recognised Constitutional Experts, which advised the Constitutional Assembly. He formed part of the technical refinement team that drafted and edited the final Constitution. At the multi-party talks in Kempton Park that led to a new, democratic South Africa, he convened a committee reviewing offensive apartheid legislation. In 1998 Van der Westhuizen coordinated the equality legislation drafting project for the justice department and Human Rights Commission. President Nelson Mandela appointed him to the Pretoria High Court in 1999.

Born in Windhoek and now living in Pretoria, Van der Westhuizen was appointed at the same time as judge Thembile Skweyiya. He studied at the University of Pretoria, receiving a BA degree in law with distinction in 1973 and two years later an LLB, also with distinction. In 1980 he completed his doctorate in law. Along the way he picked up the Grotius Medal from the Pretoria Bar for the best final-year student in law. He also received several fellowships in the United States and Germany. He was admitted as an advocate in 1976 and was with the Pretoria Bar from 1989 until 1998.

Van der Westhuizen became a professor in law at Pretoria University after completing his doctorate and was head of the department of legal history, comparative law and legal philosophy until 1994.

Date of birth: May 26 1952

Vavi, Zwelinzima

The spitfire general secretary of Cosatu, Zwelinzima Vavi, is an affable and straight-shooting unionist. He was general secretary of the National Union of Mineworkers (NUM) before taking the helm of Cosatu when Mbhazima Shilowa quit for politics.

Throughout Thabo Mbeki's time in office, Vavi ran a campaign against the growth, employment and redistribution strategy (Gear). The federation believed Gear to be a local structural adjustment policy aimed at deficit reduction and little else. For being an opposition leader within the tripartite alliance, Vavi incurred the wrath of Mbeki, who was in near constant battle with his union and communist allies during his tenure as president.

When Mbeki fired Jacob Zuma as deputy president, Vavi hoisted his colours and hitched his wagon to the fortunes of the man who is now president. He brought the support of the federation to Zuma's fight-back campaign and was key to Zuma's victory at the ANC's conference at Polokwane in 2007.

Vavi has declined nomination on to the ANC lists, indicating that he will spend another term at Cosatu. While the federation is looking forward to far more worker-centred policies, it appears that an early fight with the new government is likely. In a nutshell, Cosatu wants a higher budget deficit, firmer labour regulation to deal with subcontracted and brokered labour, and greater social spending. The federation also wants to be central to all policy formulation. Cosatu has already drawn up a document showing how the promise of Polokwane has been lost. This suggests that while Vavi may damp his fire a little, he will continue to play the role of internal opposition to government for some years.

Vavi came by his skill as a tough negotiator naturally, having spent his working life on the mines. Born in Hanover in the Northern Cape to farmworker parents, he says that neither he nor his 11 siblings know their birthdates, but he has an official date of birth and is sure of the year, 1962. He became politically involved when the ferment spreading through the country after the 1976 Soweto uprising finally reached Sala township near Queenstown, where his parents settled after their eviction from the farm where he was born.

In 1980, while in high school, he joined the Congress of South African Students (Cosas). After matric, he was hired as a clerk at the Anglo American Vaal Reefs gold mine; he became a shop steward, then moved up the NUM ladder. Vavi is a board member of the local organising committee for the 2010 Fifa World Cup, and a member of the board's audit committee.

Date of birth: December 20 1962

Yacoob, Zak

Constitutional Court judge Zakeria Mohammed Yacoob is famous in the legal fraternity for his sharp memory. Blinded at 16 months because of meningitis, Yacoob has perfected his listening and mnemonic skills to such an extent that he can remember invoice numbers during the course of a trial.

He has lived most of his life in Durban but spent three years in Johannesburg during the 1980s Delmas treason trial, alongside prominent lawyer George Bizos, appearing for members of the United Democratic Front. In the early 1990s he also defended high-ranking ANC officials who were accused of a plot to overthrow the South African government in Operation Vula, involving Mac Maharaj and the Shaik brothers. He took up his seat on the Constitutional Court in 1998.

Yacoob attended Durban's Arthur Blaxall School for the Blind from

1956 to 1966, then studied for and obtained his BA degree majoring in English and private law at the University of Durban-Westville (UDW), completing a bachelor of laws degree at the same institution two years later. While at the university Yacoob helped set up, through negotiations, UDW's first elected student representative council.

He was admitted as an advocate not long afterwards and from 1981 went into practice as a junior counsel, at the same time engaging in human rights and struggle activities. He served on the executive committee of the Natal Indian Congress and organised and participated in various protests against the apartheid government of the day. He also served on the Durban Housing Action Committee, the executive of the Durban Detainees' Support Committee, and chaired the Durban Committee of Ten, which fought for better education. He was a member of the Democratic Lawyers' Association from 1979 to 1984 and operated as a member of the ANC underground in the early to mid-1990s.

After the unbanning of political organisations in 1990 he participated in the multi-party talks to devise an interim, democratic constitution, serving on its fundamental rights technical committee. He was also a member of the Independent Panel of Recognised Constitutional Experts advising the Constitutional Assembly, which hammered out the final version of the Constitution.

Yacoob has advised local government bodies, the National Land Committee and the department of finance. He is currently the chairperson of the South African National Council for the Blind and is a member of its national management committee.

Date of birth: March 3 1948

Zille, Helen

The ANC lost a key province in the 2009 provincial elections because of the slow but determined rise in politics of the first female leader of the Democratic Alliance (DA).

A former *Rand Daily Mail* political journalist who uncovered the fact that political activist Steve Biko was tortured to death in detention, Helen Zille spent the 1980s as part of NGOs and activist organisations, including the Open Society Foundation, the Independent Media Diversity

Trust and the Black Sash. She also campaigned against vigilantism and repression in the Cape townships and was part of the peace movement that worked to bring warring factions in Crossroads together.

She obtained a BA degree from the University of the Witwatersrand and joined the former Democratic Party in the mid-1990s. She was asked to reformulate the party's education policy and stand as a candidate on its election list for the Western Cape legislature. She also acted as technical adviser to the party at the Codesa negotiations in the early 1990s when a democratic South Africa was hammered out.

The 1990s were spent first working for a consultancy where she specialised in public policy, and then serving as director of communications for the University of Cape Town. She was elected to the Western Cape provincial parliament in 1999.

Her success as Cape Town mayor was crucial in the party's turn-around from a defensive, aggressive force to a constructive critic that is now taken more seriously by the ruling party. She managed to escape the ghost of Tony Leon's combative manner quickly when she took over from him in 2006 and started to deal with the ruling party in a tough but respectful manner, which brought a sea-change in how the official opposition is seen by the ruling party.

Previously provincial education minister in the Western Cape and then mayor of the Cape Town Metro, Zille is known for her can-do attitude, rather than for spending her time taking on opponents in Parliament. In fact, she left Parliament when she became DA leader to take up the mayorship. Parliament was left to Sandra Botha, another sign of how Zille set herself apart from her predecessor, who held the reins of the party tightly from the front opposition benches.

Zille has been granted audiences with then-president Thabo Mbeki and the current ANC leadership to discuss thorny issues like the disbandment of the Scorpions, an unprecedented feat for the DA, which had previously been only at the receiving end of ANC insults.

Her stint as Cape Town mayor was not an easy one. She had to manage a fragile coalition of smaller parties which, when the going got tough, were lured to the ANC side with sweeteners and handouts. Despite this, she managed to hold the coalition together and the metro is known as the best-run municipality in the country. Under her leadership Zille managed to reduce crime by 90% in the Cape Town city centre. As Western Cape premier, she has promised to build on these successes. Again she will leave Parliament to the parliamentary caucus and get on with what she knows best – governing.

Date of birth: March 9 1951

Zondi, Musa

Quietly spoken and considered, the Inkatha Freedom Party's secretary-general, the Rev. Keith Muntuwenkosi 'Musa' Zondi, is the antithesis of the war-mongering stereotype associated with the party – an image that grew to prominence during the 1980s and 1990s when violence between the IFP and United Democratic Front/ANC was ongoing in KwaZulu-Natal and the then-Transvaal's migrant labour hostels. Political analysts concur that he was one of the few IFP leaders not to be associated with the bloodshed of that time and was therefore someone foreign diplomats were comfortable meeting.

His has been a consistent rise within party structures and Zondi remains a confidant of IFP president Mangosuthu Buthelezi. Together with national chairperson Zanele Magwaza-Msibi, he remains one of the favourites to succeed Buthelezi once Shenge retires from active politics.

An intellectual in Buthelezi's inner circle, Zondi has consistently used newspaper column space to defend both the party and its president against criticism, especially when this relates to the IFP's violent history. Zondi also served as managing editor of the isiZulu-language newspaper *Ilanga* from 1993 to 1998. Established by ANC founding president John Dube, the paper has, in modern times, been criticised as an IFP mouthpiece.

Zondi served in national government between 2001 and 2004 as the deputy minister of public works. He has been a member of the National Assembly since 1994.

Born in the Nkandla district of KZN, he matriculated from Dlangezwa High School in 1979. Zondi has a BA degree in development administration, African politics and theology from Unisa. He is reading for an MPhil in business ethics (corporate governance) at the University of Stellenbosch.

Zondi joined the IFP in 1978 when he was elected chairperson of the Dlangezwa High School branch of the IFP Youth Brigade. He served as the national chairperson of the Youth Brigade from 1994 to 1997 and has filled the position of IFP secretary-general since 2004.

Date of birth: February 19 1960

Zuma, Jacob

The man with the funny head, benign smile and the occasional burst of laughter assumes the presidency after a brilliant election campaign by the ruling party. The ANC president is a man who evokes strong emotions among South Africans. Millions of his supporters view him as a humble rural person from Nkandla in KwaZulu-Natal (KZN) who was nearly denied power by an educated elite led by former president Thabo Mbeki. But many other South Africans see him as a leader who assumes power with the dark cloud of fraud and corruption still hanging over him, as his guilt or innocence has never been tested by a court.

Only a few years ago it seemed very unlikely that Zuma would make it to Mahlamba Ndlovu (State House) as he spent most of his time in court. The fraud and corruption charges stemmed from what has been termed a generally corrupt relationship with convicted fraudster Schabir Shaik. His rape trial appeared to have dealt him a fatal blow, as not only the nature of the alleged crime but his embarrassing views about Aids and gender during the trial (a woman wearing a wrap called a kanga was presumed therefore to be asking for sex, and he was not worried about contracting HIV from the HIV-positive complainant because he took a shower afterwards) portrayed him as a person unfit to lead the ANC, let alone the country. But he was acquitted in that case, and two weeks before the 2009 elections the National Prosecuting Authority (NPA) declined to prosecute him on charges of corruption, fraud, racketeering, tax evasion and money laundering.

But most significantly, the ANC has won the elections convincingly, despite concerns that Zuma could be an electoral liability. Even the Congress of the People, the party formed by ANC leaders unhappy with his leadership, has been unable to cripple the ANC.

Zuma's resilience is testimony not only to his popularity but also to the loyalty and hard work of those who stood up for what was once an unpopular cause to defend him.

Thabo Mbeki was the architect of his own downfall, as the elevation of Zuma can mostly be attributed to failed Mbeki plans to deal with the man. Although historically Mbeki and Zuma had been allies, once the prospect of Zuma succeeding him stared him in the face, Mbeki acted. He not only gave Zuma few powers as deputy president, but in 2005, when the opportunity presented itself to get rid of him, he fired him as deputy president of the country. Zuma then also stepped down as deputy president of the ANC. But at the end of June 2005, a historic national general council in Pretoria, convened to discuss policy matters, became the catalyst of events that have resulted in Zuma becoming South African president.

At the council, province after province of the ANC went for the jugular, attacking Mbeki for firing Zuma and ultimately reversing the decision to allow Zuma to step down from the party. It was a harrowing four days for Mbeki and his associates as various proposals for organisational redesign that they tabled for the reform of the party were rejected. At the end of the conference it was clear that the tables had been turned and the Zuma supporters were beginning to take control. Mbeki used the ANC national executive committee, which was full of his supporters, to get Zuma to agree that there was no evidence of a plot against him.

But Zuma supporters were convinced that there was indeed a plot by Mbeki to make use of the NPA to defeat him by sending him to jail or just destroying his credibility. The NPA was blamed for the remarks of its head Bulelani Ngcuka, who notoriously declared there was a prima facie case against Zuma but it was not winnable in court. His path to power was plotted in the main by the ANC Youth League and tripartite alliance partners Cosatu and the South African Communist Party, who believed he was the victim of a political conspiracy.

A self-taught politician without formal education, Zuma is credited with restoring peace to KZN, with freeing King Goodwill Zwelithini from the clutches of the Inkatha Freedom Party (IFP), and bringing relative peace to troubled Burundi and the Democratic Republic of Congo.

Zuma joined Umkhonto weSizwe (MK) in exile in 1975, three years after his release from Robben Island, where he had spent 10 years in jail. In exile he is said to have brought a sense of urgency to the need to send cadres back to infiltrate the country. Then–ANC president Oliver Tambo identified him as a future leader and made him coordinator of the political council. Under Zuma's command, hundreds of young MK cadres crossed the Swaziland and Mozambique borders into South Africa. Cadres also credit him with persuading the Mozambican and Swaziland governments to allow the ANC to operate there despite considerable pressure and threats from the South African apartheid government. He then returned to the ANC head office in Lusaka, where he became chief of the intelligence department. The Motsuenyane Commission later criticised Zuma for failing to prevent human rights abuses by the ANC's security apparatus in the organisation's detention camp in Angola in the early 1980s.

Zuma was one of the first leaders to return from exile and prepare the ground for negotiations with the apartheid government. In 1991, at the first ANC national conference held in South Africa after its unbanning, he was elected deputy secretary-general. In 1994 he became ANC national chairperson. After the first national democratic elections in South Africa in 1994, he was appointed MEC for economic affairs and tourism in the KZN government. He returned to his work of bringing peace to the violence-ravaged province. As an MEC, he achieved very little, as he spent too much time preoccupied with party matters and repairing relations between the IFP and the ANC.

He was elected deputy president of the ANC at the national conference held at Mafikeng in December 1997. Mbeki appointed him deputy president of the country in 1999 after his first choice, IFP president Mangosuthu Buthelezi, turned down the post.

Date of birth: April 12 1942

Parties

African National Congress

Many South Africans remain loyal to the oldest liberation movement on the continent despite its infighting and perceptions that it has lost its moral compass. The party won an overwhelming 65.9% of the votes in the 2009 elections, comfortably keeping control of eight provinces but losing the Western Cape to the Democratic Alliance. This is a drop from the almost 70% it received in 2004, but still remains solid support, given that it had experienced a split resulting in the formation of the Congress of the People (Cope).

The new leadership, headed by Jacob Zuma, consists of many people who were sidelined during the Thabo Mbeki era or who fought with Mbeki and became his bitter foes. These include Zuma, former security chiefs who fell out with Mbeki, such as National Intelligence Agency chief Billy Masetlha and head of the defence force Siphiwe Nyanda, former Gauteng premier Mathole Motshekga, former Mpumalanga premier Mathews Phosa and businessman Cyril Ramaphosa (the last two were falsely accused of trying to topple Mbeki). Essentially what we have had since December 2007 is Zuma's ANC.

Those who wanted to continue with the legacy of Mbeki's ANC and were petrified of Zuma and his followers have moved out of the party to form Cope. These are people who felt that Zuma and his troublesome young man Julius Malema were contaminating the good name and moral integrity of the ANC. Malema was elected ANC Youth League president after the Polokwane conference and immediately declared his passion for a Zuma presidency by saying he would kill for Zuma, a pledge he made at a youth rally in Bloemfontein in 2008. Since then Malema has become the bogeyman of the party, with a number of people who left the ANC expressing outrage that the party could allow him to attack party seniors, leaders of other opposition parties and even women in general – he said that the woman who accused Zuma of rape had appeared to enjoy the sexual encounter. Generally, the party has refused to condemn Malema, saying he needs nurturing and grooming instead of condemnation. There has, however, been one exception: Malema was forced to apologise after he ridiculed education minister Naledi Pandor.

At its conference in 2007 the party had a membership of 600 000, which is still minuscule compared to the over 10-million voters it has attracted at the national polls since 1994. Its youth wing remains dynamic and rabble-rousing and keeps itself alive on campuses around the country. The Women's League continues to be lethargic, waiting to be led and showing no life at all, although the ANC has met the 50/50 requirement for gender parity in its lists.

Cope, which was expected to be a realistic challenge to the ANC for power, failed to live up to expectations. Its main weakness was an inability to mount a visible campaign, as it relied mainly on being accessible to the media while doing little work on the ground.

Under Zuma, the ANC has become closer to its partners in the tripartite alliance, Cosatu and the SACP. Until Polokwane, the alliance relationship was frosty. The partners accused Mbeki of marginalising them and implementing anti-worker policies. The soured relationship became personal between Mbeki, Cosatu general secretary Zwelinzima Vavi and SACP general secretary Blade Nzimande. Eventually the two workers' organisations joined up with Zuma to oust Mbeki from his presidency, first of the ANC and later of the country. But the *toenadering* has also caused discomfort within the ANC, as many question whether Nzimande and his comrades are not seeking to dictate ANC policy.

In early 2009, the new ANC began to make its power felt, with five new premiers being introduced in the provinces and the former Mbeki premiers being sent to the National Assembly. Under Zuma, government is set to work on implementing the tenets of a developmental state – described as government playing an active role in the economy, although the detail is still missing. According to the party, a powerful developmental state should have strong planning capacity and the ability to intervene in strategic areas. This is not a state that micro-manages

1 of the People

all aspects of government, but rather acts as an effective and continuous system of coordinating, monitoring and evaluating the implementation of government programmes and projects. State-owned enterprises have specific developmental roles to play and are fundamental to the ability of government to intervene decisively in shaping the economic and social future of the country.

Zuma has also promised that he will closely monitor the performance of government departments and will not hesitate to act against both civil servants and ANC politicians who fail in their responsibilities. He has promised to act strongly against under-spending by departments, saying there should be no justification for budgetary roll-overs when citizens remain without services.

The challenges in the new term for the ANC government include an education system that still produces young people who have no skills to match those required in the economy. Besides rampant crime, which statistics indicate has been going down but is still too pervasive, growing unemployment ensures that the poor remain trapped in a cycle of poverty. Given the deteriorating global economic situation and the closure of mines, factories and a number of small companies, the economic picture is likely to get worse before it gets better. In this environment expectations of the new government will be immense. Critics expect Zuma and his team to fail; it is up to them to prove the cynics wrong.

Congress of the People

At the time that the Congress of the People (Cope) was formed in 2008, it was hailed as the first real threat to the ANC, the most substantial breakaway since the movement was transformed into a political party. Cope opened up the possibility of challenging the ANC's electoral dominance for the first time, after several other breakaway parties had failed to shake the oldest liberation movement in Africa. In what was the biggest split since Robert Sobukwe formed the Pan Africanist Congress in 1959, the new party attracted senior ANC leaders such as former South African deputy president Phumzile Mlambo-Ngcuka, department of communications director-general Lyndall Shope-Mafole and business-man Saki Macozoma.

Born after former ANC chairperson Mosiuoa 'Terror' Lekota served 'divorce papers' on the ruling party, Cope was a product of the breakdown of relations between leaders in the ANC. The 2007 Polokwane conference, where former president Thabo Mbeki lost his quest for a third term as ANC president to his rival Jacob Zuma, created divisions that proved difficult to heal. Mbeki loyalists were forced out of key positions of power. The final straw came several months after the conference, when Mbeki was recalled by the ANC as South African president.

A good deal of excitement was created by the announcement that a national convention would be called where South Africans from all walks of life would decide whether, following the ANC's failures in its 15 years of governing the country, there was a need to form a new party. Under the slogan 'In defence of democracy', more than 6 000 delegates attended the convention, including leaders of several opposition parties that supported the idea of strengthening the opposition against the ANC. At the end of the convention, a decision was taken that a new political party would be formed.

Speculation was rife that Mbeki was behind the formation of Cope. Some senior ANC leaders such as Fikile Mbalula claimed that the former state president was instrumental in giving political direction to Cope leaders – an allegation Mbeki denied. However, all Cope founders were Mbeki loyalists. With Lekota at the forefront, and former Gauteng premier Mbhazima Shilowa and former deputy defence minister Mluleki George as founding members, more ANC national and provincial leaders resigned from the ruling party to join Cope. The breakaway faction was initially dubbed 'Shikota' – a merger of Shilowa and Lekota – because it took over a month to acquire a name for the new organisation.

At some of its first rallies, supporters arrived wearing T-shirts bearing Lekota's face with the name South African National Congress (SANC). The ANC challenged this in court and prevented the dissidents from using any name similar to the ruling party's. The next appellation was the South African Democratic Congress, or Sadec, but the name Sadeco already existed and a political party with that name was registered with the Independent Electoral Commission (IEC). The IEC – which has the last word on political parties' names – does not allow names and logos that are confusingly similar.

Then came the name Congress of the People (immediately shortened to Cope), which the ANC also contested right up to the Pretoria High Court. The ruling party argued that the ANC had initiated the 1955 Congress of the People, which adopted the Freedom Charter. Cope contested the court application on the basis that the 1955 gathering was inclusive of South Africans from all walks of life and from a number of political formations, not only the ANC. Two days before the inaugural congress of the new party, the ANC's application was dismissed with costs and Cope finally became a party with a name.

At most of its first rallies, supporters clashed with their ANC counterparts. ANC members were publicly intolerant of a breakaway faction, sending out signals that the ruling party was facing uncertainty about the effect the new party could have on its support at the polling stations. When Bantu Holomisa left the ANC to form the United Democratic Movement, the ANC had not shown any sign of concern, at least publicly. Public support for Cope increased, however, and the party became one of the few organisations to claim membership of more than 428 000 within a month and before it was formally launched.

In the 2009 national elections, the party received almost 8% of the vote, a significant shortfall from its own projection of 51%, later lowered to 30%. This means the party is the third largest behind the ANC and the Democratic Alliance, which received 16% of the vote, double the support that went to Cope. The new party is the new official opposition in the Eastern Cape, Limpopo, North West and Northern Cape legislatures and countrywide it received around 1.2-million votes cast.

Party leaders say it was only 120 days old when it participated in the elections and could still grow. However, the party will have to shift from its middle-class focus to a mass-based party if it seriously intends challenging the ruling party's grip on power.

Democratic Alliance

The Democratic Alliance (DA) performed well during the 2009 elections, showing that it is a force to be reckoned with and still has potential for more growth. Not only did it win an outright majority in the

Western Cape but it increased its support base from 12.5% in the 2004 election to almost 16.66% of the electorate. The party defied speculation that it would be overtaken by the new kid on the block, the Congress of the People, as the official opposition. The party is preparing for the local government elections in 2011 emboldened by the hope that it is starting to win acceptance not just among minority groups, but also among black South Africans.

The DA has always been a necessary evil for the ANC. Although a thorn in the flesh of the almighty ANC, the DA was needed by the ruling party to show that, unlike other liberation movements, it can successfully implement multi-party democracy. But until now, true multi-party democracy has eluded South Africa because of the poor performance of the DA at the polls. Although the party's presence in Parliament jumped from 10 MPs when it first contested democratic elections in 1994 as the Democratic Party (DP), to 50 MPs after the 2004 elections, it was still a far cry from being a considerable force in Parliament, with the power to change or scrap legislation, because of the ANC's overwhelming dominance.

The party's policies are based on creating an 'open opportunity society', where the state's role is enabling rather than interventionist and where the public service is depoliticised in order to ensure unbiased service delivery.

Along its way to becoming the official opposition, the former DP has made some political decisions that it would prefer to forget. In 2000 the DP joined forces with the National Party (NP) to form the Democratic Alliance, which contested the municipal elections with some success, winning a few key municipalities in the Cape, including the jewel in the crown, the city of Cape Town.

The relationship between the two parties soured behind the scenes before it completely broke down in 2001 when party leader Tony Leon suspended controversial Cape Town mayor Peter Marais from the party; Marais had been implicated in a number of contentious decisions and actions, including a sexual harassment lawsuit. NP leader Marthinus van Schalkwyk's response to Marais's suspension was to reconstitute the New National Party, which later was wholly incorporated into the ANC.

The DA has also had to work hard in recent years to live down the damage caused in the 1999 elections by its notorious 'Fight back' campaign, which was perceived as negative, aggressive and counterproductive by analysts and voters. Though the party's support increased then, it did not meet the expectations of voters, nor did it become a threat to the ANC. It returned 45 members to Parliament. In 2004 it opted for a more conciliatory tone with the slogan 'South Africa deserves better' and won 12% of the national vote.

Since 2004 the party has made a serious start in developing its own policies on matters like education, economies and security, to show it is more than an irritating Chihuahua – Leon's nickname in ANC circles. It wanted to shake off the image that the party merely criticises without contributing new ideas, and started referring to itself as an alternative government rather than an opposition.

Leon's departure from the throne at the party's elective conference in May 2007 made way for the former MEC for education in the Western Cape, Helen Zille, at the time mayor of Cape Town, to take over the reins. Zille came in riding on the wave of her success in holding together the political coalition that ruled Cape Town after the 2006 local government elections. As mayor, she had her hands full keeping together a fragile coalition often threatened by infighting and attempts by the ANC to unseat her by a variety of methods, including the wooing of smaller parties. Despite initial teething problems, the coalition emerged as the most successful example of how a unified approach by opposition parties could unseat the ANC. Zille has since taken office as Western Cape premier after the party's spectacular win there in April 2009.

The biggest chink in the DA's armour has always been the fact that it is seen as a white, middle-class party that does not capture the hearts of people at grassroots level. Mass-based support in South Africa is crucial to electoral victory and the DA has not been able to appeal to enough black voters to take on the ANC at a national level.

Although Zille has been credited with the party's change in tack and its relative success in appealing to the broader society, the changes started under Leon's rule. Former MP Ryan Coetzee was appointed CEO of the party and given the responsibility to revamp the DA into the well-resourced and slick election machine that it is today. The turnaround in its administration, coupled with Zille's election as party boss, has paid dividends. Gone are the days when the DA was dismissed as the annoying fly in the ointment of the ANC's plans. Zille was given an audience with former president Thabo Mbeki, at which he fixed her collar during a lighter moment, to the chagrin of some women who saw this act of endearment as patronising. Zille also met with ANC secretary-general Gwede Mantashe, who holds great respect for her, despite being on the other side of the political spectrum.

Independent Democrats

When Patricia de Lille came away from the 2004 elections with more than a quarter of a million votes, she had everything going for her and for the Independent Democrats (ID), the party she started by crossing the floor in 2003. She was the first female leader of a political party and was held in high esteem for her relentless work in exposing corruption in the multi-billion-rand arms deal. She also managed to build a name for herself; consequently the new party did not carry much baggage from her previous political home, the Pan Africanist Congress (PAC), that could haunt her.

What went wrong in five years for the ID to attract only 160 000 votes in 2009 – a small fraction of the one million that De Lille had set as its target?

It would have been impossible to maintain the 2004 momentum without the consolidation of support, an effort that needed money and clear strategies. The emergence of the Congress of the People as a black-based party that held great appeal for coloured people did De Lille's party no favours.

According to Susan Booysen, analyst from the University of the Witwatersrand, De Lille neglected her core constituency in favour of the big prize – to cut across racial barriers and play for a big national following. This created the space into which opposition parties like the Democratic Alliance (DA) could move, with great success. 'As politically incorrect as this might sound, she should have nurtured her core voters and then moved on.' Instead she decided to play with the big boys and took on a national campaign that was very expensive but failed to yield significant results. Although she crisscrossed the country during her election campaign to show she was not a Cape-biased politician, the reward for these efforts was minimal. But De Lille chose a tough crowd to please. Western Cape voters are more likely to switch allegiances and 'like to be begged' by political parties to win their votes. Voters in other provinces are more set in their voting patterns. She therefore lost on two fronts – alienating her core supporters while struggling to win over new ones in other parts of the country.

De Lille also failed to brand the ID as an organisation separate from her: voters still refer to it as 'Patricia's Party'. The ID has been at the forefront of environmental issues, but the explosive arms deal revelations have petered out for the most part. The ID's leadership has also undergone major changes in the past five years: De Lille's former confidant Avril Harding was booted out as secretary-general and chief whip of the party, while others like Simon Grindrod and Vincent Gore crossed the floor to the DA.

Like the United Democratic Movement, the new party held great promise, but when the hype was over and the real work started, it was only one person's dream.

Patricia de Lille left the PAC to give birth to the ID, the party that prides itself as clean, critical, outspoken and independent – much like the characteristics ascribed to its leader. Although the ID has been very vocal about the importance of the rule of the law and of the law taking its course, its views have not prevailed in controversies such as the parliamentary travel scam, the Oilgate scandal, and the charges against ANC president Jacob Zuma.

The 2004 elections appeared to confirm its appeal: at its debut, the ID scored better than many of the established parties, emerging as the fifth-largest party in Parliament. Very rapidly, the party underwent phenomenal growth. It has more than 130 councillors in all provinces throughout the country – De Lille noted before the 2009 elections that the party was governing 26 municipalities – and has consistently won by-elections.

Although De Lille has said she did not build the ID alone, she is central to the party. Provincial and national structures have been established in a whirlwind of activity. What carries the party is her face and her reputation as a feisty politician who does not mince her words.

After obtaining only 0.92% of the national vote in the 2009 elections, De Lille has now announced that she is ready for coalitions with other parties.

Inkatha Freedom Party

A party sometimes mistaken for a cultural movement entrenched in Zulu nationalism and traditional values, the Inkatha Freedom Party (IFP) is having to undergo a period of deep introspection after taking a battering in the 2009 provincial and national elections.

After losing key municipalities after 2004, especially in the former IFP stronghold of KwaZulu-Natal (KZN), the party attempted to recruit younger and more sophisticated urban voters nationally, but it was all in vain. Obituaries of the party are already being prepared and a drastic overhaul is necessary if the party is to remain relevant.

Even Mangosuthu Buthelezi, who has been party leader for the past 34 years, from the days when it was still called the Inkatha National Cultural Liberation Movement, has begun moving away from the image of a Zulu warrior, and more towards that of a besuited statesman in his late 70s. He has opted out of the custom of carrying traditional weapons at rallies and has told party members to follow suit. He points out that when people do carry the weapons, the media usually focus on them.

The IFP has been erratically losing power over the past decade. In 2004, it won 1.9% less of the vote than in the previous general elections, and obtained 28 parliamentary seats compared with the previous 37. And now, with ANC president Jacob Zuma becoming increasingly popular in rural KZN, a province the IFP previously dominated, and with the ANC gaining support in Ulundi and Nongoma, which it previously considered no-go areas, the party has lost even more ground.

In the greatest of ironies, the IFP's Koos van der Merwe said after the April 2009 elections that his party lost as a result of the ANC playing the Zulu nationalism card, an allegation the IFP has tried to shrug off for its entire existence. In 2009 the IFP won 4.55% of the national vote, a decline from its 7% in the 2004 elections.

As is usual at election time, flare-ups between ANC and IFP supporters erupted in rural KZN, with arguments around rallies planned for the same day, provocations in the hope of violent reaction, and even motor accidents, which the IFP blamed on the ANC. On election day, an Independent Electoral Commission presiding officer working in Ulundi was arrested for allegedly being in possession of ballot boxes with ballots pre-marked in favour of the IFP.

In 2007, the IFP joined the Democratic Alliance and United Democratic Movement in eliminating floor-crossing, which it termed a betrayal of voters' wishes. This happened after an embarrassing moment for the IFP, when its own national chairman, Ziba Jiyane, highly popular with members of the IFP Youth Brigade, left the party during the floor-crossing window to start a party of his own, the National Democratic Convention (Nadeco). To add insult to injury, Buthelezi's own son Tutu joined Nadeco and then moved from that party into the welcoming arms of the ANC, just weeks before the national elections.

While Buthelezi has mentioned that he may be handing over leadership after the elections, it's not something to bank on. Buthelezi has 'stepped down' before but held on to the position after saying he had been persuaded otherwise by his party. Potential successors in the running for the top spot are secretary-general Musa Zondi, national chairperson Zanele Magwaza-Msibi and national organiser Albert Mncwango. But Buthelezi's noncommittal attitude to the need for grooming a successor is upsetting the Youth Brigade and reformists within the party who have been lobbying for the position. They feel that mismanagement of the process of choosing a successor could create chaos in the party when the time comes for Buthelezi to hand over. This, along with the party's desire to make rural Ulundi the administrative capital of KZN, and Buthelezi's reminders of the virtue of chastity, may not prove very helpful in the IFP's drive for young urban voters.

Historically, the IFP was formed by Buthelezi in 1975 as part of his vision of a multi-party democratic opposition to the National Party. With his views on fundamental struggle issues diverging from those of the ANC, the two parties were a political contradiction of allies and yet rivals at the same time. The IFP disagreed strongly with the ANC's resort to violence and calls for disinvestment as a means to fight the apartheid government, which the IFP felt were measures not representative of the desires of the entire black population of South Africa. The divide between the parties grows wider at every election and then snaps back after the results come out. But it appears as though, this time, the elastic may be worn out and no longer able to return to its original shape.

South African Communist Party

The South African Communist Party (SACP) has enjoyed a year and a half of very warm relations with the ANC. This is a result of the departure of Thabo Mbeki and the ascendance of Jacob Zuma, who has repaid the communists' loyalty to him by drawing them in on ANC decision-making. The party hopes that some of its members of Parliament, such as its general secretary Blade Nzimande and his deputy Jeremy Cronin, will be key decision-makers in a Zuma government, helping it realise its path to power objectives.

The party is also experiencing something of a break after the bitter divisions caused by the battle over Zuma and the consequent resignations and expulsions from the party of individuals such as treasurer Phillip Dexter, Gauteng provincial secretary Vish Satgar, central committee member Willie Madisha and spokesperson Mazibuko Jara from the Young Communist League (YCL). Those critical of general secretary Blade Nzimande have called him a dictator and Stalinist for his intolerance of dissent. But the dust appears to be settling, as the party presented a united face for the 2009 elections.

As a member of the tripartite alliance, along with trade union federation Cosatu and the ANC, the SACP has had the opportunity to influence government decisions, such as those leading to the introduction of the National Credit Act and the Mzansi bank account, which caters for low-income earners.

In 2006 an SACP central committee member told the *Mail & Guardian* that 'there is massive division in the SACP over the Jacob Zuma issue ... particularly over how it has been managed'. The YCL was particularly supportive of Zuma through all his travails, from his axing as South Africa's deputy president, to his rape trial and corruption charges.

Nzimande traded his academic post at the University of Natal for Parliament in 1994 before assuming full-time leadership of the party in 1997. His support for Msholozi has come at a cost: efforts to remove him failed and several senior members left the SACP. Many people who sought political alternatives outside the SACP did so because of a dislike for Nzimande.

Perhaps in all the events of the party thus far, the most significant was the 2002 relaunch of the YCL, 53 years after its banning under the Suppression of Communism Act. When the SACP was reconstituted underground, the YCL was not.

The SACP did not contest the 2009 elections as a separate entity, but it is contemplating whether to test its electoral strength in 2011, using the local government poll. In 2007, 54% of SACP members were simultaneously members of the ANC, which poses the question of how exactly the SAPC intends to challenge the ANC at this level.

In 2009, the SACP celebrates its 88th anniversary of 'unbroken struggle for national liberation, the reconstruction and development of our country, and for an end to all forms of oppression and exploitation'. The SACP has put its weight behind the ANC and, in campaigning for the 2009 elections, pushed the ANC's clearly non-socialist manifesto.

The party has worked to uphold the legacy of the late Chris Hani, arguably the most popular SACP leader, who was assassinated in 1993.

The SACP was established as the Communist Party of South Africa in July 1921. It was the first non-racial political party in South Africa and led the call for a black majority government, believing that this was the first step towards socialism in the country.

United Democratic Movement

When the United Democratic Movement (UDM) was formed in 1997, many in the country regarded it as the future official black opposition and a potential alternative to the ruling ANC.

Armed with experienced leaders and veteran politicians like Bantu Holomisa and Roelf Meyer, the leading constitutional negotiator for the now-defunct National Party, the UDM surprised many in the 1999 national elections when, barely 20 months after its formation, it obtained

14 parliamentary seats in the National Assembly and 3.42% of the vote. It also took official opposition seats in the Eastern Cape and Limpopo and gained seats in six other provincial legislatures after the election.

The party, which billed itself as the political home of all South Africans, was seen as a threat to the ANC's political heartland in the Eastern Cape, as the province continued its slide into total chaos, troubled by a lack of service delivery. Its growing support there was even noticed by former president Nelson Mandela, who tried unsuccessfully to persuade Holomisa to rejoin the ANC.

Today, 12 years on, the party is hardly visible in various communities across the country.

It does not control a single municipality in the country, having lost King Sabata Dalindyebo in Mthatha to the ANC in June 2004. Bedevilled by defections to the ANC and the Democratic Alliance and by financial problems resulting from court battles against floor-crossing legislation, the party continued to lose substantial support throughout all provinces. The biggest blow for the UDM came when 13 of its senior members – eight MPs and five MPLs – crossed the floor to join other political parties in September 2003.

Party insiders have blamed the UDM's dismal performance over the past years to Holomisa's 'dictatorial' leadership style. Since Meyer's resignation in 2000 and the expulsion of the party's deputy president, the late Malizole Diko, the UDM has become a one-man party – a fact admitted by Holomisa himself. 'It could be termed one of the UDM's weaknesses,' Holomisa told the *Mail & Guardian*.

Perhaps one of Holomisa's major failures as UDM leader is that instead of selling his party to South African voters, he always resorted to criticising what the ANC was doing wrong. University of KwaZulu-Natal political scientist Zakhele Ndlovu sees this as a mistake many opposition parties in the country have committed: 'We are more interested as voters in what the UDM is offering, not what the ANC is doing wrong, because we already know that.'

Political analysts have predicted the UDM's dismal performance will continue, especially since the formation of the ANC splinter party, the Congress of the People, which has a strong presence in the Eastern Cape.

The UDM received a paltry 0.92% of the vote in the 2009 elections, managing to garner only about 150 000 votes across the country. Unless Holomisa acts to arrest the demise, he will have almost nothing left by the next elections in 2014.

The UDM's election strategy in 2009 was hardly different from the one it applied in 2004. The party's key policy priorities are socio-economic development with an emphasis on job creation, fighting crime with a proposal for a super-ministry of crime prevention, improving the quality of education, stemming corruption and pushing for a reform of the electoral system. Good messages as they are, the voters are deserting Holomisa.

Provinces

Eastern Cape

Nowhere else in South Africa is there a province so haunted by the ghost of apartheid as the Eastern Cape. This, the second-largest province in the country after Northern Cape, houses 6.9-million people; more than 80% speak isiXhosa and about 60% live in rural areas.

On a political level the memory of the bantustan system overshadows provincial politics and plays itself out at both provincial and municipal levels. When the boundaries of the new provinces were drawn shortly after the 1994 elections, the Eastern Cape was given both the Ciskei and Transkei bantustans as well as a chunk of the former Cape Province.

The car-manufacturing hub of South Africa, Port Elizabeth and East London, was supposed to ensure that jobs were created for thousands of people in this, the ANC's heartland. The province's other major source of income would be agriculture. But over the years politicking and access to government resources through tenders and business contracts became the main driving force of economic development and wealth creation for those individuals with government connections.

By 2004 the province was the country's basket case. Following the 2004 elections numerous attempts were made to intervene in provincial government departments that were falling apart, but to no avail. Instead of the hive of economic growth that the province was supposed to be, it has become the source of horrific tales of babies dying in filthy, understaffed hospitals.

Matric results have gone from bad to heartbreaking, with a 2008 pass rate of just over 50%, even lower than the 2007 rate when the province's matric results were the worst in the country. And those matric students were the lucky ones – formal education has completely eluded a fifth of the adult population.

The official unemployment rate in 2007 was 25.5%, counting only people who were still looking for work. The actual rate, including those who had given up any hope of a job, was estimated to be closer to 40%. Not surprisingly, in the same year, Stats SA revealed that the province had the highest percentage of people relying on social grants in the country – just over 19%.

The Eastern Cape is seen as the birthplace of the ANC because almost all its pre-2007 leaders hailed from this province, including former presidents Nelson Mandela and Thabo Mbeki. It housed the country's premier tertiary institution for black students during the apartheid years, and therefore when liberation came, it was mostly those from the Eastern Cape who stepped in and were ready to govern.

At a national level the province might have been well represented, but at home things were falling apart. Mbeki's appointment of several unsuitable premiers led to great divisions in the political class, even though everyone was committed to the ANC. But in 2004 Mbeki made his gravest mistake to date in appointing Nosimo Balindlela, a relatively unknown leader who was given the premiership position, trumping more seasoned provincial politicians who had clout with the people at the grassroots. Balindlela's reign was an unmitigated disaster. With no coherent governance plan and severe infighting in the ANC's provincial executive committee (PEC), she engaged in damage control rather than governing. She had support from some leaders and communities, but not enough to give her the respect a premier of such a vast and poor province needs for success.

In 2006 new leaders were chosen at a provincial ANC conference and the previous chairperson, sports minister Makhenkesi Stofile, was removed. Former provincial education minister Stone Sizani won in a showdown with former Eastern Cape Development Corporation CE Mcebisi Jonas.

As the new chairperson, Sizani was immediately tasked by the PEC to start lobbying for Mbeki to stand for a third term as ANC president. He set about convincing the branches in the provinces to support Mbeki's bid, despite having lost his job on Mbeki's orders in 2000 because of the president's suspicion that Sizani was one of the 'ultra-leftists' opposed to his macroeconomic plan. Sizani saw the Mbeki campaign as a way to re-enter politics, but his campaign to win the province for Mbeki met with fierce resistance in some of the biggest regions, like the OR Tambo region, which embraces the former Transkei. Ironically Mbeki grew up there in Idutywa, where his mother, Epainette Mbeki, still resides.

Residents of the former Transkei were of the opinion that they were being marginalised in the development of the province in favour of the former Ciskei, where the provincial legislature is housed in Bisho, close to King William's Town. They opted to support then-ANC deputy president Jacob Zuma because they felt a change in leadership would bring them back into the fold.

The divided support for Mbeki in the Eastern Cape should have been a weathervane of things to come. When the province voted to determine its choice for ANC president, Mbeki managed to secure the most votes, but by a margin that was too close for comfort. Mbeki lost his presidency at Polokwane and the Mbeki-ites had to admit defeat.

Deputy defence minister and Amathole region chairperson Mluleki George soldiered on, however, and continued lobbying support in the region. After the sacking of Mbeki in September 2008, his efforts came in handy. He joined defence minister Mosiuoa Lekota in a live press conference announcing they were 'divorcing' the ANC, and the following he continued to enjoy in Amathole became the first support base of the Congress of the People (Cope). This was important because any party that thought it could take on the ANC had to gain significant support in the Eastern Cape, and with Amathole as the second-biggest region in the province, Cope was off to a promising start. Most of the PEC members elected in 2006 defected to Cope, leaving Sizani and the deputy provincial secretary and provincial health minister Pemmy Majodina to steer the ship through its most troubled waters so far.

With the Eastern Cape the heartland of both the ANC and Cope, it was to become a hotbed of activity and a barometer of the parties' support at a national level. ANC and Cope leaders took to the rural villages, wooing chiefs and kings in a bid for support. The ANC went on a witch-hunt to sniff out Cope moles and threw all its resources behind fighting by-elections in the province caused by ANC councillors defecting to Cope. The plan worked. The rebel party has yet to win a single by-election here.

The April 2009 election results have seen most of the ANC's support intact with 19 seats, while Cope and the Democratic Alliance have to be content with three seats each in the provincial legislature. What was a promising start to a real opposition came to a crushing end as Cope's leaders realised the support they had was closely tied in with their political clout, without which they couldn't dent the deeply entrenched loyalty for the ANC.

Free State

The Free State has enormous potential. It is South Africa's breadbasket, producing most of the country's sorghum, and much of its wheat and maize. Its economic strengths include mining and manufacturing as well as agriculture – one-third of the country's gold production takes place in the Free State, and the petrochemical giant Sasol is based in the province. Free State was one of only two provinces that did not report a rise in unemployment in 2008; at 26.5%, it has the third-lowest unemployment rate in the country, after the Western Cape and Gauteng, and in 2008 its economy grew by 4.2%. Its youth are geared for success: the 2008 matric pass rate, at 71.8%, was higher than the national average.

There's only one serious problem: infighting in the ruling party, which has not let up since democracy arrived in the province. However, after over a decade spent waiting in the wings, Ace Magashule, longtime chairperson of the ANC in the Free State, has found 2009 the year when he finally gets to be premier. Magashule had been repeatedly overlooked by the ruling party for the post of premier. A Jacob Zuma supporter, he had difficult relationships with each of the pro-Mbeki premiers, particularly the original premier, Mosiuoa Lekota. After Lekota was forced to resign as premier – he was sent to chair the National Council of Provinces – and his replacement, Ivy Matsepe-Casaburri, fell from grace, the premiership went first to Winkie Direko and then, in 2004, to Beatrice Marshoff.

In 2007 Direko and former Mangaung mayor Papi Mokoena were involved in a bitter campaign to end Magashule's run as ANC chairperson, but Mashagule emerged unscathed. At the beginning of 2008, the ANC's Free State secretary Charlotte Lobe resigned, citing disillusionment with the party's conduct in the province. But eventually amity was restored: at the party's provincial conference in Parys in 2008, all five nominees for the top provincial posts, including Magashule, were elected unopposed.

After the Polokwane conference, ANC leaders agreed that certain premiers should be redeployed. When the ANC announced its candidate list for the 2009 elections, five of the party's eight provincial premiers, including Marshoff, would be sent to the National Assembly. This was seen as an attempt to remove her from internal power struggles.

The Democratic Alliance (DA) has been struggling to transform itself into a formidable opposition. But the arrival of the Congress of the People (Cope), which is now the new official opposition, could add a bit of spark to the competition for votes. In the 2009 elections the ruling party lost 10% of the votes in the province, dropping from 81.70% in 2004 to 71.10%. Most of the votes lost went to newcomers Cope, which received 11.61% of the votes, compared with the DA's 11.60%.

The Free State is the third-largest province in the country but has the second-lowest population density, after the Northern Cape. It is home to 2.8-million South Africans, of whom 84% are African, 13% white and 3% coloured. Sesotho is the dominant language, spoken by 57% of the population, followed by Afrikaans and a smattering of isiXhosa, Setswana and isiZulu.

The province ranks third in the country for basic services: 90% of the population have access to clean water, 91% have access to free basic electricity, 87% to sanitation, and 30% to telephones. Service delivery has not been without its hitches. In 2006, the Mangaung municipality, which includes Bloemfontein, Thaba 'Nchu and Botshabelo, was mired in controversy. The Scorpions arrested the mayor, the late Papi Mokoena, his wife, his political adviser, the city manager, the chief operations officer and the speaker after a string of corruption allegations and tender scandals came to light. According to the Scorpions' report, corruption consumed R150-million, or 10 % of the municipal budget. And Mangaung, where more than half of all households live beneath the poverty line, desperately needs its budget. The case is ongoing.

In 2009 Marshoff denied allegations that the Free State's healthcare system was 'in tatters' but confirmed that it was experiencing severe financial constraints. In the 2007/8 financial year, the province set up eight new sites to dispense antiretroviral (ARV) drugs, but the health department revealed that because of its poor financial situation, it could not supply ARVs to all patients. The department had to be bailed out by USAid, Pepfar and pharmaceutical companies.

There is a strong emphasis on education in the province. At primary level, the province has been driving intervention programmes to increase the number of no-fee schools and improve the standard of maths and science education, while at tertiary level the most prominent issue seems to be one of race. Underlying racial tensions at the University of the Free State (UFS) bubbled over in early 2008 after the surfacing of a racist video shot by UFS students. The video came in the wake of the university's attempts to integrate student housing.

When one thinks of the Free State, the image of maize comes to mind. There's so much of it that the provincial government had planned to back an ambitious private-sector biofuel initiative to be based in Bothaville, but the deal stalled after Cabinet decided to exclude the use of maize in biofuel production. However, the impetus for biofuels is still there and stakeholders are looking for alternatives to build the industry.

The Free State has the infrastructure, the people and the business backbone to drive real growth. Now that Magashule has finally got his hands on the premiership, he will be under pressure to produce the goods.

Gauteng

Gauteng remains the mecca of the country, constantly attracting thousands of migrants to its cities. It is home to South Africa's biggest city, Johannesburg, and three of the country's six metropolitan councils, Tshwane, Ekurhuleni and the City of Johannesburg. As with six other provinces, the ANC has had a firm grip in Gauteng, ruling it since 1994 and likely to continue at least for another term. In 1994 the election result was close but the ANC, with 57% of the vote, outmuscled the National Party. In subsequent elections the ruling party increased its majority to 67% in 1999 and 68% in 2004, and the ANC has again been returned to power in the province in 2009 but with a smaller majority, receiving 64% of the votes. Some of the lost support went to the Congress of the

People (Cope), which won almost 8% of the vote in its debut contest. The Democratic Alliance increased its support to almost 22%.

Gauteng lost its premier, Mbhazima Shilowa, in October 2008, six months before his term came to an end, when he joined Cope. Shilowa had run a stable, coherent team for two terms, although he came under attack for protecting some of his provincial ministers, including finance MEC Paul Mashatile and education MEC Angie Motshekga, after they were exposed in conflicts of interest with companies to which their departments awarded tenders. Shilowa had to leave after he criticised the party's sacking of former president Thabo Mbeki. He is now the deputy president of Cope.

The other parties which have occupied not more than three seats each in the past 15 years include the Inkatha Freedom Party, the United Democratic Movement and the Pan Africanist Congress.

Gauteng has the smallest land area (only 1.4% of the country) but the largest population of the nine provinces of South Africa. According to Stats SA, Gauteng's population stood at 10.4-million in 2007. This accounts for approximately 21% of the national population. In the period 2001–7 the province's population increased by an estimated 13.9% from 8.8-million. Of the current population, approximately 7.8-million are over the age of 15 years and some 2.6-million are under the age of 15 years.

The province's ever-increasing population is mainly attributed to in-migration from other parts of South Africa and the continent. Local government demarcation shifts have also resulted in an increase in Gauteng's population. The area of Merafong, which includes Khutsong, has recently been reincorporated into the province, after being shifted to North West five years ago.

Gauteng's high population growth rate puts pressure on public services, housing and other infrastructure. In the face of a growing demand for housing, the province has seen a slight decrease in the percentage of informal dwellings, from 23.5% to 22.6% between 2001 and 2007, as well as an increase in the percentage of people owning their own houses. However, the province has over 200 informal settlements, making it one of the provinces with the highest number of informal settlements.

Gauteng has the largest economy of South Africa's provinces and is showing sustained and robust growth. In 2006, the province contributed 34.8% of gross domestic product (GDP), thus retaining its position as the country's economic hub. The provincial economy grew at a rate of 6% in 2006, higher than the national average. While the global economic crisis is expected to impact on the province's growth rate in the short term, the outlook for the period to 2014 remains positive. Foreign direct investment grew from R450-million in 2001 to R1.5-billion in 2003, increasing to R3-billion in the period to 2008.

While traditionally the Gauteng economy was based on mining, agriculture and manufacturing, the primary sector has continued to decline, with the secondary and tertiary sectors accounting for more and more of GDP and employment. The key sectors contributing to the province's GDP are finance and business services (21.3%); manufacturing (19.6%); government and other services (19%); wholesale, retail and hospitality (13%); and transport, communications and storage (7.7%). Increased tourism, investment in the film industry and the hosting of international sporting, arts and cultural events have also made a contribution to economic growth in the province. A significant number of multinationals and conglomerates have chosen Gauteng as the base for their business activities and for expansion into South Africa and the rest of the African continent.

Economic growth and development have resulted in an increase in the number of jobs, a decline in unemployment levels and an increase in per capita income.

- The number of people employed in Gauteng increased from just over 2.8-million in 2002 to over 3.4-million in 2007.
- Unemployment dropped from 30.4% in September 2001 to 19.5% in September 2007.
- Gauteng's labour absorption rate is above national trends, increasing from 48.2% in September 2001 to 54.6% in September 2007.
- Increased employment levels resulted in an increase in per capita income from R41 243 in 2004 to R44 230 in 2006.
- A key challenge, however, remains the high level of youth unemployment, with people aged 20–34 representing 65% of the unemployed.

South Africa's legacy of inequality and a skewed distribution of wealth based on race continue to plague the province. Figures for 2005/6 showed that:

- 10% of the population earned over 50% of the income.
- 40% of the population earned less than 7% of the income
- While black Africans represented 79% of the population, their share of expenditure increased only minimally from 42.9% in 2000 to 44.3% in 2005.
- Whites represented 9.5% of the population and their share of expenditure declined slightly from 44.1% to 42.9% between 2000 and 2005.

This is a clear indication that the level of poverty remains high and that efforts to bridge the gap between rich and poor in the province must be intensified. Key household income sources are salaries, rent and business activities, while key household expenditure items are housing, water and electricity (24.8%); transport (20.6%); and food (12%).

The profile of Gauteng reflects, on the one hand, the noteworthy economic growth and achievements in the provision of social and basic services; on the other hand, it shows that poverty, unemployment and inequality levels remain unacceptably high and need to be more effectively addressed.

KwaZulu-Natal

KwaZulu-Natal (KZN) is slowly emerging from the wreckage of its violent past, which, prior to the 1994 elections, threatened to destabilise the country. The political squabbling between the Inkatha Freedom Party (IFP) and the ANC in the build-up to the 2009 general elections, while deplorable, was nowhere near the levels of violence of the 1980s and early 1990s, during which the Institute for Race Relations estimates that around 250 000 people lost their lives. Then, political intolerance was so severe that merely wearing the wrong T-shirt could get one killed and the inhabitants of entire villages were murdered with impunity.

To a degree, KZN has moved away from its reputation as a killing field, and with relative peace has come development, increased investment and, between 2004 and 2008, a 4.1% economic growth rate. Yet economic upliftment is not very widespread, especially in rural areas. Of the close to 10-million people (20.9% of the total South African population) who live in the province, 5.3-million are living in poverty, according to the provincial department of agriculture. Conservative estimates put the number of people barely surviving on less than R200 per month at around 1.2-million people. At the same time, growing urbanisation is placing an increasing strain on urban infrastructure – many municipalities have only recently woken up to the need for maintenance – and seen the mushrooming of informal settlements.

The chasm between rich and poor, urban and rural, has also not been adequately addressed because of incompetence and corruption at local government level and a malaise that extends to the province's financial institutions which are responsible for powering more broad-based development, especially in the SMME sector. Ithala Bank, which should essentially be KZN's development bank, has often been criticised for being the 'piggy-bank' of the province's political elite – the errant debt servicing of many of whom has raised concerns about Ithala's current financial capacity.

While the province has a very good infrastructure development strategy, its outcomes have been pitiful. The European Union-funded Gijima scheme, for example, managed by the provincial treasury since 2004, aims to create opportunities for the poor, but only two of its projects got the go-ahead from government in the past two years – at a cost of R130-million. KZN has spent big on infrastructure development, with multi-billion-rand projects including the Dube Trade Port and King Shaka Airport, expected to cost over R7-billion, the building of better roads in northern KZN, and the Moses Mabhida World Cup stadium in Durban.

Traditionally, the lush subtropical province has relied on tourism and agriculture (sugar cane and fruit) as its main economic activities. Both are being impacted upon by the rampant development of housing estates, golfing estates and other residential and hospitality developments that appear to be eating up the land.

Agricultural activity has also been affected by unresolved land claims (of which there is a serious backlog, with cases dragging on for years). The South African Cane Growers' Association estimates that almost 50%

of the land in the province is under claim – of which only 4% has been settled – leading to insecurity amongst farmers about future development of their farms. Farmers also raise issues of crime and safety. According to Stats SA, the number of commercial farmers in KZN dropped from 6 000 to 4 500 between 1997 and 2000.

After winning 41 out of a possible 81 seats in the 1994 elections and initially ruling the province, the IFP has experienced serious electoral decline. After the 1999 election it just edged out the ANC with 41.9%, compared to the ANC's haul of 39.38%, and was obliged to share power. In 2004 the ANC won the province for the first time with 47.47% of the vote, compared to the IFP's 34.87%. Although IFP president Mangosuthu Buthelezi warned his supporters against casting sympathetic votes for ANC president Jacob Zuma, this is exactly what happened in the 2009 elections. When the final results were released, the IFP had continued its decline, winning only 22% of the votes against the ANC's 63%, a massive increase which ensured the party an outright majority.

Much of the declining IFP support can be attributed to the emergence and popularity of ANC president Jacob Zuma – a Zulu traditionalist, populist and social conservative who strikes all the right chords with this Zulu heartland. Expectations are especially high in KZN that as president of the country Zuma will ensure, because of his rural economic background and ethnicity, a better roll-out of services (or patronage?) to the province.

Limpopo

The rural province of Limpopo derives its name from the evocative Limpopo River, which marks its northernmost border and the international boundary between South Africa, Zimbabwe, Botswana and Mozambique. Limpopo markets itself as the gateway to Africa, specifically the Southern African Development Community. But, in the past decade, the province has become a portal for tens of thousands of Zimbabweans seeking refuge in South Africa from the economic meltdown in their country. The collapse was sparked at the turn of the century by Zimbabwean president Robert Mugabe's controversial land reform policies, which forcibly removed white commercial farmers from their land. By the end of 2008,

Zimbabwe's inflation rate had soared to 13.2-billion percent a month and it had lost its status as the breadbasket of Africa.

A ramshackle refugee camp has been established in Limpopo's border town of Musina to accommodate fleeing Zimbabweans. From late 2008 and into early 2009, the provincial health department also had to erect emergency medical tents for desperate Zimbabweans seeking treatment following a massive cholera outbreak that began in the country's capital, Harare, where water and waste management services had collapsed. The pandemic inevitably spread throughout poor communities in Limpopo and to other South African provinces where residents in underdeveloped areas continue to rely on dams, rivers and wells for water.

The exodus from Zimbabwe has put a strain on Limpopo's resources. The provincial treasury complained in 2009 that cross-border migration, combined with the current global economic crisis, had reduced the province's baseline allocation for the 2009/10 financial year by R372-million. Budget allocations for the following two years have been reduced by R568.9-million and R870.1-million respectively. This does not bode well for a province that, according to 2004 figures, remains one of the poorest in the country. Limpopo made the fourth-lowest contribution to the national gross domestic product in 2004, at 6.7%, beating only the North West (6.3%), Free State (5.5%) and Northern Cape (2.2%). It also has the lowest per capita income at an average of R16 253 a year.

The province enjoyed an annual average growth of 4% between 1996 and 2005, higher than the national average, but the global economic crisis is expected to reduce this. The recession is also likely to reverse gains made in reducing the province's unemployment rate, which dropped from a high of 39.4% in 2003 to 29.5% in the third quarter of 2008.

The provincial government has been working hard to stimulate its key sectors of agriculture, mining and tourism.

Agriculture is the second-largest employer in Limpopo, where 88.2% of the province's total land area is farmland. Of this 70% is owned by white commercial farmers and 30% by smallholders in former homeland areas. Limpopo provides more than 45% of the R2-billion annual turnover of the Johannesburg Fresh Produce Market. The indisputable breadbasket of the province is found around Magoebaskloof and Tzaneen, but investment has dwindled sharply since 1996 because of conflicting land claims to 168 prime fruit and tea farms worth an estimated R3-billion and forestry land worth another R3-billion. Following the collapse of some land reform projects, which saw once-thriving commercial farms fall into ruin, the provincial department of agriculture has come to recognise the need for better communication and more effective support for new farm owners.

In terms of mining, Limpopo is home to the nation's biggest diamond, copper and open-pit platinum mines, and contains 50% of South Africa's coal resources. Of the country's mining labour force 13%, or roughly 64 000 workers, are employed in Limpopo, and this is projected to grow by another 90 000 in the next 20 years with a massive expansion drive in the sector.

The province is building the R7-billion De Hoop Dam and associated waterworks to enable the expansion of platinum mining in central Limpopo. The expansion is expected to involve investment of some R20-billion.

There has been some controversy over proposals to establish an open-cast coal mine and power station in the pristine World Heritage site of Mapungubwe, while construction of the R100-billion Medupi power station in Lephalale, which falls in the scenic Waterberg area, is already under way. Once completed in 2015, Medupi will be the 22nd-largest power plant and fourth-largest coal plant in the world. Transnet has announced that it will spend R10-billion to upgrade its Waterberg line by 2025 to increase the transport of coal to fuel the country's power stations.

Limpopo will have to balance its industrialisation with its status as a leading wildlife tourism destination and host to two important transfrontier parks – the Limpopo-Shashe Transfrontier Park, which straddles the borders of South Africa, Botswana and Zimbabwe, and the Great Limpopo Transfrontier Park, which takes in portions of South Africa, Zimbabwe and Mozambique. The bulk of the Kruger National Park also falls within its borders. Southern Africa's largest, most pristine floodplain is also found here, in the Nylsvley nature reserve. Nylsvley, which covers 16 ha when it floods, is on the Ramsar list of wetlands of international importance. The Eurasian bittern, a bird highly sensitive to environmental change, was last seen here 20 years ago.

The province also has a rich cultural history that includes the aura of 'Rain Queen' Modjadji, the Mapungubwe and Thulamela archaeological sites, which reveal an ancient trading empire predating Great Zimbabwe, and the battlefields of the Sekhukhune wars of independence. There are plans to turn Moria City, which attracts over one million Zionist Christian Church pilgrims every Easter, into a tourist destination, attracting visitors in the same way as other religious sites, such as the Vatican City.

In 2006, the number of national tourists grew by 22.5%, from 3.1-million to 4-million trips. The number of international arrivals grew by 9.2% to 509 577 between January and September 2007, compared to the same period the previous year. The province also accounts for roughly 80% of all trophy-hunting operations in the country.

Another drawcard is that in a country with a high crime rate, Limpopo accounts for the fewest murders, rapes and armed robberies. The province recorded 14 murders per 100 000 people in 2006/7, compared to the Western Cape's 60.7 murders per 100 000 people.

Limpopo remains South Africa's most rural or least urbanised province – some 89.3% of people still live in rural areas. Covering roughly 10% of South Africa's land mass, the province is divided into five municipal districts: Capricorn, based in the provincial capital of Polokwane; Waterberg, based in Modimolle; Vhembe, based in Thohoyandou; Mopani, based in Giyani; and Sekhukhune, based in Groblersdal. A sixth district, the Bohlabela district, was dismantled when a decade-long border dispute finally resulted in the return of the Bushbuckridge area to Mpumalanga, in the south, following municipal elections in March 2006.

While the most recent figures from Stats SA indicate that Limpopo has a population of about 5.4-million people, these do not account for the loss of about a million people when Bushbuckridge was returned to Mpumalanga. This is unlikely, however, to affect the province's standing as the fourth most populous province, accommodating roughly 11% of the entire South African population. It is also unlikely to change the fact that more than half of Limpopo's people are women (54.6%) and more than half (52.1%) speak Sepedi, followed by Xitsonga and Tshivenda. Only 0.5% are first-language English speakers, though most white people are Afrikaans first-language speakers.

The voting population predominantly supports the ANC, which won 38 seats in 1994, 44 in 1999, and 45 in 2004. In 2004, the ANC secured 89.18% of the total votes. The Democratic Alliance followed with 3.59% and the Nasionale Aksie with 0.14%. There were 1.6-million voters registered in the province in 2004, while 2.2-million were registered to vote in 2009; of these 1.3-million were women. In the 2009 elections the ruling party was again returned with a huge majority of almost 85%, while the Congress of the People received 7.53% and the Democratic Alliance 3.4% of the vote.

In December 2007 the province hosted the Polokwane conference, or 52nd national conference of the ANC, where for the first time an ANC president was asked to step down before completing his term in office.

Mpumalanga

Mpumalanga's population grew by almost one million people or 28% in 2008 when, after a decade of often violent campaigning, the sprawling Bushbuckridge region in Limpopo was finally incorporated into the province. Situated just 80 km north of the provincial capital, Nelspruit, the network of deep rural villages and peri-urban settlements are amongst South Africa's most densely populated pockets of poverty.

Mpumalanga's trepidation at the incorporation appeared justified in 2009, when Bushbuckridge became the epicentre of South Africa's worst cholera outbreak in living memory and forced the province to redirect massive resources to begin building proper water and sanitation systems.

It wasn't just the infrastructure backlogs or poverty that caused trepidation. The new Bushbuckridge region brought with it a militant political tradition that regularly erupts into violent public protests and attacks on public figures. The unrest soon spread to another rural border hotspot, Moutse, where desperately poor communities revolted when the national government tried to transfer them to Limpopo as part of a wider 'alignment' of provincial boundaries.

Even without its new territory, Mpumalanga's population of 3.6-million is growing slightly faster than the national average, at 8.2% per year. The increase includes a continuing influx of young entrepreneurs, migrant workers and the rural destitute. Drawn by the opportunities created by Mpumalanga's booming mining sector and a number of massive, government-led infrastructure projects, the migrants are transforming former sleepy farm towns into bustling service centres. The most ambitious of the projects, the R8.6-billion Moloto Corridor, seeks to use new high-speed rail and road networks to transform Moutse and the surrounding apartheid-era dumping grounds into a major agri-industry and mining hub. Government has simultaneously injected R500-million into the venerable Maputo Corridor to kickstart new development along the 400 km highway and has launched a R1.2-billion venture capital fund to draw new investors into growth industries ranging from biofuels to hydroelectricity plants.

But, despite all the economic stimulus, Mpumalanga's contribution to national gross domestic product has remained static at 6.8%, while its latest available annual economic growth rate slipped below national averages to 4.4% in 2006 and its per capita income of R29 332 remains stubbornly below the World Bank's 2007 estimated national average of R55 730.

Prior to Bushbuckridge's incorporation, Mpumalanga was predominantly siSwati- or isiNdebele-speaking, with sizeable Xitsonga-, Sepedi-, and isiZulu-speaking communities. Although no official statistics are available yet, Bushbuckridge will have dramatically boosted the numbers of Xitsonga- and Sepedi-speaking residents, and will have created an enclave of South Africa's largest 'invisible' language, Sepulana. English- and Afrikaans-speaking communities remain stable, while a decade of growing trade with neighbouring Mozambique has made Portuguese an essential second business language. According to Stats SA's mid-year 2008 estimates, a higher-than-average 35% of Mpumalanga residents are under the age of 15 years.

Although the fertile breadbasket of the old Eastern Transvaal formed the core of Mpumalanga, it is the dusty apartheid-era bantustans cobbled on to it that continue to define the provincial psyche. Even 15 years after their supposed demise, the old homelands of KaNgwane, KwaNdebele and slivers of Gazankulu, Lebowa and Bophuthatswana have yet to be fully subsumed within Mpumalanga. If anything, ethnic identity and the politics of identity appear to be on the rise. The bruising 2008 contest for chairmanship of the provincial ruling party, the ANC, saw candidates stressing their regional roots. The eventual victor, David 'Hurricane' Mabuza, campaigned on a militant 'Mpumalanga first' platform that disparaged his competitors' links to neighbouring provinces. Grassroots opposition to migrant workers from Mozambique and Swaziland also remains strong, though Mpumalanga escaped the worst of the wave of xenophobic purges that swept the nation in 2008. The deep-seated xenophobia appears linked to competition for jobs, with Mpumalanga's unemployment rate on a par with the national average at 23.2% per annum.

Nelspruit's investor- and trade-driven economy saw the city double the physical footprint of its CBD over the past five years, while industrial centres such as Witbank experienced similar unprecedented commercial and residential property booms, which appear more resilient to the global recession than elsewhere in South Africa. Central to this economic buoyancy is Eskom's R140-billion emergency expansion of its electricity generation in the province, and the linked R100-billion expansion of privately owned coal mines to fuel the network of refurbished as well as new power stations. Mpumalanga currently generates roughly 70% of the nation's electricity; it has 14 power stations and produces 80% of South Africa's current coal. The 2009 Mining Indaba heard that although there are already 65 active coal mines in the province, investors are looking at spending R140-billion to establish 40 more in the province simply to keep pace with demand.

But it isn't just coal mining that is booming in Mpumalanga. Although temporarily interrupted by the global recession, there are significant investments in expanded mining for platinum, vanadium, gold, iron and magnesite, while Sasol continues to invest in its petrochemical plants in Secunda. The mineral renaissance has, in turn, sparked massive renovation of both rail and road networks, alongside construction of major new water and gas pipelines, and has created boom towns in places as disparate as Mashishing (formerly Lydenburg) and Standerton.

The economic growth comes, however, at a price. Air quality on the industrialised Mpumalanga highveld was officially classified as among the worst in South Africa in 2008, while water pollution has deteriorated so rapidly that the neighbouring states of Swaziland and Mozambique have expressed official concern.

And it isn't just neighbouring states that are complaining. The Kruger National Park has reported mass crocodile and other riverine die-offs along the crucial Olifants River due to chemical pollution, while conservation authorities elsewhere in the province warn that entire river systems are being sterilised by chemicals leaching from mines and factories. Even where industrial pollution is not a factor, untreated human effluent from burgeoning informal settlements and crumbling municipal treatment plants are contaminating ground water across the province and turning rivers, from the mighty Crocodile, Vaal and Inkomati to smaller tributaries, into toxic cholera reservoirs. Provincial authorities acknowledge the problem, and speak of better water management, but have presented few concrete plans, despite a decade of increasingly shrill warnings about the growing crisis.

Also in crisis is Mpumalanga's forestry industry, which supplies 72% of the nation's mining timber, 40% of its sawed or veneered logs, and 49% of its charcoal sales. Vast land claims, the increasing costs of labour and water, growing global competition and the second devastating wildfire in five years have impacted significantly on the province's pulp and paper giants, Sappi and Mondi. Both companies, plus scores of smaller foresters and even commercial farmers, have responded by mechanisation in their plantations and modernisation of their mills in an attempt to curtail costs. Foresters are also exploring joint ventures with land claimants in a bid to secure their stocks. They remain unrepentant, though, about odious sulphur emissions from mills and processing plants, despite campaigns by infuriated tourism operators and conservationists who complain that they have difficulty selling the concept of a 'pristine African wilderness' that smells of hell.

Tourism continues to grow, all the same, with the reinvigorated Mpumalanga Tourism and Parks Agency (MTPA) reclaiming the province's position as South Africa's fourth most popular tourism destination after a 10-year slide down the ranks to eighth position on the back of corruption scandals and a failure to invest in either marketing or tourism infrastructure. The revitalised MTPA has combated the malaise with renovations of key public game reserves, a massive public marketing campaign, and support for private sector initiatives. The provincial government also awarded Mpumalanga's fourth and final casino licence in 2009 and injected new funding into the provincial airport, while international operators such as Dubai World ploughed over R2-billion into new lodges, hotels and conference centres ahead of the 2010 World Cup.

Preparations for the World Cup have, however, been anything but a happy experience. The host city, Nelspruit, ignored private sector advice and insisted on building Mpumalanga's R1-billion stadium on community-owned farmland just outside the city limits – without consulting the owners. The municipality instead cited 'over-riding public interest' and paid the Matsafeni clan a nominal R1 for the land, demolishing the province's oldest independent black school in the process, and accusing outraged community members of being unpatriotic. Community activism, bolstered by legal assistance from human rights lawyers, soon exposed a litany of contractual and procedural irregularities that saw the city's mayor, municipal manager and 2010 manager all axed in 2008. Instead of addressing community demands for fair compensation, the provincial government weighed in to support efforts to reverse the Matsafeni land claim and to steamroller the 'donation' of the land back to government. The strong-arm tactics backfired, however; a 2008 damning court ruling branded government's machinations as an apparent attempt to 'hoodwink' the Matsafeni in a scheme that was no different from historical cases when settlers or colonial authorities robbed native people of their land in return for mirrors or 'shiny buttons'.

Simultaneous efforts by the city's whistleblowing speaker Jimmy Mohlala to root out suspected corruption in the deal ended in his assassination in early 2009. Police investigations into the murder remained unresolved at the time of publication, as did increasingly acrimonious negotiations between the Matsafeni and government.

The Matsafeni deal was not the only contested land reform project in Mpumalanga. Regular corruption and maladministration scandals saw two provincial land claims commissioners and scores of officials fired over the past five years. Only an estimated 20% of the province's 646 land reform projects were still classified as productive farms in 2009. A 2008 department of land affairs report noted that 20% of assessed restitution projects in Mpumalanga were non-operative, 26% were in decline, a further 34% were in the balance – and only 20% were classified as successful. Public frustration with the inept management of land reform saw large public protests across the province, as well as mounting criticism by organised business, labour and tourism bodies.

The widespread public dissatisfaction with government delivery, and the lacklustre leadership of two premiers deployed by former president Thabo Mbeki, have done little to erode the ANC's outright dominance in Mpumalanga. The party has enjoyed a two-thirds majority in the provincial legislature since democracy in 1994, winning 80.7% of the 30 legislature seats in 1994, 84.8% in 1999, 86.3% in 2004 and 85.55% in 2009.

North West

The third term of the ANC government in the North West did not bring sufficient change to the lives of its citizens living in poverty. The provincial government was still preoccupied with rebuilding parts of the province affected by an exodus of businesses after the demise of the former homeland Bophuthatswana, in particular the capital city Mafikeng. The collapse of economic activities had led to the deterioration of infrastructure in several areas.

The province is still predominantly rural, 70% of the population living in rural areas and the unemployment rate standing at 27.4%. With the exception of the key economic player – the mines – the economy is characterised by small, medium and micro enterprises (SMMEs). The province contributed 6.4% to the national gross domestic product in 2007 and has, through Invest North West, attracted R6.8-billion of investment since 2003.

But it is the politics of the ANC that has kept North West in the news. The ruling party in the province mainly supported former president Thabo Mbeki's failed attempt to occupy the ANC's presidency for the third time at the party's Polokwane conference in 2007. Long after Polokwane, the scars of that conference remain and factionalism has prevailed. Divisions within the party's provincial leadership, the ongoing fight for power, as well as the loss of trust between the national executive committee and the provincial executive committee (PEC), have overtaken the running of the province, in turn affecting service delivery. In Ipsos Markinor's government performance barometer, the province scored 51% in satisfaction ratings in 2008, down from 70% in 2007.

The province's second premier, Edna Molewa, survived the chop when the newly elected PEC voiced dissatisfaction about her taking decisions without consulting the ANC's provincial leadership. Molewa was also accused of not providing leadership as the province was preparing for the ANC's national elective conference. Unlike other premiers she did not publicly declare whether she supported Mbeki or his rival Jacob Zuma. Molewa's stance also cost her the post of ANC provincial chairperson, which was won by Nono Maloyi at the Sun City conference.

Opposition parties used this opportunity to garner support, resulting in 16 political parties contesting the 2009 general elections in the province, and making competition for votes fiercer than before. Only 12 parties had fought for seats in the province's legislature during the 2004 elections, with the ANC taking 27 seats, followed by the United Christian Democratic Party (UCDP) with three, the Democratic Alliance (DA) with two and the Freedom Front Plus only one.

The formation of the Congress of the People (Cope) created hopes that the new party would give the ANC a hard time in the province, but it struggled in the North West to get off the ground and was not visible enough for the voter.

It was the UCDP that used the opportunity well by reminding the people of the North West what they once had when their area was the homeland of Bophuthatswana. The party governed the homeland from 1977 until South Africa was democratised in 1994. The UCDP claims that, given another chance, the party could resuscitate the province and its economy. 'We are a tried brand in the North West, we subsidised the industrial areas because we wanted to create jobs,' said deputy leader of the UCDP Kgomotso Ditshetelo.

However, in the 2009 elections Cope mustered enough votes to become the new official opposition, just ahead of the DA. Cope took 8.33%, the DA 8.25% and the UCDP 5.27% of the vote while the ANC won 72.89%, which, while still high, was a sharp drop from the 86% in 2004.

The revival of the economy has begun to produce results, though it has been concentrated in the already developed towns of Rustenburg, Klerksdorp and Potchefstroom. 'It shouldn't be happening the way it's happening, but you can't stop businesses when they're interested in certain areas,' said Invest North West CEO Gaba Tabane. Tabane said that what was negatively affecting employment opportunities was the ANC government's inability to sustain industrial parks built during the time of Bophuthatswana. 'They were heavily subsidised, but now they stand empty,' said Tabane. According to the ANC's local government and housing MEC, Howard Yawa, the bulk of investments in the province still go to areas that are well developed. 'There is a congestion of resources in areas whereas – if planned properly – they can be channelled to poor areas,' he said.

It is estimated that in 2005 there were still some 300 000 people in the province over the age of 15 with no formal education. The poverty situation was exacerbated further by the transfer of several developed townships from North West to Gauteng as part of the disestablishment of cross-boundary municipalities. The province lost 617 914 people from townships such as Ga-Rankuwa, Mabopane, Temba and Fochville in this exercise. That accounts for R2-billion of the province's share of revenue raised nationally and allocated as a block grant to provinces. 'One thing that was not considered when these municipalities were removed was that most of the North West people live in rural areas. There is still a need for infrastructure development, roads and schools,' said Yawa. The population stands at just over 3-million, although it is expected to decrease, because of the towns that the province lost to Gauteng.

The Mafikeng air route, which was resuscitated at the end of 2003 after being closed for three years, is still underutilised, with two flights per day between Johannesburg and Mafikeng. The Mafikeng Airport, which boasts the second-largest commercial airstrip in the world, only introduced Sunday flights in June 2007.

Revenue from casino money decreased when the province suffered the loss of two casinos – the Carousel outside Hammanskraal and Morula Casino in Mabopane – which now both belong to Gauteng. The two casinos contributed about R70-million per annum to the province's economy.

More than 440 000 people in the province live with HIV and Aids, while there are 0.8 doctors per 10 000 people, according to information provided by the North West government. It is the sixth-largest of the nine provinces in the country, covering an area of 116 186 square kilometres (9% of South Africa's land area).

Northern Cape

The Northern Cape is South Africa's largest and emptiest province, where less than 2% of the country's population is spread out across some 30% of the land area. Carved out of the less-populated regions of the former Cape Province, it is known for the beauty of its broad, windswept desert vistas. Africa's first transfrontier game park, the Kgalagadi, is here, a combination of South Africa's Kalahari Gemsbok and Botswana's Gemsbok. The Ai-Ais Richtersveld is another park that crosses borders, this one shared with Namibia and home to spectacular rugged scenery. The Karoo National Park and the Fish River Canyon, the second largest in the world, draw travellers from South Africa and abroad, as do the hectares of Namaqualand daisies blooming in the springtime.

It is one of the places that harried urban South Africans dream about, envisaging slow, simple country lives – returning to the close-knit communities of one's forebears and tilling the soil; or opening a B&B in a Victorian-style house, with a deep stoep and broekie lace, from which one can watch the world go meandering by; or buying a smallholding and farming a few sheep to keep the grass trimmed.

The reality is somewhat different.

Some of the worst crime rates in the country occur in the Northern Cape. The province has the lowest police-to-population ratio in South Africa. This is reflected in the third-highest murder and attempted murder rates in the country. More than 18% of all murders in South Africa take place in the Northern Cape.

In part because of its small population, the Northern Cape has few hospitals – and they are much needed, because HIV/Aids and TB are serious health problems. Up to 2003, 10% of all natural deaths recorded were due to TB, and in 2006, the latest figure available, the prevalence of

HIV was 15.6% – below the national rate, but still too high for comfort. The Northern Cape has historically battled with high rates of foetal alcohol syndrome (FAS). The *American Journal of Public Health* has called FAS in South Africa an 'epidemic', and notes: 'The prevalence rates of more than 40 cases per 1 000 children in … the Northern Cape province … represent some of the highest rates … in the world.' Asbestos is also a serious problem. Asbestos mining was banned in the mid-1990s but has left its legacy: dozens die every year from the asbestosis contracted on the mines or in the mining towns. The mining sector is also blamed for high TB rates.

Mining, specifically diamond mining, once created great wealth – along with great hardship – in the Northern Cape. Kimberley was the site of the world's greatest-ever diamond rush. The discovery of five diamond-bearing Kimberlite pipes in close proximity in the 1870s lured thousands of prospectors to the diamond fields to work small claims in hot, dusty conditions, and the Great Hole which they excavated, now largely filled with brackish water, has become a major tourist site. Before long, the individual claims were amalgamated by the De Beers Consolidated Mines Ltd, formed by Cecil John Rhodes and Barney Barnato. Today most of the world's diamonds are still sold through De Beers' Central Selling Organisation.

It's not only diamonds that are mined in the Northern Cape. There are substantial deposits of zinc, lead, manganese, iron ore and copper as well as an impressive array of semi-precious stones – rose quartz, tiger's eye, verdite and others. It is a cause of some irritation to the provincial government that most of the metals and minerals dug out of the Northern Cape earth are processed elsewhere; beneficiation plants inside the province could seriously cut the unemployment rate. The official rate in 2007, the latest statistic available, is set at 26%.

The province has the third-lowest literacy rate in South Africa, at 83%, and 18.2% of the population has no schooling. Those who do get to school do well; in 2008, 72% of Northern Cape grade 12 students passed their matric, close to the Western Cape's 78% and Gauteng's 76%, and well above the national average of 62.7%.

Some 68% of the population speaks Afrikaans, the largest percentage in the country, and in 2008 nearly a third of the population was under 15 years. Overall, life expectancy for men is 52 and for women 62.

The province boasts the country's largest population of Khoisan, whose historical claim to the area can be shown by the abundance of San paintings and engravings, some very old indeed.

The ANC dominates the Northern Cape, but there are other parties jockeying for position. Also active in the province are the Congress of the People (Cope), the Democratic Alliance (DA), the Independent Democrats, the African Christian Democratic Party and the Freedom Front Plus. Cope has become the new official opposition, winning 16.67% of the vote, while the DA took 12.57% and the ANC 60.75%.

Western Cape

The Western Cape is readily reduced to cliché, both by its admirers and its detractors – the result of both its outrageous physical beauty, and the knotted complexities of its demographic and political landscape. The Cape, we hear from politicians and government officials shuttling back and forth to Parliament, is 'slow to transform', or 'not really African'. International documentary crews are fond of panning their cameras over the shack settlements that line the N2 highway, and then cutting to the cliffside mansions of the Atlantic seaboard in this 'most divided of South African cities'. Answers to what 'transformation' or 'Africanness' on the continent's southern tip would look like come less trippingly off the tongue. Clearly, policies to share more equitably the region's extraordinary wealth have to respond to a set of realities that are starkly different from those of Gauteng.

There is no escaping the fact that the province's ethnic mix sets it apart dramatically from the rest of the country and strongly shapes its politics, but the dynamics of race are greatly complicated by the boundaries between social classes, language groups, city and countryside. Migration, too, is constantly altering the terms of any calculation, from hospital budgets to likely voting patterns.

As of 2009, the province had just more than 4-million residents, some 2.2-million of them coloured, around 900 000 African and 700 000 white. Although the proportion of whites in the mix has been steadily declining since the end of 'influx control' and job reservation laws designed to keep Africans out of the region, it remains unusually high compared to other provinces, and there will be a substantial coloured majority for the foreseeable future. Meanwhile, concerns about the impact on budgets and service delivery of migration to the province from the impoverished Eastern Cape, driven by the relative abundance of jobs and the availability of better hospital care and schools, are so tinged with racial anxieties that policy-makers find it difficult to address them head-on.

It is not surprising, then, that the ANC has never won a provincial election in the Western Cape. In the uhuru election of 1994, urban working-class coloured voters and conservative whites gave the National Party 53% of the vote, and even a decade later, when it finally took control of the provincial legislature, the ANC was able to do so only with the help of floor-crossers. Things have sharply deteriorated for the ruling party since then, not least because of an exceptionally vicious series of internal battles – for precedence within the provincial party, and for the spoils of power that have accrued to empowerment companies with the right party connections.

The ousting as premier of Ebrahim Rasool in 2008, long planned by ANC provincial chair Mcebisi Skwatsha and his right-hand man Max Ozinsky, was ultimately made possible by local powerbrokers whose influence at national level was boosted after the ANC's Polokwane conference: Tony and Lumka Yengeni, and former Cape Town mayor Nomaindia Mfeketo. Rasool's ouster closely mirrored the sacking of president Thabo Mbeki, and had similar effects – branches defected wholesale to the new Congress of the People (Cope), and confusion prevailed over who would lead the provincial party into the 2009 elections. Would the party pick a coloured premier candidate like Rasool's successor, the low-key Lynne Brown, or Chris Nissen, or would Skwatsha finally get his hands on the prize?

By 2009 the anger and disillusionment within the ANC had left rich electoral pickings for its rivals, principally the Democratic Alliance (DA), Cope and the Independent Democrats (ID), all of which won council by-elections in formerly ANC-held wards.

White votes had by 2004 largely consolidated behind the DA, and in the 2006 municipal elections the party, under the new leadership of Helen

Zille, took control of the strategically crucial Cape Town metropole. Zille has used that position to present an image of incorruptibility and efficiency, and campaigned hard to attract coloured and African voters, with some success. She was effective in deflecting blame for the city's housing crisis onto the ANC provincial government, and exploiting anger over the perceived neglect of coloured areas by the ruling party. She has had difficulties of her own with a fractured party – regional kingpins like Western Cape leader Theuns Botha are dead set against her efforts to remake the DA in a more liberal mould, but she has thus far managed to contain them.

The ID profited in 2004 and 2006 from the popularity of its leader, Patricia de Lille, and after a disastrous decision to go into coalition with the ANC in the city council, it reversed itself and joined Zille's ruling coalition. The question for the party, as ever, was whether it could move beyond De Lille's personal appeal and a narrow coloured-nationalist voter base to win a more significant share of the vote.

Cope, which emerged almost fully formed in the Western Cape after an ANC congress which excluded hundreds of Rasool-aligned branches, has strong field commanders in key ANC-supporting areas like Langa, and financial backing from some of the powerful black business players who came to constitute a rival elite for the city's white establishment after 1994.

The final provincial votes in the 2009 elections showed that the DA under Zille had won an outright majority, the first time an opposition party had won control of that province. The ANC lost massive support, from 45% in the 2004 election to a mere 31.55%. The DA almost doubled its support from 27% in 2004 to 51.46% in 2009. Cope came a distant third, garnering 7.74% of voter support. Zille has now relinquished her Cape Town mayoral seat to become the new premier of the province, where her party intends showcasing 'real delivery' as opposed to the ANC's 'slow-moving machinery'.

All this plays out against the backdrop of an economy that is powerfully exposed to the global economic downturn. Long-haul tourism, advertising and film-making, ship chandling and repair, wine and fruit growing, are all buffered by a weaker rand, but not enough to offset plummeting global demand. Financial services, another traditional mainstay of the province, are in deep decline. High property values, which for a decade have underpinned a major construction boom, are now in real decline.

All this will make it even harder to repair a seriously frayed social fabric: a housing shortage which the provincial government puts at 400 000, a health system cracking under the strain of HIV/Aids and tuberculosis, and the worst substance abuse and violent crime problem in the country.

That said, the Western Cape has better prospects than many of its neighbours: sound infrastructure, a diverse economy, relatively high levels of education, and a degree of political competition that limits the scope of provincial and municipal governments for corruption and under-performance. Either way, the place is increasingly difficult to reduce to cliché.

Issues

Black Economic Empowerment

Black economic empowerment is a key plank of South African economic policy. Regulated by the Broad-Based Black Economic Empowerment Act, the legislation is aimed at transferring equity and wealth to formerly excluded South Africans. The Act empowers black South Africans including Africans, Indians and coloureds as well as all women. Court action by the Chinese community has ensured that they are also classified as black.

A complex law, the Act sets targets for the achievement of equity ownership and black management across the economy. It also sets targets for preferential procurement (whereby big companies seek to buy from small and medium-sized black companies); enterprise development (whereby big companies catalyse the creation of small-scale black-owned enterprises); and socioeconomic development (through the stipulation that big sectors develop the communities in which they operate).

There is no watertight measure of progress as no exhaustive survey has been done, but various measurements suggest black ownership constitutes between 10% and 15% of listed wealth.

Employment equity, or affirmative action, has been a far more empowering form of wealth transfer. A KPMG survey suggests that the target for employment equity is well on the way to being met. This is, however, disputed by the Black Management Forum.

Preferential procurement and enterprise development targets are not even out of the starting blocks yet, say critics, who complain that not even state-owned enterprises are acting as catalysts for small black businesses.

Generally, the recession has not been kind to BEE. Because most deals are financed by debt and paid for through dividends, various analysts say the biggest deals are under water.

Until now, the most effective transfers of wealth have been public share offers to the black public by Sasol, MTN and Vodacom.

The most controversial aspect of BEE has been the creation of a generation of oligarchs who benefited through serial deal-making. They include ANC national executive committee members like Cyril Ramaphosa and Tokyo Sexwale as well as former activist and national executive member Saki Macozoma and the former ANC head of the presidency, Smuts Ngonyama.

It is likely that new president Jacob Zuma will order a review of black economic empowerment as required by the Polokwane resolutions of the governing party. His allies on the left want it to be far more redistributive and broad-based, whereas the present incarnation is business-oriented and aimed at creating a black business class.

Corruption

Corruption has come of age. No more the bastard babe hidden even from relatives during the National Party's hypocritically puritan rule; no more the noisy toddler, its destructive lurches overlooked by polite society in the Mandela years; and no more the teenager, sure-footed but shy to show its gawky features in the presence of its ever-disapproving patron, former president Thabo Mbeki. As South Africa installs its fourth democratic Parliament, corruption confidently demands attention and hogs public discourse. What has changed?

The question may be addressed at levels both of perception and of measurable reality.

Corruption as a topic has been thrust to the fore by a confluence of often-related factors: internecine blood-letting during the succession battle; the tug-of-war over the Scorpions, the directorate of special operations tasked with probing organised crime and corruption; the police chief under investigation; the president-in-waiting awaiting trial on corruption and fraud charges; and further investigations into the arms deal.

Research by Media Tenor, which monitors media coverage, found constantly rising levels of reporting on issues of corruption between 2004 and 2008. Significant reporting spikes occurred in mid-2005 when Schabir

Shaik was convicted and Mbeki fired his deputy, Jacob Zuma; in late 2007 when the ANC held its Polokwane conference where Zuma ousted Mbeki as party president; and during August 2008 – the highest level yet – when arms deal bribery allegations were levelled at Mbeki personally, shortly before the ANC forced him to step down as the country's president. The freeing of debate after years of Mbeki's intellectual hegemony, and the mere fact that comrades were prepared to dish dirt on each other as the succession struggle intensified, arguably emboldened South Africans, media practitioners included, to speculate about the probity of their leaders.

The increasing volume of the discourse on corruption is likely to have fed perceptions that corruption levels themselves have risen. But is South Africa sliding into the abyss of endemic sleaze, fraud and bribery?

An easy answer is to say we have always been there, at least from the time that Jan van Riebeeck conned the Khoi out of their prime beachfront estate, or when Cecil John Rhodes swashbuckled his way across the Vaal and the Limpopo, provoking war and conquering territory for the Crown as much as for the mining interests of his company, De Beers.

Or the decades of National Party rule, when the original sin of apartheid obscured a system of institutionalised criminality set up to beat the oil and arms embargoes, soon spreading its rot to the system's architects themselves.

Or the Mandela and early Mbeki years, when bribers and beneficiaries of apartheid were embraced and reinvented – and when the poisoned chalice of the arms deal was concocted and first covered up.

Reality is hard to measure. Are we sliding deeper into the abyss?

One attempt at scientific measure is found in the Global Integrity Report, a United States-based study of quantitative and qualitative indicators applied to countries around the world. South Africa scored a respectably 'moderate' 79 out of 100 in the 2008 report, down from a 'strong' 81 in 2006. The above-average score was thanks in part to South Africa's sturdy legislative and formal institutional environment: yes, there are free and fair elections; yes, there are anti-corruption agencies; yes, there is anti-corruption legislation covering all bases; yes, politicians have to report their interests; and yes, the head of state is subject to the law.

But already the 2008 score was dragged down by issues of implementation – the 'in practice' questions the report also tries to answer. While the law shielded the heads of anti-corruption bodies from political interference, their de facto independence was not equally clear, as evidenced by Mbeki's suspension of national prosecutions boss Vusi Pikoli, the decision to disband the Scorpions, and doubts about public protector Lawrence Mushwana's objectivity. Next time around, the Scorpions will have been dismantled and Pikoli fired, unless the courts gainsay the executive and Parliament. Zuma will have been installed as the next president and, in his case, the law did not run its course. These are among the indicators that will drag South Africa's ratings down more.

But this kind of study finds it easier to look at the structural context in which corruption occurs and is confronted, rather than counting its actual incidence. Are we sliding deeper into the abyss? Do our politicians and officials seek 'rent' from the positions they occupy? Is there a privileged class of cronies who pay that rent in return for contracts and opportunities directed their way? Do our political parties fund themselves through their access to state power?

Anecdotally, and in some instances through exposure, the answer to each of the above tends towards 'yes'. But there is another measure. Next time a traffic officer proposes a 'spot fine', will you pay?

* The author was a paid contributor to an earlier edition of the Global Integrity Report. At the time of writing, judgment was pending in a High Court review application brought by M&G Media, the author and others against the public protector.

Crime

One of the most emotional issues South Africa has battled with and failed to address is crime. Some researchers such as David Bruce, Amanda Diessel and Sasha Gear of the Centre for the Study of Violence and Reconciliation have suggested that this is due to the politics of crime. Those who are privileged enough and have big pockets are able to shout the loudest about crime, they say, whereas those on the periphery of society are probably the most plagued by crime.

In line with the latest government epiphany that violent crime is most prevalent among those who know one another, Bruce and colleagues suggest that the government pay more attention to policing poverty-stricken areas rather than wealthy areas where affluent members of society live. They argue that it is in the best interests of all South Africans to police poverty-stricken areas because that will eventually take care of the larger crime problem in the country.

The crime situation is further puzzling because South Africans, as an independent 2007 study by the Institute for Security Studies showed, are convinced that crime is worse than it was during 2004. However, the very same South Africans are the ones who are reporting an improved crime environment – and yet say they do not feel as safe as they felt about five years ago. This suggests, according to some, that crime is driven more by perception than reality, and that the irrationality brought on by the trauma of past experience compounds the situation.

The study, called the Victims of Crime Survey, was used to verify the official crime statistics delivered by the department of safety and security and to check the crime-reporting patterns of South Africans, who, it has been suggested, are too crime-weary to report incidents to the police. The tracking study, which compared data between 1998 and 2007, supported the notion that crime was declining or, alternatively, stabilising.

This is exactly what the police told South Africans when the department released official statistics for the period between March 2007 and April 2008. The police reported that the murder rate was at its lowest in 14 years. The statistics also showed that crime had declined in all the serious crime categories including murder: that out of every 100 000 South Africans some 38 were murdered, down from 40 in the previous period. As the Freedom Front Plus party rightly pointed out, this was not low enough: the world average per 100 000 citizens is a lowly five people.

In the same period the police reported that attempted murder was down by 7.5% and indecent assault and rape were also down. (However, rape statistics were only collected for nine months because of a change in the country's rape laws.) On the up were house robberies, car hijackings and business robberies, which increased by 13.5%, 4.4% and 47.4% respectively. More concerning in the statistics was an unusually high murder rate among children, which was up by close to 24%. Although coming off a small base, this trend, which was most prevalent in the Western Cape, is disturbing. The police and independent researchers alike attributed the trend to gang activity.

At the announcement of the statistics, former minister of safety and security Charles Nqakula was unrepentant in his belief that policing in South Africa was not the responsibility of the police alone and that other parts of society, such as families, and the government's social cluster should also play a role. This is probably what informs the latest thinking on addressing the crime scourge, which holds that the police will only win the war on crime if there is a single helicopter view of the crime situation across all relevant government departments such as social development, justice, and safety and security.

In a bid to deal better with the crime situation, the government embarked on an extensive review of the criminal justice system holistically, from the moment a crime is reported, all the way to its appearance on the court roll and onward until the sentencing of offenders. The review, headed by deputy minister of justice and constitutional development Johnny de Lange, revealed that the South African criminal justice system is dysfunctional. The report noted that police do not have new age investigative capabilities such as high-tech crime forensic labs and DNA analysis. It also revealed that crime-fighting efforts were hampered by the inability to integrate all government databases into one for enhanced crime fighting.

The police, for example, could not get access to the 30-odd-million fingerprints at the disposal of the department of home affairs. The closure of certain specialist units, the review showed, had depleted the police of competent detectives who could ensure that offenders met their fate. The methods employed by the police, according to the review, were archaic and harked back to the apartheid era when confessions were literally beaten out of suspects.

At the court level the study revealed a backlog of 70 000 cases and showed that the court system was not efficient enough in prosecuting cases. At the correctional services level the study revealed that the jails were crowded by prisoners who had committed minor offences but stayed in jail because they could not afford bail set as low as R200.

Following these findings, the government then took a decision to invest over R5-billion to overhaul the whole system and build a new database, enhance the crime labs in terms of both financial and human resources, buy new high-tech equipment to allow the police to do their jobs, and build a new DNA database to allow for scene-to-scene matching of DNA from possible offenders. The budget will also ensure much better pay for highly skilled policemen such as detectives and will also lead to prosecutors being paired with detectives to screen cases in an effort to ensure a better conviction rate.

This project is already under way and, barring a lack of political will, should revolutionise the way crime is fought in South Africa.

The 2010 World Cup has also bolstered crime-fighting efforts by ensuring an increase of the police force to over 240 000 officers by 2012, the acquisition of high-tech surveillance planes and helicopters, and the boosting of the South African Police Service's crowd management capabilities.

The Economy

If the South African economy were a person it could be described as schizophrenic. In a continent of underdeveloped countries, South Africa's economy stands out as pre-eminent. No other African country has the sheer national wealth or diversity of businesses, including some of the continent's biggest homegrown multinationals.

Visitors to the country are often surprised by the sophistication of the road and rail networks and highways, and electrification in the urban areas, which compare well with the rest of the world, not to mention Africa. The tap water is drinkable. Mobile phone coverage is good, backed by a workable fixed-line service. Internet coverage is increasing and costs are coming down, with long-delayed competition in telecommunication finally making itself felt. Add to this a functioning commercial legal system and a business environment that scores 32 out of 181 on the World Bank's ease of doing business index.

In terms of gross domestic product, the value of all economic activity in the country, and adjusting for the buying power of the local currency,

South Africa rubs shoulders with countries like Argentina, Thailand, Pakistan and Greece. GDP purely in US dollar terms at the end of 2008 was around $283-billion (almost R2-trillion at current prices). Yet the physical infrastructure is not matched by human development, and wealth is concentrated in a few hands. The population of 49-million is sharply divided along economic and racial lines.

Desperate rural poverty, a legacy of apartheid's predatory neglect, persists. The unemployment rate is stubbornly high, around 22%, and this excludes those so discouraged by a lack of job opportunities that they have given up looking for work altogether. Income inequality, still racially based, is matched only by countries in Latin America. The disparities are summed up in the metaphor of South Africa being a country with two economies, one belonging to the First World and the other to the Third World.

In human development, according to the United Nations, South Africa compares with little-known Vanuatu, the island whose flag is uncannily similar to South Africa's, and the small, landlocked, former Soviet republic of Tajikistan. Many people are completely reliant on the state, and are financially excluded, with coverage of the population through health, life and short-term insurance all low.

According to the Centre for Social Science Research at the University of Cape Town, around a quarter of the population earns below the equivalent of US$1 per day (adjusted for local purchasing power), compared to about a half in countries such as Kenya, Swaziland, Uganda and Senegal, but the figure is much higher than for other middle-income countries.

That South Africa's people experience the economy in vastly different ways is potential ammunition for populists. Advances in the general well-being since 1994 and the advent of democracy have been slow and hard-won. A contraction in the economy by almost 2% in the fourth quarter of 2008 marked the end of a decade of generally low but positive growth, a big contrast to the roller-coaster economy of the apartheid years.

The conservative approach can be defended by arguing that South Africa's ANC government had to be cautious precisely because of its redistributive agenda. It had to persuade foreign firms and funds that it was not financially irresponsible. Consequently, until the global economic crisis broke, South Africa pursued a policy of fiscal and monetary conservatism, under the leadership of finance minister Trevor Manuel at the National Treasury and governor Tito Mboweni at the Reserve Bank.

The Treasury reined in public spending and moved towards a budget surplus; the Reserve Bank doggedly pursued a policy of inflation targeting. Both have met with a torrent of criticism from the union movement. At the same time poverty has been ameliorated by a system of social grants with old age pensions at its centre, but extending as well to child support.

The result of the fiscal conservatism has been that when the global crisis hit, the finance minister could announce that the infrastructure programme could go ahead and he could increase the number of people getting social grants, without raising taxes or pushing the national budget so far into deficit as to mortgage the prospects of future generations. The projected budget deficit – the gap between what government rakes in and what it spends – for 2009/2010 is manageable at around –4%.

The deficit on the current account of the balance of payments, South Africa's chequing account with the world, is another matter. The Treasury expects this gap between our income from abroad and foreign spending to average around 7% a year for the next few years, despite a lower foreign-exchange value of the rand putting pressure on imports. This is high compared with other emerging markets, and likely to be worrying for investors.

The volatile rand currency unit is also of concern. The stated policy of the central bank is not to intervene in the currency market as it did disastrously in the Asian crisis. The floating currency does, however, provide a natural shock absorber for external financial disruption, allowing the bank to focus on inflation.

Though South Africa has evolved from being entirely dependent on exports of gold bullion into an economy where services dominate and exports are more diversified though still commodity-based, South African exports have underperformed relative to those of other emerging markets. This has meant that while the economy has grown, it has not grown strongly enough to make a real dent in unemployment.

Nonetheless, the overall wealth of South Africans has started to improve, even if it is unevenly shared. In 2007 gross national income per head had risen to its highest since the central bank started recording the figures. The figure stands at almost R40 000 in current prices, very roughly around $2 600 per head unadjusted for purchasing power parity (the *World Bank Atlas* method gives a figure of $5 760, close to Brazil and other Latin American countries).

The global financial and economic crisis is bound to throw some obstacles in the economy's path, which is already rockier than it should be because of high crime and HIV/Aids infection rates, and there may even be some reversal of steady economic progress. But the acknowledged sound governance of the financial sector and the fact that South African banks are capitalised in the local currency are important armour against the crisis. Also, South Africa is still a significant gold exporter, and this is one area where its economy has thrived before on bad news in the rest of the world.

Education

The education system has, broadly speaking, gone through three cycles since 1994. The years 1994 to 1999 were a period of policy overhaul. Under then-education minister Professor Sibusiso Bengu, new laws were conceptualised and written. Creating a new legislative framework for education was done with remarkable speed. From 1999 until 2004, with Kader Asmal cracking the whip as minister, the lagging implementation of policies picked up. But this period could perhaps be more appropriately defined as one in which the unintended outcomes of policies started to surface, demanding reviews and refinement. The last four years, since 2004, have been about consolidation, with minister of education Naledi Pandor placing heavy emphasis on getting the basics right.

In this period the education authorities have been prioritising the quality of education from the level of early childhood learning right through to the education they receive at university level, and putting systems and plans in place to make it happen. This could also be seen as a response to pressure from the National Treasury, which has been allocating the lion's share of the national budget to education year after year with a disappointing return on investment.

In addition to concerns about the quality of education, in particular for the poorest children, access to education has been prominent on Pandor's radar. Increasing the number of no-fee schools to 60% to prevent children from being excluded on the basis of their socioeconomic conditions has been one of the strategies to tackle access. But the distinction between schools that charge fees and no-fee schools has highlighted the class dimension that education has acquired in South Africa. Those who can pay for schooling buy quality, whereas those without the means have limited options.

Another strategy to improve access has been an ongoing focus on inclusion, which should be interpreted in the widest possible terms to mean providing access to education for children notwithstanding the barriers they may experience: whether disability, poverty, disease or sexual orientation. This approach applies across the board, starting with early childhood development (ECD). Recognising that the phase of learning from birth to nine years is critical for educational success, the government undertook in 2008 to speed up delivery. The target is to ensure that all children who enter grade one in 2010 should have had access to an accredited grade R (the reception year prior to grade one) programme. In 2008 only about half of the number of eligible grade R children were benefiting, but at the same time there were positive signs that provincial departments of education were setting up more sites.

Building on a firmer ECD foundation, the department of education launched its Foundations for Learning campaign in 2008 to bolster the reading, writing and mathematical skills of children in grades R to six. The campaign provides for clearer guidelines for educators to teach these areas as well as additional resources in the poorest schools. This strategy is a response to the fact that South African learners have consistently come out at the bottom of the heap in a number of international studies.

The targeted teaching of reading, writing and mathematical skills has also been seen as a response to shortcomings in the outcomes-based curriculum. After the initial introduction of outcomes-based education in 1998, many teachers wrongly assumed they no longer had to teach the three Rs. This misconception has, by and large, been addressed by the department, together with other shortcomings that were identified in the review of the curriculum in 2000. These included the overcrowding of the plan, which meant teachers had too much to teach, and the under-specification of the curriculum, which meant they did not have enough detail of the content they had to tackle.

The revised national curriculum statement up to grade nine was introduced from 2004 and paved the way for the new grade ten to twelve curriculum that was introduced in 2006. Consequently, the first national senior certificate examination in 2008 replaced what was commonly known as 'matric'. It was the first time a truly national examination was written in South Africa, and it yielded a pass rate of 62.5%.

In an effort to provide more opportunities for tertiary study, in particular in critical skills areas such as construction, financial management and tourism, the department has been paying special attention to further education and training (FET) colleges. A total of R1.9-billion has been allocated to the recapitalisation of the 50 FET (technical) colleges over three years, a period which has just ended. This involved the drafting of a more relevant and modern curriculum for the sector as well as the refurbishment of campuses. But the FET college sector still battles on, not being, in the system's lifelong learning-speak, adequately connected to open pathways to the higher education university sector, still having poor pass rates and struggling to attract the best teaching staff. And despite the best efforts from various ministers to make delivery in education a reality, these plans continue to be bedevilled by weak provincial education departments, many of which don't have the management capacity to support the centrally initiated projects to improve quality and broaden access.

Like the general and further education bands, higher education in South Africa underwent dramatic changes from about 2004 after former education minister Asmal announced the merger of institutions, reducing the number of universities and technikons from 36 to 23. The intention was to form a single, coherent education system accessible to many students and to move away from a fragmented system where institutions were divided on the basis of race.

In the new higher education landscape, some research universities like Cape Town, Stellenbosch and the Witwatersrand were left untouched, while others were merged, like the (historically white) University of

Natal with the (historically Indian) University of Durban-Westville. Technikons merged with each other (Technikon North West, Technikon Northern Gauteng and Technikon Pretoria), while comprehensive universities which offer degrees and diplomas were formed through the mergers of technikons and universities. A case in point is the University of Johannesburg, a merger between (historically white) Rand Afrikaans University, (historically white) Technikon Witwatersrand and the Soweto campus of (historically black) Vista University.

The higher education sector is divided into three.

Universities: Cape Town, Fort Hare, Free State, KwaZulu-Natal, Limpopo, North West, Pretoria, Rhodes, Stellenbosch, Western Cape and Witwatersrand.

Universities of Technology: Cape Peninsula, Central, Durban, Mangosuthu, Tshwane and Vaal.

Comprehensive universities: University of Johannesburg, Nelson Mandela Metropolitan, University of South Africa, University of Venda for Science and Technology, Walter Sisulu University, and University of Zululand.

The merged institutions have struggled to come up with a new identity as they are an assimilation of different institutional cultures, work ethics and academic standards, and a mish-mash of new and old infrastructure. While R2.1-billion was allocated up to 2007 to support direct recapitalisation and the infrastructure costs of merged institutions, and to alleviate the previous debt of some of these institutions before the mergers, problems persist.

In some cases there are unequal services across campuses, a difference in the state of infrastructure and the quality of courses on offer, while students tend to continue life without interacting with their counterparts on other campuses. Student protests have occurred as a result of poor service delivery, while management structures are also problematic. Experience of university mergers in the UK shows that it can take up to 20 years for issues and problems to be bedded down. The ANC government has hinted at a review of some of these mergers, which are seen as marriages of convenience.

Meanwhile, a physical renaissance is occurring at several universities:

R3.9-billion was allocated to construct new buildings and refurbish older ones, as well as improve teaching and learning resources and library facilities. The funds are also earmarked to boost graduate outputs and produce more science, engineering and technology graduates. This is the first major government allocation to institutions in the past 30 years. There was no major infrastructure investment in the sector during the 20 years prior to the demise of apartheid, or during the first 10 years of democracy, when the new education department was finding its feet. The sector creaked under the pressure to increase student enrolment, with inadequate facilities to support this growth.

The R3.9-billion is being allocated to universities according to their needs, with a bias towards historically black universities. The object is to upgrade facilities so that disparities in learning, teaching and research infrastructure are evened out. Furthermore, another R3.2-billion is being allocated to universities in 2010/11–2011/12, earmarked specifically to help the higher education sector achieve national social and economic development goals.

Despite this huge expenditure on public higher education, a high student drop-out rate haunts the sector. Nearly 50% of undergraduate students either drop out or fail, due to a range of socio–economic problems and a school system that does not prepare them adequately for higher learning. This is costing the taxpayer billions of rands and Pandor has asked her advisory body, the Council on Higher Education, to investigate the viability of a four-year undergraduate degree, where students are taught basic literacy and numeric skills. Some universities already offer extended degree programmes to cater for ill-prepared students.

In 2009, more first-year students than before were accepted into universities as a result of the new national senior certificate exam, which some critics say allowed learners to achieve higher-than-normal pass rates in mathematics. Some universities have had to scramble to accommodate these students and the system has experienced the 'massification' of the sector. Whether these new students, who are the first to pass a school exit exam under the controversial outcomes-based education system, have the skills to cope will be revealed in the June and November examinations.

Academics are meanwhile leaving the sector for the corporate world, which entices them with higher salaries. While their workloads have increased, they are under pressure to publish, and Pandor has often said that she admires the fact that many continue to put up with the strains and demands of the sector.

The declining subsidisation of universities from about 2000 to 2006 could be changing, with government putting in more funds for block grants or subsidies. Finance minister Trevor Manuel has announced that universities will receive an extra R700-million over the medium term to cope with student growth, while the education department has announced that an additional R337-million is being given to universities to help keep tuition fee increases down.

Many analysts are hopeful that if additional funds are directed to universities, this may assist them in realising national goals of boosting research and graduate outputs. But for this to happen, the increase in subsidisation needs to occur steadily over the next 10 years.

Environment

South Africa has more biodiversity than most countries, with 299 species of mammals and 858 species of birds, and a floral kingdom in the Cape that is both the smallest and the richest among the five such kingdoms worldwide. But despite its wealth of flora and fauna, the impact of climate change and South Africa's international profile in that area, environment still takes a back seat in South African politics and is seen as one of the weakest Cabinet posts.

Environmental legislation has strengthened since the ANC took office, and some of the laws to protect the environment are among the most progressive in the world. The governmental custodian of the environment is the department of environmental affairs and tourism, which has done useful work in revising old legislation around pollution and waste, as well as managing development. But in many ways the environment is still seen as a soft political issue and many of the laws pay only lip-service to severe challenges. Environmental protection in South Africa still equals anti-progress and anti-prosperity for many businesses and, sadly, for many politicians.

Despite their efforts, there are still gaps in the law. The environmental impact assessment (EIA), for example, required for a development to take place is often just seen as a rubber stamp by developers. Critics have raised fears that the EIA process is open to abuse because the consultants who conduct the assessments are paid by the developers.

The department of minerals and energy oversees the EIAs related to the mining industry. Sceptics have pointed out that the environment will always be the loser in this process because the department's mandate is to promote mining, not to protect the environment. Even though this law is set to change in the near future, quite a lot of damage has already been done by mining projects that were approved without the necessary oversight from the department of environmental affairs and tourism.

A mining licence was granted to an Australian mining company in the biodiverse hotspot of Pondoland, despite ferocious objections from environmentalists and much of the community affected. In Mpumalanga mining houses are also queuing up to mine coal in some of South Africa's most vulnerable wetland areas and, far from regulating them, the minerals and energy department is encouraging their operations, citing South Africa's growing economy and thirst for coal as an excuse to approve the operations. A mining licence has also been granted to mine coal on the doorstep of one of South Africa's World Heritage areas, Mapungubwe.

Blackouts that stretched over several weeks in early 2008 have encouraged the opening of new areas for coal mining. Eskom provides 95% of the country's power, most of it produced by coal. The crisis was caused by a number of factors, including poor maintenance, a lack of planning, and low coal reserves, and was so serious that the country's largest gold, platinum and diamond producers had to shut their underground mines for a week when they were told their electricity supply could not be guaranteed. Businesses and households were then subjected to a round of 'load-shedding', or planned blackouts on an announced schedule, lasting several hours, several times a week. The blackouts sparked a national crisis when it emerged that the government had been warned about the problems as early as 1999 but had done little to improve infrastructure during a period of rapid economic growth.

South Africa's appetite for coal-fired power plants comes up against the country's prominent stand in dealing with climate change. Under the leadership of environment minister Marthinus van Schalkwyk, South Africa has embraced the concept, promoting it to the forefront of environmental politics.

South Africa's environment will suffer from the effects of climate change, with the east of the country destined to become wetter and more prone to storms and floods, while the west of the country will dry out and be more prone to droughts. South Africa's poor will be the most vulnerable. The Cape floral kingdom's biodiversity is also threatened by climate change. At the same time South Africa, with its addiction to a coal economy, is Africa's biggest carbon emitter and will have to cut down on its greenhouse gases if it is going to limit the effects of climate change.

At the end of 2009, South Africa is expected to be a star negotiator at the United Nations climate change conference in Copenhagen, when a new treaty (to follow that of the current Kyoto protocol) is set to be launched. Under the Kyoto protocol only developed countries have to cap their greenhouse gas emissions, but under the expected Copenhagen protocol, developing nations such as China, India, Brazil and South Africa, whose economies are growing at a rapid pace, will also have to take on some form of an emissions cap.

It is not only about appearing as a major player on the world stage. South Africa's water infrastructure faces an 'Eskom situation'; climate change is exacerbating problems caused by municipalities, especially in rural areas, allowing the infrastructure to deteriorate in their water treatment plants. Cholera appears in scattered locations from time to time: in Delmas, Mpumalanga province, three years ago; in Eastern Cape villages in 2007 and again in 2008; and in 2009 in Limpopo province, allegedly imported from Zimbabwe, where water treatment systems had broken down completely.

Several environmental reports have indicated that South Africa's rivers are not up to scratch, with pollution killing crocodiles in Kruger Park rivers and some of the rivers running through the game reserve dry during winter months. A controversial report by Dr Anthony Turton, a senior researcher at the Council for Scientific and Industrial Research (CSIR), warned that the country had run out of surplus water, with 98% of it already allocated. With many rivers and dams already highly polluted

– from, among other causes, gold and coal mining and an accumulation of nutrients encouraging the growth of algae, depleting shallow waters of oxygen – there was no capacity to dilute these effluents. Turton – who was suspended by the CSIR and his paper withdrawn by his employers because, among other reasons, it was disturbing – warned of a future of social instability unless the crisis was dealt with.

The South African Institution of Civil Engineering and the Water Institute of Southern Africa have reported that the recruitment and education of engineers and water scientists are up against a 'crucial bottleneck'. About 12% of the population, or 1.34-million households, still lack water services. The bucket system of sanitation still operates in some provinces and 5% of municipalities do not meet drinking-water quality standards.

Early in 2009, the International Union for the Conservation of Nature (IUCN) revealed that many species of freshwater fish, amphibians, shellfish and insects in southern Africa were at threat. A study of 1 279 freshwater species across southern Africa found that 7% are at risk of extinction. Of the 94 threatened species, 78 are found in South Africa.

Environmental reports in South Africa suggest a number of rivers whose quality is highly suspect. They include the Vaal, Magalies and Jukskei rivers in Gauteng, the Olifants River in Mpumalanga and KwaZulu-Natal's Umgeni River. Several of these rivers contained unacceptably high volumes of *e.coli* bacteria. A major danger is that pollution in some areas can well have filtered into ground water already.

There is some hope on the horizon: in early December 2008, the South African Cabinet approved the implementation of phase two of the Lesotho Highlands Project, in which water will be supplied from Lesotho to Gauteng and the Vaal River.

Although so far the environment is still a relatively small player in local politics, the search for resources and the legacy that current political decisions about the environment will leave for future generations will only increase the important role of the environment.

The hope is that the new global market which arises from the ashes of the global credit crunch will be much greener and incorporate the environment much more thoroughly. New industries incorporating renewable energy will create jobs out of solar- and wind-power manufacturing – so-called green jobs.

Foreign Affairs

For the past five years South African foreign policy has focused heavily on the promotion of South–South relationships, an emphasis driven by the government's desire to create a stronger platform for countries of the South to voice their opinions and influence matters at a global level. This objective has been pursued through the creation of new alliances such as the India-Brazil-South Africa (Ibsa) forum, as well as through vocal leadership roles in the Group of 77 and the Non-Aligned Movement, and in the lobby for the expansion of the United Nations Security Council to include permanent representatives from Latin American and African countries.

South Africa has also maintained good relations with countries from the North such as the United Kingdom, the United States and various European countries, although these relationships are to a great extent dictated by the imperatives of trade relations and agreements.

Within Africa, South Africa has invested significant time and resources in conflict management and mediation, and in contributing to post-conflict reconstruction. South Africa continues to be the single largest financial contributor to the African Union and is a strong proponent of strengthening the continental body. It has not, however, supported Libyan leader Muammar Gaddafi's push for the immediate creation of a United States of Africa.

South–South relations

The Ibsa formation was created in 2003 and is intended to provide a vehicle for coordination on key multilateral issues facing India, Brazil and South Africa. South Africa is by far the smallest of the three members, both in terms of population size and economic strength, with both Brazil and India having economies four times the size of South Africa's. Analysts agree that the Ibsa forum has yet to have any real impact. Still, South Africa's association with these two political and economic heavyweights is seen as an important boost for the country's image and influence in the

257

rest of the world. South African trade with Brazil amounted to $1.3-billion and trade with India amounted to $2.3-billion.

South Africa in Africa

Former president Thabo Mbeki made South Africa's involvement in the rest of the continent a priority of his foreign policy. The country has provided technical and financial input in the areas of security sector reform, civil service reform and election management in the Democratic Republic of Congo (DRC), and Mbeki also frequently intervened in order to keep the arduous 2003–6 transition on track.

South Africa continues to play a key role in the Burundian peace process through the facilitator, former minister for safety and security Charles Nqakula. South Africa's success in Côte d'Ivoire has been more limited; after years of shepherding the peace process, Mbeki withdrew from his role as mediator in 2005 largely as a result of regional dynamics and a perception that he was too close to Ivorian president Laurent Gbagbo.

South Africa has peacekeeping troops with the United Nations mission in the DRC, the United Nations–African Union hybrid mission in Darfur and the United Nations mission in Côte d'Ivoire. The new ANC government is expected to be less involved in foreign, especially African, matters.

Relations between South Africa and the continent's other economic giants – Nigeria and Angola especially – have occasionally been tense, with the governments of the two sometimes resentful of South Africa's presumption that it is the only candidate for the role of 'elder statesman' on the continent. Relations with Angola are particularly tense, especially as Angola's economic and military strength allows it to forge its own strong unilateral links to key African countries.

Although it is among the most stable countries in Africa, and has the most liberal Constitution and the most transparent and democratic institutions, South Africa has not always acted as a champion of good governance. Aside from its support for the government of Robert Mugabe in Zimbabwe, South Africa has shown its support for Sudanese president Omar al-Bashir and has resisted transparency in the African Peer Review

Mechanism's report on South Africa. The Mbeki government was also the first to congratulate Umaru Yar'Adua, the winner of the seriously flawed 2007 presidential election in Nigeria. Change at the top made little difference: in March 2009, at the behest of China, the government headed by Kgalema Motlanthe refused to issue a visa to the Dalai Lama, who had been invited by fellow Nobel laureates to attend an international peace conference in Johannesburg. As a result, the conference was cancelled.

Zimbabwe

Much has been written about South African policy – or what some see as a lack thereof – towards Zimbabwe. The long-standing political and economic crisis in Zimbabwe has seen millions of Zimbabweans flee to neighbouring South Africa since 2000, and there is little doubt that the crisis next door has had a negative impact on South Africa.

Nonetheless, the Mbeki government maintained an apparent sense of loyalty towards the Mugabe government, refusing to criticise the president outright or to call for a change in government. Pursuing an official policy of 'silent diplomacy', South Africa has doggedly insisted that Zimbabwe must find its own solution to its problems. It has also resisted international urging, in particular from the UK and the US, to increase pressure on Mugabe.

By 2009, a government of national unity had been formed, and there were tentative hopes that Zimbabwe was back on the road to recovery. Jacob Zuma has been a vocal critic of the Mugabe government, but it is not clear whether his government would pursue a policy less pro-Mugabe than its predecessors.

South Africa at the United Nations

South Africa's voting record at the United Nations over the past few years has disappointed human rights activists from countries such as Burma (Myanmar) and Zimbabwe, and placed it at odds with the UK and US over issues such as Iran.

In 2007 South Africa voted against a UN Security Council resolution criticising the Myanmar military government. South Africa has also consistently blocked attempts by the UN Security Council to impose sanctions on Zimbabwe or to censure Mugabe. South Africa's apparent decision to side with the leaders of oppressive governments and its argument that domestic issues must be resolved internally have surprised many, especially as international support and activism contributed significantly to its own struggle to overthrow the apartheid regime.

South Africa spearheaded opposition to imposing sanctions on Iran for evading UN attempts to investigate its nuclear programme, angering the US, UK and European nations. Its attempts failed, but in the process it won the approval of many developing countries which felt that it demonstrated to the five permanent Security Council members that less powerful nations are also a force to be reckoned with.

Gay Rights

Public perceptions of the Constitution, and how its provisions filter down to all citizens, were subjected to a surprisingly severe test when the Constitutional Court told Parliament to find a remedy for same-sex couples whose rights were being denied if they were unable to marry. The issue of same-sex marriage highlighted the gap between some social attitudes and a Constitution frequently declared the most progressive in the world, while offering a test case for the extension of equality jurisprudence based on the founding document of our democracy.

Judge Albie Sachs handed down the judgment on December 1 2005, noting that the exclusion of same-sex couples from the provisions of the Marriage Act of 1961 (for which marriage, by definition, is a bond between a man and a woman) contributed to social prejudice. He gave Parliament a year in which to provide a remedy, which ultimately came in the form of another marriage law, the Civil Union Act – with Parliament making the judge's deadline by one day.

In the meantime, that year's delay had led to an outpouring of distaste at the notion of same-sex marriage when the legislation passed through Parliament, for the process included public submissions. Organisations ranging from conservative religious groups to the Congress of Traditional Leaders of South Africa (Contralesa) and groups such as Doctors for Life vehemently opposed the very idea of same-sex marriage. Often the debate degenerated into an expression of deep distaste for lesbian, gay, bisexual, transgender and intersexed (LGBTI) people in general.

Contralesa had put on its own road show tackling the issue before the legislation even got to Parliament. In Parliament, Contralesa called for an amendment to the Constitution to prevent same-sex marriage or, failing that, for a national referendum on the issue. Other public hearings, mandated by Parliament, took place elsewhere in South Africa, with more vociferous opposition expressed, alongside fierce lobbying by LGBTI activists.

The religious discourse was based on the idea of sin (homosexuality) and the 'sanctity of marriage' (for heterosexuals). The African traditional objection was based on the notion that such rights would contribute further to the breakdown of family bonds, the assault on traditional African culture (in the form of institutions such as lobola), and the decline of the patriarchy – though the issue was not always stated that way. The ANC's parliamentary caucus had to bring its whips to bear to ensure that the legislation, in its final form, was passed.

Yet the Civil Union Act was the culmination of a long campaign for LGBTI rights, one that went back to the earliest days of the negotiations towards a new democracy. The issue of gay rights seemed an important test for the new state's commitment to human rights in general – those that protect minorities are often the litmus test. In 1990, the first lesbian and gay pride march agitated publicly for such rights, while behind-the-scenes lobbying continued. In 1997, soon after the final Constitution was ratified, the common-law crime of sodomy (historically used to persecute gay men) was struck down. From that date to the promulgation of the Civil Union Act on November 30 2006, a series of cases forced the law to accommodate the rights of LGBTI people – in emigration, pensions, adoption, and other areas.

The logical end-point of that series of cases was the same-sex marriage case, which sprang from the desire of a lesbian couple, Marié Fourie and Cecelia Bonthuys, to marry in church and with the same rights as a straight couple. Supported by the National Coalition for Gay and Lesbian Equality, their case went from the Pretoria High Court to the Supreme Court of Appeal, which affirmed their right to equal treatment, and then finally reached the Constitutional Court and led to the Sachs ruling.

In the year during which Parliament developed the requisite legislation, the draft Bill went through several changes. There was opposition to simply reading the words 'or spouse' after 'husband' or 'wife' into the Marriage Act, which would have been one legal remedy. So Parliament drafted new, non-gender-specific legislation, and, after some confusion and, ultimately, frank consultation with activists and legal experts, it reached its final form as the Civil Union Act. Earlier drafts had not, in fact, given same-sex couples precisely equal marriage rights (such as the capacity to regard such a union as a marriage and not just a civil union).

In Parliament, the Bill was opposed by the Inkatha Freedom Party, the Freedom Front Plus, and the African Christian Democratic Party, whose leader Kenneth Meshoe declared that the existence of the Bill made this 'the saddest day of the 12 years of our democratic Parliament'. The Independent Democrats opposed the Bill because it felt it was still discriminatory. It was supported by the Democratic Alliance, and in the end by the ANC's parliamentary majority. Leaders such as then-minister of defence Mosiuoa Lekota spoke out in favour of it. The ruling party realised there was no way around the Constitution, even if many of its members and representatives were scandalised by the Bill; the ANC did its duty and forced it through.

For many in the LGBTI community, the Civil Union Act was a triumph; it felt like an affirmation long denied, and a rush of same-sex marriages followed. Some of its provisions, however, left unhappiness: it provided opt-out clauses for home affairs officials to refuse to marry same-sex couples, while they would not, under the Marriage Act, be able to refuse to marry a heterosexual couple. Further, it required religious bodies to apply for certification for its marriage officers as a denomination, disallowing the application of individual marriage officers. This meant that the mainstream Christian churches (not to mention Muslim religious groups) did not apply and simply let the matter fester in most cases, though on occasion it led to increased internal debate and consideration of the rights of LGBTI people within such religious communities. One prominent Methodist minister, at least, left the church because it refused to entertain the idea of same-sex marriages.

Most troubling, though, is the apparent increase in violence perpetrated against LGBTI people, particularly lesbian women, which seems to have come along with the greater visibility and social legitimacy afforded by the Civil Union Act, and perhaps by the tempers raised during the parliamentary process. Several such hate crimes have been perpetrated within the last few years, some of which have come to court. The murder of Sizakele Sigasa and Salome Masooa on July 7 2007, just one of many such crimes, led to the 07-07-07 campaign to stop violence against LGBTI people; it is continuing.

Health

South Africa has the shame of being one of the few stable countries in the world to have seen a worsening of key healthcare indicators, as life expectancy has continued to fall while maternal and child mortality rates have risen. Much of this is due to the ever-increasing spread of HIV and the accompanying rise of an epidemic of TB.

Even apart from these two devastating epidemics, South Africa's healthcare system is under attack from two sides. The infectious diseases typical of a developing country continue to take their toll, but increasingly so too do the so-called 'lifestyle' illnesses associated with growing affluence, such as obesity, diabetes and hypertension. It is estimated that approximately 75% of black women in South Africa are overweight or obese, as are 42% of white women. More than half of white men (56%) are estimated to be overweight or obese; so are 49% of black men.

The HIV and TB epidemics have continued to spread and to facilitate each other. TB cure rates in South Africa are abysmal at about 57%, while the country is estimated to have the fourth highest burden of TB disease in the world. Poor patient treatment and management have contributed to the spread of drug-resistant forms of TB, which are frequently spread in healthcare settings due to poor infection control. The 2008 South African Tuberculosis Conference heard that there is no information on almost a third of TB patients nationally. The department of health has failed to react swiftly to the TB epidemic, despite repeated calls for greater integration of HIV and TB treatment and community-based treatment in order to improve both patient discovery and care.

The failure to adapt to the resources available has also been seen in the development of the antiretroviral programme. Although now the largest in the world, the system had been close to reaching capacity due in part to departmental insistence that clinicians, rather than trained nurses, continue to monitor patients who are healthy and stable on chronic treatment. With approximately 5.5-million South Africans estimated to be living with HIV, South Africa's antiretroviral programme needs to expand hugely in order not only to soak up existing need but also to adjust to the demands of patients who will sicken in the future. It presents a management problem of unprecedented proportions, and much of the progress made to date has been due to the resources supplied by external funders rather than by the department of health itself.

The department suffered a steady decline of both skills and reputation under the leadership of former minister Manto Tshabalala-Msimang. The good news is that the past five years have seen an increase in public healthcare staff to approximately 251 000. The bad news is that this is roughly the same head count as in 1997, while the demands on the public healthcare system have rocketed.

An ongoing issue for the national and provincial departments of health has been poor financial and strategic planning. Even when the department of health has strategic plans, implementing them has been an ongoing problem because of lack of capacity and accountability. Another persistent problem has been lack of accountability at all levels of the healthcare system, as demonstrated by outbreaks of infectious diseases in healthcare facilities – including the transmission of drug-resistant TB. A third issue was highlighted by a study that estimated that in 2008 approximately 260 mothers, babies or children died every day – representing an infant death approximately every eight minutes. Infectious diseases and malnutrition are the biggest killers of children, but a large proportion of infant and maternal deaths could be prevented by better medical care.

One of the high-profile planning or management failures came in late 2008, when the Free State department of health placed a moratorium on new patients starting antiretroviral therapy. The causes of this decision have yet to be clearly revealed, but the furore that erupted over that example of curious healthcare rationing both followed and preceded a steady trickle of tales of shortages of basic medical supplies at facilities around the country.

A problem South Africa shares with many other developing, and some developed, countries is a difficulty in retaining healthcare workers. The closure of nursing colleges led to a shortage of these critical workers, a situation compounded by the better salaries paid in the private sector and the lure of working overseas. Working outside South Africa, or working in the private sector, has also resulted in a gross shortage of specialist healthcare workers in the public sector. The problem is aggravated because the loss of senior, experienced specialists means there are fewer people to pass on their skills and to provide mentorship.

The government has instituted various measures to deal with these problems, such as the requirement of two years of community service for a range of healthcare workers upon graduation. However, the shortage is so gross and the time lag for training is so extended that the healthcare sector can expect a shortage of skilled workers for some years to come.

Much of the problem in retaining staff lies not just in the salary differentials, but also in the environment in which they work – again reflecting the impact of poor management.

Regulation of the private healthcare sector has been a major point of discussion over the past five years but is still very much in progress. Legislation has repeatedly failed to be enacted, either because it has not made it through the parliamentary process or because of court challenges from stakeholders.

The erratic pronouncements of Tshabalala-Msimang on a range of issues, including evidence-based medicine, and most notoriously the potential role of beetroot, lemon juice and garlic in helping Aids patients, added to the low morale of the department of health. Her replacement as minister by Barbara Hogan was seen as something of a new start for the department.

Intelligence

If corruption is the rhino of our democracy – large, noisy and causing havoc everywhere – then intelligence is its elephant cousin: no less weighty, but less visible, thanks to a combination of camouflage and convention.

The impact of the intelligence services on South Africa's transition was immense. Intelligence was a covert shaper of events, from the information scandal leaks in the late 1970s that ushered in the era of P.W. Botha and his Military Intelligence backers, to the clandestine meetings involving senior figures of the old National Intelligence Service with Thabo Mbeki and Jacob Zuma, which began the process of a negotiated settlement.

But if there were hopes that the post-1994 constitutional era would deliver a more open politics, less driven by the machinations of intelligence agencies – public or private – then the period since 2004 has comprehensively dashed those expectations.

The dark clouds had already gathered around the Hefer Commission of late 2003. That piece of political theatre was supposed to vindicate prosecutions boss Bulelani Ngcuka and humiliate those accusing him of having been an apartheid spy: struggle stalwarts Mac Maharaj and Moe Shaik. Instead the commission exposed the political impact of spies and spying as well as the way our security services might easily be politicised and abused despite their constitutional fig-leaf. Since then the storm has truly broken. Factional strife has infected the conduct of intelligence in profound ways.

After the 2004 election the security services were purged of those perceived as not sufficiently loyal to Mbeki. Out went minister Lindiwe Sisulu, moved from intelligence to housing; out went Vusi Mavimbela, retreating from his position as director-general at the National Intelligence Agency (NIA) to bide his time in Tokyo Sexwale's Mvelaphanda corporation; out went defence force chief Siphiwe Nyanda, taking 'early retirement' to regroup in the arms business.

The purges backfired: the dismissal of Jacob Zuma as deputy president in mid-2005 brought together a 'coalition of the wounded' that drew strength from the historical ties of its main players to the intelligence community. The coalition launched a highly successful campaign to discredit the one agency it did not control: the National Prosecuting Authority's Directorate of Special Operations, better known as the Scorpions.

In December 2004 Mbeki had chosen a perceived loyalist to head up domestic intelligence at the NIA: Billy Masetlha, who had previously led the presidential support unit, a de facto presidential intelligence unit.

It was a remarkable error of judgement. By August 2005 Masetlha was involved in a stand-off with police commissioner Jackie Selebi – perceived as another Mbeki man – outside ANC headquarters at Luthuli House. The two were jockeying for access to the building after a mysterious fire that might have exposed sensitive documents in the office of ANC secretary-general Kgalema Motlanthe.

By then Masetlha was also deeply embroiled in a hoax email saga. The emails – a bizarre concoction of fact and fantastic misinformation – purported to be intercepts of messages between Mbeki's most prominent backers: businessman Saki Macozoma, intelligence minister Ronnie Kasrils, deputy president Phumzile Mlambo-Ngcuka and her husband, who had retired hurt from the political fray, stepping down as national director of public prosecutions after the bruising public confrontation with 'Mac & Moe'. The emails supposedly revealed a political plot against Zuma involving Mbeki's supporters, together with a weird right-wing grouping and members of the Scorpions unit, regarded by Zuma supporters as part of the conspiracy against him.

On October 19 2005, Masetlha played his hand, making a secret report to Mbeki about the anti-Zuma 'plot'. He was suspended the next day and later dismissed, after a report by the inspector-general of intelligence accused him of misusing his powers to launch a politically motivated intelligence operation. He became an influential figure in the growing mobilisation of anti-Mbeki forces.

In 2007 the tempo of intelligence intrusion into the domestic political realm increased markedly. In May, the anti-Scorpions campaign – part of a drive to discredit the charges laid against Zuma by the unit – received a considerable fillip when the oddly named 'Browse Mole' report was leaked to trade union federation Cosatu, one of Zuma's key allies in his power struggle with Mbeki. The document showed the Scorpions were engaged in intelligence gathering in relation to Zuma, in particular about allegations that he was receiving funding from Angola and Libya. It had almost certainly been leaked from within the NIA or the police and was seized on as evidence that the Scorpions were engaged in a political campaign against Zuma and were acting outside their legal mandate by gathering intelligence.

Then in October, another internal Scorpions memo found its way into the newspapers – again apparently courtesy of police crime intelligence or the NIA. This memo purported to be a record of a management meeting of the Scorpions held in the wake of the mid-2007 ANC policy conference, which had resolved to disband the unit. It revealed a discussion, led by Scorpions boss Leonard McCarthy, of ways in which the unit could lobby to safeguard its continued existence. But the Scorpions' investigation during 2007 of Selebi, by that time Mbeki's most powerful remaining ally, removed any remaining political insulation the agency might once have enjoyed. Mbeki's bid to protect Selebi led to the extraordinary suspension of Vusi Pikoli, the national director of public prosecutions, who had refused to back off.

At the start of 2008 the country was also treated to the spectacle of the deployment of new NIA director-general Manala Manzini and acting head of crime intelligence Mulangi Mphego in what appeared to be a bid to suborn the main witness against Selebi.

By the beginning of 2009, the counter-purge was in full swing. Mbeki, ousted from the ANC leadership at the party's national conference in December 2007, had been recalled as president before his term was up. Pikoli, who had demonstrated his willingness to resist pressure as much from Mbeki as from the Zuma lobby, had been dismissed by the new ANC leadership, which cited his handling of the Browse Mole report and other spurious security concerns. Mphego, regarded as too much of an Mbeki man, was in court fighting against what he said was a bid to gerrymander the selection process for a new crime intelligence boss in order to appoint a Zuma loyalist.

Both Masetlha and Nyanda seemed set for a return to positions of power in the security establishment. Zuma ally Dr Siyabonga Cwele had replaced Mbeki ally Ronnie Kasrils as intelligence minister and – of more concern – had quietly buried an independent review commission report prepared in the aftermath of the hoax email debacle. Central to the report was the recommendation that the NIA's broad mandate, which allowed it to get involved in domestic political issues, be considerably tightened. But it appears that mandate is a tool too powerful for the incumbent political faction to discard.

In the past five years we have witnessed enough to realise that the intelligence elephant is a rogue that should be penned and tamed. Instead it seems we may expect its rampages to become even more brazen and widespread.

Labour

Retrenchments and shorter working hours are fast becoming a reality in South Africa and the world over. Since the news of the global financial meltdown in 2008, job losses instead of job creation have taken centre-stage, as most companies battle to cut costs in the quickest and easiest way to deal with the challenges of the crisis. The International Labour Organisation has predicted that more than 20-million workers throughout the world will lose their jobs before the end of 2009. In South Africa, it is expected that more than 300 000 jobs will be shed in the same period. Already, over 60 000 jobs in the mining, manufacturing and automotive sectors have been lost between June 2008 and February 2009.

Statistics show that the number of unemployed in South Africa has nearly doubled, from 2.4-million in 1994 to 4.4-million in 2008. Although Stats SA has put the official unemployment rate at 25% of the economically active population, labour unions estimate the figure to be around 40%.

With the country's economic growth slowing down, it looks more and more unlikely that the government's goal of halving unemployment by 2014 will be realised. Figures released by Stats SA in February 2009 showed that in the fourth quarter of 2008, the country's economy contracted for the first time in 10 years, indicating that South Africa may slip into recession. The country's manufacturing output dropped by 11.1% from January 2008 to January 2009 – the biggest fall in one year since 1991. Manufacturing production for the three months up to January 2009 fell by 8.1% compared to a 5.8% fall in the previous three-month period.

The deteriorating economic situation forced Reserve Bank governor Tito Mboweni to take the unusual move of cutting the repo rate by 1.5% in two stages after December 2008, down to 10.5%. Mboweni increased interest rates to 11.5% in 2008 as a result of rocketing food, electricity and fuel prices. This pushed the inflation rate to over 10%, way over the 3–6% official target range.

With the impact of the financial crisis starting to hit South Africans, markets are betting on further cuts of up to a cumulative four percentage points before the end of 2009. Labour federation Cosatu believes that cutting the cost of borrowing will help sustain and promote investment and thus save and create jobs. 'We have repeatedly warned that the Reserve Bank's obsession with "inflation-targeting" would lead to slower economic growth and far too few new jobs. Tragically this was an underestimate of the danger. It has now in fact led to economic decline and hundreds of retrenchments,' says Cosatu's spokesperson Patrick Craven. 'This could have been far less serious if the Bank had heeded our call years ago to base its policy on growth-targeting and employment-targeting as well as fighting inflation.' Craven says that continued retrenchments across various sectors of the economy are likely to reduce union membership going forward.

Earlier in 2009, government, labour and business took a bold step by adopting a framework agreement to counter the effects of the world recession. The agreement includes a package of measures, including a review of interest rate policy, an effort to save a maximum number of jobs and to promote future growth, particularly in manufacturing and the labour-intensive sectors.

Cosatu general secretary Zwelinzima Vavi in March 2009 told a national bargaining conference of the Chemical, Energy, Paper, Printing, Wood and Allied Workers' Union that the time for unions to review their bargaining strategy had come. 'As always, but particularly in these difficult times, we may have to make difficult, even painful compromises in the bargaining chambers, to safeguard the best interests of our members. But our top priority must be to make sure that workers do not bear the full brunt of the crisis,' he said. However, Vavi said Cosatu rejected the argument by some employers that the answer to the financial crisis was to reduce the cost of doing business by cutting wages. 'South Africa still has one of the highest levels of inequality in the world, as a result of the apartheid wage gap. We cannot expect workers to take cuts in their living standards while their employers continue to rake in huge salaries and bonuses,' he argued.

Among the cost-cutting measures that many companies are using to deal with the financial downturn are the freezing of posts, the cutting of executive bonuses and workers' annual wage increases, a reduction of working hours, and the offer of retrenchment packages to employees.

Craven said that Cosatu expects the new ANC administration led by Jacob Zuma to adopt radically different economic policies 'if we are to implement the ANC manifesto pledges to build and accelerate a sustainable, equitable and inclusive economic growth path and create decent work opportunities'.

Land

The issue of land has always been an emotional one for South Africans. In 1994 the government promised to transfer 30% of the 85-million hectares of white-owned agricultural land to South Africa's black majority by 2014. But land reform is progressing at a snail's pace. Although some land may have changed hands on the open market, only 4.3% of agricultural land has been redistributed through government processes.

Many rural communities were removed from their land during apartheid and the land was sold cheaply by the government to white farmers. The department of land affairs claims that land restitution, restoring land to the communities who lost it, is in its final phase, with more than 90% of claims gazetted. But the process is far from finished. In fact the deadline for lodging claims was shifted from the original date of 2005 to the end of 2008. Statistics from farmers' organisations such as AgriSA indicate that only 20% of land claims have been finalised.

New farmers are suffering from a lack of post-settlement support from the department of agriculture. Some organisations fear that up to 50% of land reform projects might have failed, and the department has admitted that there are huge problems with assisting farmers who have re-acquired land. In early 2009 land minister Lulu Xingwana issued the threat that restituted communities would lose their land if they did not farm it optimally. The 'use-it-or-lose-it' principle has drawn criticism from across the agricultural spectrum, but its impact would be minimal: at this point it can only be applied to communities who lease land from the government and those few communities who have already received back their land.

It is questionable whether all land claims will ever be settled. Land affairs director-general Tozi Gwanya has said that land is just too expensive and speculated that he would need at least R15-billion to settle all claims. White farmers have also been threatened with expropriation when they proved unwilling to sell for the price offered by government. The department has tried to get a Bill through Parliament that will allow the government to expropriate land 'in the public interest' without going to court first. But so far organised agricultural and other civil society groups have held up the Bill, declaring it unconstitutional. Farms have been expropriated already, but through a difficult and cumbersome process. The new law would give the minister much greater power to expropriate land to facilitate land reform.

Land activists have accused the department of a lack of direction and of leadership, despite firebrand Xingwana's threats and statements. The department is notorious for its poor capacity and it has a high staff turnover. Land analysts believe that much of the blame for the slow pace of land reform can be put at its door: there is endless red tape which communities wanting to claim land, and sellers willing to sell it, must cut through.

The issue of food security has also entered the equation. Organised agriculture in particular questions whether the way land reform is currently being handled by the department can still enable South Africa to produce its own food.

Another controversy surrounds the Communal Land Rights Act, which will hand communal land management to tribal leaders to manage. The intention of the legislation – scheduled to come into effect at the end of 2009 – is to give millions of rural South Africans security of tenure. The Act will affect about 21-million people living under traditional leadership and has been challenged in court already by communities who claim it will disempower them.

Land reform has also been haunted by a host of scandals, involving especially the Land Bank, which revealed that government officials might have pocketed some of the cash meant for land reform. Not only does the bank suffer from a huge turnover of staff, but many staff face disciplinary hearings, a host have been fired already, and the Scorpions and police are investigating multiple cases of fraud and other related economic crimes.

The Land Bank's performance has been so poor that it was yanked away from Xingwana's ministry and given to Trevor Manuel to manufacture a turn-around strategy for it.

The Media

The print media are under attack from a range of sources – the rising price of paper, the shrinking pool of advertisers in a global meltdown, the rise of the 'new media'. For if a reader – who already pays a monthly fee for internet access – can click on to a story online, why buy a newspaper? But none is as dangerous as the threat of government censorship – and it will apply to all media, including new media.

The print media fought, and won, the censorship battle in the 1990s, but new media arrived in the country well after the battle. And the first draft of the Films and Publications Amendment Bill, drawn up in 2008, would apply to all media. The Bill – meant to replace the 1996 version, which in turn replaced the archaic one of 1974 – provides for the pre-publication vetting of every broadcast and every publication.

This could mean a 20-minute delay on live soccer matches, and every newspaper vetted by government censors before it was printed – not unlike government attempts to control the flow of information during successive states of emergency from 1985 to 1990.

The South African National Editors' Forum (Sanef) made representations in opposition to this Bill. A concession was then proposed: that the pre-publication screening of newspaper copy would not apply to registered members of Sanef. While this would allow established magazines and newspapers to publish without any restrictions, work done by smaller media organisations, such as community newspapers or websites, would still be subject to pre-publication scrutiny. Sanef rejected it.

As a practical matter, the publication boards would probably not have the capacity to screen every publication, but if the draft Bill became law, there would be the potential to intimidate media organisations into toeing the line. Melissa Moore, head of the Law Clinic at the Freedom of Expression Institute (FXI), called the Bill 'arrogant' and a 'viperous assemblage of executive authoritarianism'. Writing in the *Media Magazine*'s November 2008 issue, Moore said that the 1996 Act had sought to prevent harm, rather than protect morality. It did not tamper with the creation and possession of material, while the new Bill was now attempting to introduce a morality test for films and publications.

Parliament sent the Bill to president Kgalema Motlanthe, who sent it back, expressing reservations about the unconstitutionality of certain sections. There have been no further calls for submissions, and as Moore says, the Bill as it stands now 'doesn't deal with half the problems we [the FXI] had'. 'Our first concern is the damaging and suppressive effect it is going to have on our hard-won right to freedom of expression, and secondly, it will probably necessitate a proliferation of court cases to challenge the infringing provisions before the courts.

'If the Bill is passed in its current format it would be a classic case of Parliament being let off the hook for failing to perform their constitutionally mandated function of passing legislation that is in keeping with the aims and objectives of the Constitution.'

Online publishers can sleep easy, however, if they're not worried about the looming shadow of government censors. Internet pundits have described 2009 as the year of the internet. The $600-million Seacom undersea cable is expected to dock in South Africa in June 2009 and the EASSy submarine cable in 2010, a development that will see broadband prices go down by as much as half.

Already internet usage in South Africa has grown phenomenally. In 2008 the country's internet users grew by 12.5% to 4.5-million. The submarine cables will make more international bandwidth available to South Africa, which is certain to increase the country's new media footprint. As the internet becomes cheaper and more accessible, there will be a migration from slow dial-up internet connections to permanent, high-speed broadband connections. Downloading podcasts and watching video content will become cheaper. The demand for video content will rise as broadband becomes more available and less expensive. In 2002, a standard broadband package cost the consumer over R900 a month; at present rates, a similar package costs in the region of R200.

This is a further shake-up of the industry. In 2004 dial-up subscribers numbered 1.08-million and broadband subscribers around 51 000. In 2008, dial-up subscribers dropped to 700 000 and broadband subscribers grew by 2 000% to 1.05-million.

Seacom's president Brian Herlihy said that South Africa needs about 50 gigabits of international capacity to service the one million broadband subscribers in the country. The country has about 10 gigabits. This is why the expected surge of 80 gigabits of international bandwidth via the cable from June 2009 will make a massive difference to the country's new media.

According to a technology conference held in Cape Town, the real change for 2009 will be seen in the cellphone sector, which is increasingly going to be integrated with the web. The second network operator, Neotel, and cellphone giant MTN are working together in laying a 5 000-km national fibre-optic network that will connect the country's major cities.

Online publishers expect 32% growth in 2009, and according to World Wide Worx, a technology research and strategy organisation, they view social media and networking sites like Facebook and Twitter as 'a great opportunity, along with video sharing, reader-generated content and citizen journalism'. Industry experts expect that Facebook and other social networking applications will be integrated into the traditional new media. A surge is expected also in the number of people who download and listen to podcasts. Blogs, a sibling of podcasts, are expected to grow in 2009 and are tipped to be one of the strongest areas for online revenue in 2010.

In 2008 South Africa's online advertising grew by 32% (R319-million was spent), the highest growth in the English-speaking world. The only mature internet market outperforming South Africa is Brazil.

Opposition Politics

Until the evening of Sunday, September 20 2008, the South African political landscape had frozen in what Robert Schrire, professor of political studies at the University of Cape Town, once described as an 'unproductive tableau'. The picture looked something like this: while fewer South Africans had been turning out to vote since 1994, the ANC kept returning to government with ever-increasing majorities (62% in 1994, 66% in 1999, and 69% in 2004). The ruling party's comfortable dominance was further entrenched during episodes of 'floor-crossing' when several members of opposition parties defected to the ANC.

Meanwhile, the fractured and weak opposition – which collectively received about 30% of the vote in 2004 – appeared to have reached a political cul de sac, with little hope of increasing support outside perceived racial enclaves or interests. And while some parties were at times highly effective and vocal in attempting to strengthen parliamentary oversight and hold the executive to account, opposition parties seemed perpetually trapped in an existence in relation to the ruling party rather than independently of it.

In 2004, the Democratic Alliance (DA), under the leadership of Tony Leon, managed to secure 12.37% of the vote, positioning it as the country's official opposition, followed by the Inkatha Freedom Party (IFP) with 6.97%. Bantu Holomisa's United Democratic Movement (UDM) gained 2.28% while Patricia de Lille's Independent Democrats (ID), launched in 2003, attracted 1.73%. The rest of the opposition vote was spread among a number of smaller parties including Kenneth Meshoe's African Christian Democratic Party with 1.6% and the Freedom Front Plus with a minuscule 0.89%. The now-extinct New National Party (a tepid shadow of the whites-only party that had ruled the country for 48 years) picked up 1.65% of the vote before it finally imploded in 2005, with all its surviving members absorbed into the ANC.

While opposition parties fared better in the 2006 municipal elections – the DA, in coalition with smaller parties, took the strategically important Cape Town Metro and governed in coalition in at least 30 other municipalities – politics on a national and regional level had become stale and moribund. Researcher Collette Schulz-Herzenberg, who crunched 12 years' worth of electoral data for her PhD at the University of Cape Town's Centre for Social Science Research, found that not only was the ANC losing support among voters but opposition parties were losing support as well. She defined the trend as 'asymmetrical dealignment'.

Her figures also revealed a new phenomenon, one that in retrospect may have been an early indication that South African voters were ready for something new and may have in fact been ahead of the country's politicians and political parties. Schulz-Herzenberg found a growing number of 'independents' in all voting groups or blocs, people who said they felt no particular allegiance to any party. She described this as 'a silent revolution' and noted it was taking place particularly among the youth.

Support for the ruling party had been waning – but not necessarily haemorrhaging – because of a variety of factors including the arms deal scandal, dissatisfaction with service delivery, attacks by members and supporters on the Constitution and the judiciary, as well as ongoing allegations of corruption against ANC president Jacob Zuma, and the internal dissent and disruption this caused in the party.

Then one Friday afternoon in mid-September 2008 in the Pietermaritzburg High Court, Judge Chris Nicholson delivered a judgment that altered the course of the country's history. Nicholson, a former human rights lawyer, ruled that charges of taking bribes brought against Zuma in 2007 be set aside on a legal technicality.

Nicholson's controversial judgment, which also suggested that there was truth to Zuma's claim that he was a victim of a political conspiracy masterminded by then-president Thabo Mbeki, was subsequently overturned and dismissed in January 2009 by a unanimous Supreme Court of Appeal bench led by Louis Harms. But the fallout from the September 12 judgment was immediate. A week later, Mbeki was forced by the ANC's newly elected national executive committee to hand in his resignation. On Sunday night, September 20, he bade a sombre farewell on national television nine months before his term was due to end.

Earlier, tensions within the ANC had bubbled to the surface at the party's watershed 52nd national conference in Polokwane in December 2007 when Mbeki lost a bid to run for a third term as president of the party. Zuma, whom Mbeki had fired as deputy president in 2005, received around 60% of the vote to Mbeki's 40% – the result paving the way for the subsequent rupture of the almost 100-year-old liberation movement.

The political realignment or split to the left that political pundits and armchair commentators had been predicting for years failed to materialise. Instead 'leftists' in the ANC gained control of the party and, within a few months of Mbeki's 'recalling', a group of disgruntled members, led by former minister of defence Mosiuoa Lekota, former Gauteng premier Mbhazima Shilowa and former deputy minister of defence Mluleki

George, announced their intention to form a breakaway. Emboldened by the move, hundreds of ANC members across the country resigned from the party to support the new venture. Later, after much national canvassing, consultation and legal wrangling about a name, the Congress of the People, or Cope, was formally founded on December 16 2008. It registered for the 2009 general election shortly afterwards.

There is unanimous agreement that the birth of Cope has irrevocably altered the nature of South African opposition politics. It has reinvigorated the political milieu while offering an alternative home for black swing voters not yet ready to make the ideological leap required to support established opposition parties. An indication of the current political reanimation is the record number of people – 1.6-million – who registered to vote during the Independent Electoral Commission's first registration weekend in November 2008. The bulk of new registrations, 77.9%, were young people.

The key players in South African opposition politics operate on relatively narrow centrist ideological turf. And while the electorate has grown increasingly savvy and sophisticated, parties still tend to campaign around personalities rather than policies and issues. Although the IFP offers a unique hybrid of Zulu nationalism and traditional British conservatism, there are few major differences between the DA's 'new liberalism' and the social democratic principles of Cope, the ID and the UDM – or the ANC, for that matter.

The DA, with its leader as mayor of Cape Town, had an opportunity to prove it could govern successfully and effectively in coalition with other parties. The DA-led coalition's survival after at least 10 attempts to unseat it by the ANC boosted the morale of opposition parties.

All parties accept the Constitution as the supreme law of the country, essentially support the free market, black economic empowerment, the independence of the judiciary, and good, transparent, and open and accountable government. They all agree that poverty, unemployment, crime, health, housing and education are massive challenges that need to be addressed. Where parties do differ is around issues of implementation and style of governance.

While it remains to be seen how those who form coalitions will work together, there is no doubt that the grip on power that the ANC once enjoyed can no longer be taken for granted.

Transformation of the Judiciary

The transformation of the South African judiciary is a constitutional imperative and still remains a priority for the ruling ANC. This much was evident in resolutions taken by the party at its Mafikeng and Stellenbosch conferences and more recently at the watershed Polokwane conference in 2007. The delegates at Polokwane again expressed their displeasure with the pace of the transformation of an institution that has assumed great importance in South Africa's political landscape.

The judiciary has in recent times not only had to dispense justice to ordinary South Africans but it has also had to adjudicate in cases involving high-profile political figures such as Jacob Zuma, Thabo Mbeki, Vusi Pikoli and Jackie Selebi as well as one of their own, Cape judge president John Hlophe. Increasingly, in the interest of promoting socioeconomic rights such as housing and water as set out in the Constitution, the judiciary has had to issue orders against the executive and legislative arms of government, which were seen as an encroachment on the principle of the separation of powers.

At Polokwane delegates resolved to create a 'single, integrated, accessible and affordable court system', a single body that appoints both judges and magistrates, and a single complaints-lodging mechanism for both types of judicial officers. The delegates also resolved that the Constitutional Court should become the apex court in all matters and not just in those matters involving the Constitution. This would mean that the Supreme Court of Appeal (SCA) becomes an intermediate court and no longer the court of last instance in criminal matters. The chief justice should be the head of one single judiciary that includes the magistracy. Thirdly, it was resolved that full Bench decisions at the High Court level, such as the unprecedented bench of five judges of the Johannesburg High Court in 2008 sitting in the Hlophe case, should fall away. Moreover, the integration of the Labour Appeal Court into the SCA was also proposed. The delegates laid great stress on the importance of judicial training in order to create a sufficient pool of judges from South Africa's diverse society. Perhaps the most contentious of the resolutions was the proposal to put the administration of the courts under the control of the Cabinet member responsible for the administration of justice – the minister for justice and constitutional development.

To give effect to proposals like these, two pieces of legislation were prepared and tabled in Parliament for discussion and public debate: the Superior Courts Bill, first proposed in 2003 and now revived, and the Fourteenth Amendment Bill, an attempt to amend the Constitution to allow the chief justice to assume leadership of the judiciary. The Fourteenth Amendment Bill also proposed that the administration of the courts be taken away from the judges and instead be put in the hands of government technocrats under the minister of justice and constitutional development. The judges would nevertheless still be responsible for the adjudication of cases.

The two Bills caused an uproar in the legal fraternity: some leading members of the judiciary and legal profession complained that a number of the suggestions in the proposed legislation were a threat to judicial independence. Leading lights such as respected human rights lawyer George Bizos and former chief justice Arthur Chaskalson raised their objection to the Bills. It was not long until then-president Thabo Mbeki intervened and ordered justice minister Brigitte Mabandla to shelve the legislation until proper consultation with the judiciary had been completed. Discussions around the passing of the Bills continue and the interim justice minister, Enver Surty, has indicated that most of the hurdles have been overcome and that the laws should go through after the 2009 elections.

Nothing exposed the ruptures in the judiciary as clearly as the two cases involving Cape judge president Hlophe. In the first instance he was accused of improperly taking money from a private company, Oasis, for his consultancy work and also allowing the same company to sue his junior colleague, judge Siraj Desai. Hlophe claimed that he had received permission to consult for Oasis from the late justice minister Dullah Omar; Mabandla denied knowledge of a letter from Hlophe furnished to her predecessor. Hlophe was investigated and put through an inquiry by the Judicial Service Commission (JSC) but was narrowly spared impeachment when chief justice Pius Langa and others on the JSC who were not prepared to have the first judicial impeachment in post-apartheid South Africa that of a black senior judge, voted against the recommendation.

And then at the height of ANC president Jacob Zuma's running battle with the National Prosecuting Authority and an appeal before the Constitutional Court, Hlophe was at it again when he was accused of attempting to influence two Concourt judges to help find in Zuma's favour. A complaint was laid against him with the JSC. Soon thereafter Hlophe laid a complaint of his own and also sought a declaratory order from the Johannesburg High Court, claiming that some of his rights had been infringed. That court, in a 3-2 split along racial lines, found in his favour. An appeal to the SCA was lodged by the judges of the Constitutional Court. Hlophe also sued 13 judges of the Constitutional Court for R10-million.

The whole saga exposed the split within the judiciary, with a black solidarity Africanist group in the judiciary rallying around Hlophe and another liberal bloc calling for his impeachment. Politicians from the ruling ANC, as part of their strategy of defending Zuma, also entered the fray and accused Constitutional Court judges of a counter-revolutionary agenda. Later, a white female judge of the SCA, Carole Lewis, also upset the black solidarity bloc when she made a speech calling for merit and experience over affirmative action in the appointment of judges. In her speech Lewis pointed out that the heads of all South African courts were now all black males, barring the head of the specialist Competition Court, Cape High Court judge Dennis Davis. Although this is true, it is the lack of enough female judges in the judiciary that is most troubling; only one female judge, Jeanette Traverso, occupies a leadership position in the judiciary, as deputy judge president in the Cape division. The appointment of female judges is taking place at an alarmingly slow pace.

Urbanisation

South Africans are streaming to the cities in what housing minister Lindiwe Sisulu calls 'an avalanche of urbanisation ... While the international trend in migration to urban areas is estimated at an averaging

2.7%, we occupy the upper end of the spectrum.' The minister credits the provision of free houses to the very poor as attracting migrants to South Africa's cities and towns. 'Human beings are the most rational species of all animals,' she told Parliament in 2008. 'Why would any remain on the impoverished land when there is little prospect of employment and when in fact in towns, they can get free houses?'

In the cities, houses are free only for the disabled or for indigents with an income between zero and R1 500; those in the next bracket, from R1 501 to R3 500, have to put in R2 479 of their own money, up front, to qualify for a R2 479 subsidy, on a product – a basic house on a serviced stand – worth R43 506; and for those who earn beyond that princely monthly wage, there is a grant ranging from R3 501 to R7 000, intended as part of a down payment on a mortgage-linked house. (Perhaps in an effort to entice people to stay on the land, the situation is easier in the rural areas; there even those who bring in R3 500 a month need contribute nothing except, depending on the programme, their labour.)

In the 2007/8 financial year, the department counted 248 850 houses either delivered or in construction, and in the past 15 years the total comes to about 2.6-million. It's not all new houses and flats; included in the figure is the upgrading of shack settlements into the 'sustainable human settlements' which the national policy calls for – ideally, serviced stands, bricks and mortar, schools, clinics and other amenities.

Yet there are people crowded 15 to a flat in city centres. Illegal shack settlements spring up wherever there is a patch of green or a deserted factory; in Cape Town alone, there are an estimated 150 000 shacks in 222 informal settlements. The backlog nationally is 2.4-million. The department has to keep running just to stay in the same place.

A lack of accommodation doesn't deter people from pouring into the cities. Humans are rational, as the minister says; they go where the work is. In South Africa, 21 urban areas cover only 2% of the land but account for almost 70% of the national geographic value-added product. These areas encompass not only Johannesburg, Cape Town, Durban, East London and Port Elizabeth but smaller cities with good employment prospects, like Rustenburg, Richards Bay, Nelspruit, Sasolburg, Kimberley and Middelburg.

Between 1996 and 2001, South Africa's cities grew by over 10%. On the basis of 2001 figures, UN Habitat notes that more South Africans now live in cities than in rural areas and puts current population growth in the urban areas at 3% per annum. Cities can barely keep pace with the need for services.

Part of the problem is the increase in the number of households – 30%, according to the minister – with a concomitant drop in household size. The figures are contested, but there is some indication that in 1990 the average household size was 4.5 people, while by 2001 it had shrunk to 3.8. The figure varies from province to province: urbanised Gauteng, for example, shows a household size of 3.3, according to Stats SA's 2007 Community Survey, while the largely rural KwaZulu-Natal has a higher-than-average household size of 4.6.

While the figures vary, the reasons don't: family units are shrinking because of HIV/Aids, declining fertility, and an economic climate that impels the core family unit to move to the cities to find work while those on the periphery – elderly relatives especially, perhaps one or two children – remain in the rural areas, surviving on social grants. A family so divided requires more houses to live in – a point that perhaps has not escaped the notice of families crowded into shacks much too small for their needs.

The department is not doing too badly – there's been a slight drop in the share of the population who live in shacks, from 16% in 1996 to 14.4% in 2007, according to the Institute of Race Relations, and at the same time the percentage of families living in formal houses – including RDP houses – has increased from 64.4% to 70.6%. Around 20% of the population lives in subsidy housing.

There are, however, two major issues. One is what happens to the shack dwellers occupying land they have settled on because it's close to where the work is. There is a new emphasis on upgrading informal settlements *in situ* rather than moving shack dwellers out, razing the settlement and building small new units.

The experience of the Gateway development in Cape Town shows what can happen in such a scenario. The pilot project, then Cape Town mayor Helen Zille told the United Nations, 'accessed prime housing land for rental stock, moved shack dwellers in phases, spent huge subsidies on middle class housing, while the poor were pushed to the periphery of the city and put into subsidised housing elsewhere. The result was major clashes over access, resistance to moving, and housing delivery came to a standstill.' Now the city is planning to spend $4-billion on new developments in the CBD, putting in one-third of the finance, while the rest is to come from the private sector.

The Johannesburg CBD is also alive with development – office blocks turned into upmarket residential hotels; areas paved, greened and pedestrianised; a whole district devoted to the rag trade; hawkers herded, whenever possible, into markets. The big cities can do this sort of thing. Smaller cities and towns throughout the country cannot, because in many, if not most, cases, they don't have the capacity to carry out adequate planning and delivery.

According to the Constitution, housing is a power shared concurrently between the national and provincial governments, but a clause allows for the delegation of responsibility to the tier where it is best delivered. In 1997, the Housing Act gave local authorities the opportunity to become accredited to administer housing programmes. They only had to put in place the systems and capacity to deliver housing, and then housing resources would start flowing to the municipal government instead of the province.

The national department's Breaking New Ground policy, published in 2004, noted that municipalities should be accredited so they could plan, implement and maintain projects in accordance with their integrated development plans (IDPs). The theory was that city governments, which prepare IDPs, are best placed to know what their needs are, in accordance with the national department's Housing Sector Plan, setting out national objectives. However, out of more than 280 local authorities, there are only approximately 50 that have housing departments, and very few of them have the capacity to plan and implement housing programmes, according to housing policy analyst Mary Tomlinson. Not surprisingly, outside the big cities the provinces do the planning, procurement and project management, and the local authorities get the blame when things fall apart. In all but the metros and a few smaller cities, the provinces have either held on to the housing function or taken it back.

Were local authorities to become accredited, the money would go straight from the national government to the municipalities. Currently, it is funnelled through the provinces, and so the housing projects that the province is willing to fund do not necessarily reflect the projects the local authority has asked for.

Urban areas need a variety of housing forms. Catherine Cross of the Human Sciences Research Council's Centre for Poverty, Employment and Growth has identified 40 categories of self-built and formally delivered housing in the country, from thatched rondavels and shacks to flats for rent in the city centres and RDP houses. In the key economic spaces – the city centres – she says, 'the dominant constituency … is that of younger unmarried male work-seekers and employed workers, who generally fit the profile for a shack settlement constituency, but are somewhat younger and better educated than the related grouping living in the outer shack settlements'.

Urbanisation and urban growth have traditionally fuelled economic growth. The current acknowledgement of urbanisation and the focus on *in situ* upgrading of informal settlements indicate that housing, this time, is following the economy.

Xenophobia

One Sunday night in May 2008, gangs of young men swept through Alexandra township in northern Johannesburg attacking people they deemed to be foreigners – hostel residents and shack dwellers, men, women and children, even South Africans who could not remember the Zulu word for 'elbow' to prove they belonged there. The attacks continued nightly for three weeks and spread to other provinces with a history of violent xenophobic incidents: KwaZulu-Natal and the Eastern and Western Cape. In all, 62 people were killed, one-third of them South Africans, and tens of thousands lost their homes and meagre possessions.

The violence that shot through Alexandra was not unusual – only the scale of it. There have been organised attacks on refugees, illegal aliens and permanent residents, some of whom have lived in South Africa for decades, since December 1994, when gangs of armed youths destroyed homes owned by foreign nationals in Alexandra. African foreigners have been beaten, thrown to their deaths from trains, shot, or set on fire. Their shops have been looted, their shacks dismantled, their homes appropriated. There have been major incidents wherever they have settled – in townships and informal settlements in the Free State, in North West and Mpumalanga as well as in those provinces hit by violence in 2008.

Reasons given by the perpetrators range from a perception that foreigners are taking their jobs (and, bizarrely, 'their women') to the claim that they are responsible for crime. Competition for a small pool of resources – jobs and housing – has fuelled anger in many places. The conviction that corrupt local authorities are assigning scarce housing to foreigners is a frequently heard complaint in townships. Accusations that foreign informal traders are undercutting local hawkers give violent youths an excuse to attack.

Although foreign nationals are not always welcomed with open arms, in much of the country they coexist peacefully with their South African neighbours. A study by the Forced Migration Programme at the University of the Witwatersrand found several factors contributing to the outbreak of violence in those settlements where it has flared, among them the exclusion of foreigners from political participation and justice; a lack of prompt, effective conflict-resolution mechanisms; and a culture of impunity with regard to public violence in general and xenophobic violence in particular.

Another major factor was also highlighted: micro politics. In many areas where violence has occurred, the study found a vacuum in or competition for community leadership, encouraging the emergence of an alternative local leadership – unofficial, illegal and often violent – that enhanced its authority by playing to residents' resentment towards foreign Africans.

The department of home affairs' counter-xenophobia unit identified major sources of violence as a lack of service delivery, unemployment, poverty, competition for business, and crime.

There is no agreement on how many foreigners live in South Africa, since so many of them are illegal and, in effect, fly under the radar. Estimates range from a sober 1.2-million to a fanciful 12-million. The 2001 census recorded 2.3%, or close to one million people, as having been born outside South Africa. In Gauteng the percentage was 5.3%; and in Johannesburg alone, 6.7%. The numbers are certainly higher now. Stats SA's 2007 Community Survey identified 2.79% of the population, or 1.2-million residents, as foreign-born.

A head count of people crossing the borders does not shed much light on the issue. A Southern African Migration Project survey of cross-border traffic in 2006 found that out of six million border crossings, up to half that number were small-scale traders, entering South Africa to buy but not to stay. However, the meltdown of Zimbabwe has sent a large part of its population south – estimates range from 500 000 to three million. South Africa is a major draw for its neighbours, including Mozambique and Lesotho, but it is also host to Somalis, Nigerians, Kenyans, Eritreans – in fact, every African nationality is represented.

With few exceptions, they don't find it easy. Home affairs counts illegal immigrants by how many they have deported. The 2007/8 annual report noted that volumes had been growing by an average of 18% over the previous five years, but in 2007/8 the number of deportees jumped 25%; the department estimated that some 370 000 were put on trains and sent back to their home countries.

Lawyers for Human Rights notes that some 200 000 asylum seekers have applied for refugee permits in the past 15 years, and most have been turned down. In 2007, only 29% of migrants who applied were given refugee status.

Zimbabweans are particularly at risk, perhaps because there are so many of them. The asylum system remains effectively closed to new arrivals fleeing the violence and economic meltdown in Zimbabwe, according to the Consortium for Refugees and Migrants in South Africa (CoRMSA), which says that border officials turn away Zimbabweans trying to enter South Africa. They report that police regularly arrest and deport would-be asylum seekers before they can travel to Johannesburg or Pretoria and formally apply for refugee status.

Refugees and asylum seekers who manage to evade deportation and try to regularise their status can look forward to days in queues at reception centres. Only Johannesburg has opened a migrant help-desk to ease migrants through the resettlement process, though other cities are making moves in that direction.

A major reason to seek papers is to qualify for a bank account. The Banking Association of South Africa cites government's Fica regulations when explaining why most banks insist on seeing an official ID document, passport or 'acceptable other trusted document' before they will open an account. Two banking groups have begun extending basic banking services to refugees – one group will even help asylum seekers, if they have been issued with valid permits – but for the most part, migrants must keep their money close by, making them 'mobile ATMs' for thieves and policemen soliciting bribes.

Other problems are universal: accommodation is hard to come by, employers are likely to underpay migrants, especially illegal ones, and for those who come with qualifications it is difficult to register them. The South African Qualifications Authority charges for its service, and immigrants with employment rights are often turned away by employers who do not recognise either their papers or their qualifications.

One-third of 'non-national' children are not enrolled in schools in South Africa, either because they and their parents cannot pay fees or the cost of transport, uniform and books, or because administrators turn them away. Health care is also hard to come by; non-nationals are regularly refused treatment, including access to ARVs, by hospital staff.

Organisations working in the field say that even once the department of home affairs gets through its backlog, the major problem remains: government policy reflects a migration-control mindset. CoRMSA recommends 'a thorough review of immigration policies in accordance with the deputy minister's recent comments that South Africa needs to move from a migration-control to a migration-management policy framework'. Qualified refugees could help enormously in seriously understaffed areas like education and health care.

Contributors

Justin Arenstein is the publisher at African Eye News Service and its affiliated publishing company, Homegrown Magazines, and is on the board of MPowerFM and the SA Press Council.

Adriaan Basson is an investigative journalist with the *Mail & Guardian*.

Belinda Beresford is a freelance journalist, covering health issues.

Maureen Brady is a freelance writer, copyeditor and proofreader.

Stefaans Brummer is an investigative journalist with the *Mail & Guardian*.

Matthew Burbidge is editor of *Mail & Guardian Online*.

Shaun de Waal is the *M&G*'s chief film critic and the co-editor of *To Have and to Hold: The Making of Same-Sex Marriage in South Africa*.

Nic Dawes is editor-in-chief of the *Mail & Guardian*.

Monako Dibetle is a *Mail & Guardian* education journalist.

Lynley Donnelly is a business reporter for the *Mail & Guardian*.

Maya Fisher-French is a freelance financial journalist who is a regular contributor to the *Mail & Guardian*, focusing on economics and personal finance topics.

Drew Forrest is deputy editor of the *Mail & Guardian*.

Lloyd Gedye is a business and arts journalist at the *Mail & Guardian*.

Primarashni Gower is associate editor: education at the *Mail & Guardian*.

Yolandi Groenewald is the *Mail & Guardian*'s environmental reporter.

Ferial Haffajee, former editor-in-chief of the *Mail & Guardian*, is editor-in-chief of *City Press*.

Sharon Hammond is editor of African Eye News Service and associate editor at the agency's affiliated publishing company, Homegrown Magazines.

Pearlie Joubert is Cape Town correspondent for the *Mail & Guardian*.

Mara Kardas-Nelson is a *Mail & Guardian* reporter.

Qudsiya Karrim is a journalist with *Mail & Guardian Online*.

Karabo Keepile is a *Mail & Guardian* journalist.

Matuma Letsoalo is the *Mail & Guardian's* labour reporter

Barbara Ludman is a former *Mail & Guardian* associate editor.

Percy Mabandu is a journalist with *Mail & Guardian Online*.

David Macfarlane is a freelance journalist.

Mmanaledi Mataboge is a senior reporter at the *Mail & Guardian*.

Thabo Mohlala is a reporter for the *Mail & Guardian* and *The Teacher*.

Rudo Mungoshi is a reporter for BigMedia online publishers.

Nosimilo Ndlovu is a reporter at the *Mail & Guardian*.

Faranaaz Parker is a *Mail & Guardian* journalist.

Cornia Pretorius is associate editor: education at the *Mail & Guardian*, editor of *The Teacher* and co-editor of *Higher Learning*.

Ilham Rawoot is a *Mail & Guardian* reporter.

Mandy Rossouw is a senior political reporter at the *Mail & Guardian*.

Sello Selebi Alcock is the *Mail & Guardian*'s justice and crime reporter.

Reg Rumney is the director of the Centre for Economics Journalism in Africa at Rhodes University.

Lucky Sindane is the *Mail & Guardian*'s sports reporter.

Sam Sole is an investigative journalist with the *Mail & Guardian*.

Rapule Tabane is deputy editor-in-chief of the *Mail & Guardian*.

Marianne Thamm is a freelance columnist, journalist and editor.

Niren Tolsi is Durban correspondent for the *Mail & Guardian*.

Thembelihle Tshabalala is a *Mail & Guardian* journalist.

Stephanie Wolters is a freelance journalist, political analyst and former Africa editor of the *Mail & Guardian*.

Percy Zvomuya is an arts and features reporter for the *Mail & Guardian*.